ROADS

ARCHAEOLOGY AND ARCHITECTURE

ROADS

ARCHAEOLOGY AND ARCHITECTURE

Richard K. Morriss

TEMPUS

For Lucy

Roads go on
While we forget, and are
Forgotten like a star
That shoots and is gone.

On this earth 'tis sure
We men have not made
Anything that doth fade
So soon, so long endure.

(From *Roads*, by Edward Thomas (1878-1917))

First published 2005

Tempus Publishing Limited
The Mill, Brimscombe Port,
Stroud, Gloucestershire, GL5 2QG
www.tempus-publishing.com

© Richard K. Morriss, 2005

British Library Cataloguing in Publication Data.
A catalogue record for this book is available from the British Library.

ISBN 0 7524 2887 X

Typesetting and origination by Tempus Publishing Limited
Printed in Great Britain

Contents

Preface

In spite, or perhaps because, of modern society's apparently never-ending love affair with the motor car, the roads and road infrastructure that it needs are seldom seen as being of any historical interest. Some may be vaguely aware of a Roman road here and there, but most motorists probably do not know that they have just passed over a 600-year-old bridge still in everyday use or are travelling on a route that has been in existence for several thousand years.

If roads are thought about at all by the busy road users of the twenty-first century, it is usually in regards to what is needed to make them better: to ease traffic congestion; to improve busy junctions; to speed up journeys. Considering the amount of time most of us spend in our cars, often in traffic jams, this is not surprising. Usually, therefore, roads are thought about in a negative, rather than in a positive, way, and the fact that they have, for thousands of years, helped shape the development of our society is generally not appreciated.

Other historic forms of transport, on the other hand, are seen as having a distinct history and a cohesion that the roads do not. There have been hundreds of books about railways and canals, and although most of those concentrate on the trains and the barges respectively, there are at least many others that concentrate on their infrastructure – the stations and bridges, the aqueducts and locks.

Whilst there are also hundreds of books about road transport, the vast majority are concerned with cars (and particularly about very fast cars); others concentrate on other road vehicles – motorbikes, lorries, traction engines, buses and trams, for example, or the history of roads in a particular area or period. Far rarer are the books on specialist aspects of the infrastructure such as signposts and milestones, or bridges and ferries, and rarer still any book that attempts to encompass the whole of the road transport infrastructure and consider it as a single entity.

1 This quiet Wiltshire lane now leads to a farm and then becomes a track up Avebury Down in the distance. Yet until it was bypassed in the eighteenth century it was one of the most important highways in Britain, a part of the Great West Road; before that it was a *herepath*, one of the main Saxon roads or 'army roads' and, given the fact it begins on the edge of the prehistoric stone circle of Avebury, could have been in use for thousands of years

This book is not a book on the history of roads or on the techniques of archaeology. It is simply an attempt to outline and catalogue the very rich archaeological and architectural resource that is directly or indirectly related to Britain's roads. Some of this resource is well protected, but much of it is not; some of it is worth protecting, and much of it is not. However, all of it is part of our common heritage and as such worthy of at least appropriate study, understanding, and recording.

PART I

INTRODUCTION

CHAPTER 1

What is road archaeology?

Before asking the question 'what is road archaeology?' a more important question is 'what is a road?'. That may seem an odd question at the start of a book pertaining to be about the archaeology and architecture of roads, but is not as simple a question as it may first appear. It also needs to be answered before an obvious second question – 'what is archaeology?' – can even be attempted. Yet how does a road differ from, or equate to, a highway, a lane, a track, a path or a street? The etymology of the various words used to describe 'roads' over the years is fascinating and too complex to delve into for this particular work, but can be briefly summarised.

The use of the Standard English word 'road' as it is now commonly understood – a fixed link between places for all forms of pedestrian and wheeled traffic – is surprisingly modern, dating only to the late sixteenth century. The word stems from the Old English *rád* – to ride – and in the medieval period could simply mean riding on horseback. That meaning is fossilised in the name of Chester's historic race course, the Rodee; the word could still literally mean a raid by marauders on horseback as late as the mid-seventeenth century. It could, and still can, mean a place where ships could ride at anchor and in the Saxon epic poem, *Bēowolf*, the sea itself is the *swan-rād* (swan-road).

An older word for a road is a 'way', derived from another Old English word, *weg*, which meant to move, or to journey, or to carry – the latter meaning evolving into our modern word 'weigh'. By the late medieval period, the term 'roadway' had come into being to complement the older terms 'highway' and 'by-way' – used for important and not so important routes respectively. Even then the term 'highway' was not confined to land transport; the important navigable rivers of Britain, such as the Severn, Wye and Thames, were classed as 'King's highways'.

The oldest English word for a road is now limited mainly to those in towns. 'Street' is also derived from an Old English (i.e. Teutonic) word, *stræt*, but that was, in turn, derived from the Latin – *strata* – as used by the Romans in the term *via strata*, specifically 'paved street or road'. In the Saxon period this seems to have been a term used for the crumbling Roman roads that still formed important elements in the landscape, and useful boundaries between territories, landholdings or parishes. The word became incorporated into the place names of settlements along the lines of Roman roads – *Stretton, Stretford, Stratford, Street, Streetly, Stratfield, Streatham* etc.

The word 'street' is thus the only one that originally had a specific meaning of a deliberately engineered route dedicated to traffic. 'Road' and 'way' historically simply meant a route, the bounds of which were ill-defined if defined at all. Depending on a number of geographic and economic factors they could be yards, or miles, wide. In modern parlance and legal statute however, the definition has, by and large, been restricted to a specific type of made-up way for wheeled traffic within set boundaries.

In recent years there have been attempts at a more definitive meaning of 'road' as an archaeological monument type. One of the biggest schemes to categorise and to produce long-term management strategies for the archaeological heritage was the Monument Protection Plan set up by English Heritage. In their official definitions, produced in 1990, a 'road' is described as 'an artificial way having a constructed bearing surface, providing a means of communication suitable for wheeled traffic, between places and features'.

Such a definition excludes the unsurfaced drove roads or ridgeways and contrasts with the given definition of a 'trackway', which is 'a routeway linking two or more places together which has not been deliberately constructed as a bearing surface but which has been worn down through prolonged use, and which has defined boundaries'. Whilst this book is mainly concerned with roads, the distinctions are still blurred.

Having, hopefully, at least agreed what a road might be, there is a need to understand what 'archaeology' is. Again, the initial answer might seem easy. Archaeologists, surely, are those sartorially-challenged individuals scraping the ground with well-worn trowels and triumphantly reconstructing a whole Roman city on the evidence of a single sherd of pottery. Of course, no one really has that image anymore, even though most people still believe that archaeologists do work mainly on excavations – a belief fostered by the surprising amount of television programmes on the subject that have sprung up in the past 10 years or so.

Archaeology is far more than that. Archaeology is one of the two main strands of History – the other being the documentary research of primary archive material. Archaeology is the objective study of physical remains, of the material culture of the past. These two elements of history are, and have to be, mutually compatible. Neither can be used without the other if any meaningful conclusions are to be drawn. However, it has to be said that if the material culture is properly studied and assessed through appropriate archaeological techniques it should provide the more reliable evidence – simply because structures and buildings are their own record. An archaeologist can, of course, make a mistake or come to the wrong conclusions, but the evidence will not be at fault; however, if a clerk made a mistake in a fourteenth century deed it is far more difficult for the documentary historian to identify it – and even a simple mistake can thus devalue such a document as a piece of reliable historical evidence.

Virtually all of the many different archaeological techniques can and often need to be used in the study the road network, from the simplest survey to the most technologically advanced forms of ground-probing radar. On the broadest scale, landscape archaeology can assess the position of the road in the landscape and its affect on the settlements on its route – or, conversely, the effect of settlements on the road. For example, the creation of a new road or the diversion of an old one can lead to the development of a completely new settlement or the demise of an old one. Several settlements were the direct result of Roman road planning in the first century AD, for example, and others a direct result of the abandonment of a Roman road centuries later.

In other cases, the development of a new settlement could lead to the diversion of an ancient route to serve it. The site of Shrewsbury appears to have been ignored by the Romans, whose main city was further to the east at modern Wroxeter. A Roman road passed to the south of the site of Shrewsbury but when its defended site led to the creation of a Saxon *burh* it attracted the main roads to it, including, presumably, a *herepath* or 'army road', and later, the main road from England into mid-Wales.

Later still, the deliberate creation of a planned medieval market town could lead to a main road being diverted to go through it – and a similar thing happened when Old Sarum was abandoned in favour of a new city, Salisbury, in the valley below. Even minor changes, such as the destruction of a Roman bridge or the construction of a medieval one, could have effects on the urban morphology of a town or a village. This has continued over time, even into the twentieth century when the development of motorised transport led to the spread of suburbs around the major towns and unwelcome ribbon development along the main roads leading out from them. Bypasses from the 1930s onwards have formed a magnet for further development, and now many a bypass around a town forms almost a *de facto* development boundary.

Landscape archaeology on a more intense and localised level also recognises the roads and the traces of roads in the landscape itself, identifying and making sense of what once were once rather disparagingly called the 'lumps and bumps in the ground'. It is, perhaps, the only form of archaeology that can attempt to assess the development of the earliest prehistoric trackways, especially where these are spread out over a swathe hundreds of yards wide in a typical braided pattern of *holloways*, for example. The lateral expansion of a track or road was very common throughout Britain and, apart from the Roman period, seems to have continued until areas were gradually enclosed and the roads confined. Even in the modern era, there are examples of this. The first modern road was built north of Blair Atholl to Inverness in the 1920s; it was superseded by a better one on an often different alignment in the 1960s and that has, in turn, been superseded in the 1980s by the modern A9 which runs on yet another alignment. Thus, there are now, in places, three separate roadways in the landscape all built in the same century, and to confuse matters, there are occasional traces of a military road of the eighteenth century.

2 Centuries of travellers finding the best ways along generally unsurfaced routes, together with the effect of rainwater, often lead to the creation of braided holloways, especially in hilly areas such as this section of a road in Radnorshire

3 Modern abandoned roads in the Drumochter Pass in the Scottish Highlands. The first proper road through the pass was by General Wade in the 1720s and much of that route was followed by Telford in the early nineteenth century. A new tarmacadamed motor road was built in the 1920s, and can be seen on the right. It was bypassed in sections by an improved road in the 1960s (in the centre) and that, in turn has been bypassed by the present road (on the extreme left – itself partly on the course of Wade's original road)

In contrast, many roads have been on more or less the same alignment, albeit sometimes intermittently, for 2,000 years – if not longer. Many Roman roads still carry modern traffic and some were themselves probably based on pre-Roman routeways. As successive generations have repaired such roads, layers have built it up to the present level which can be well above the original. Such an archaeological resource contrasts markedly with the unsurfaced prehistoric and medieval holloways that effectively formed themselves through wear and erosion.

When ancient roads are identified, and where the need arises and the resources are available, the 'traditional' techniques of archaeological excavation come into play. Cross-sections through roads are especially useful in understanding the manner in which they were constructed and subsequently maintained and used – and even help, through various dating techniques, in assigning dates to the various phases thus identified. In this way the skilled archaeological excavator will be able to use stratigraphy to identify the relationships between the various

4 and 5 When a road is kept in use and
constantly maintained, the successive
applications of new surface materials
can lead to the road level rising. This
can be seen in these two photographs of
consecutive milestones on the Shropshire
section of the Holyhead road, rebuilt in
the early nineteenth century by Thomas
Telford; the base of the first stone has been
buried whilst the second has been reset to
its original height

layers within the excavated areas and then, if there any dateable finds – pot sherds and the like – use those to add a reasonably accurate chronology to the development of the road.

The combination of such techniques in a fairly small but well-targeted area can add enormously to our knowledge not only of that particular area but sometimes, because of the linear nature of roads and their purpose, of a whole region. Thus the archaeological work carried out on the Roman road between Old Sarum and Dorchester where it crosses the Hampshire/Dorset border demonstrated its relationship with the Bokerley Dyke, a Romano-British defensive earthwork that crosses it. When the Dyke was first built in the late fourth century AD it blocked the Roman road; one reason may have been to halt a well-documented attack by Saxon raiders in AD 367. Subsequently the road was reopened, and repaired, possibly indicating that the danger was over. Some time later, in around the early fifth century after the end of Roman rule, the road

6 Archaeological recording of this complex of earthworks revealed a small story in the decline of Roman Britain and its defence against the Saxons. This Hampshire section of the Ackling Dyke, the Roman road south of Old Sarum, was blocked by the late fourth-century AD Bokerley Dyke on two separate occasions and reopened and repaired during a time of relative peace in between

was blocked again and never reopened. The archaeological study of a small area produced a microcosm of the end of the Roman era in Britain.

The roads form only a part of the road infrastructure and they are related to other aspects of civil engineering – bridges, tunnels, causeways etc. – along their routes. There are also many different types of buildings that are directly or indirectly related to the road network, from the ancient pilgrims' inn to the modern motorway service station or from a bus garage to a car factory. These can also be studied archaeologically in various ways. The cost of such work is not necessarily very great and is certainly cheaper, usually, than excavation.

In addition, this type of study is often well within the capability of the individual enthusiast. Such study is usually non-destructive and, where appropriate, fairly straightforward. It could range from a simple understanding of various construction breaks in the fabric of a bridge or of the insertion or removal of features in a building to a fully detailed stone-by-stone analytical drawing.

7 Techniques of building archaeology are often needed to understand the built heritage associated with the road network. The Pen-y-bengog bridge on the modern A5 in Snowdonia is three bridges in one; the odd rough arch is a remnant of the bridge of the first turnpike of 1802–08. Telford's original bridge was built alongside it in the early nineteenth century and was subsequently widened in the twentieth century by a new arch on top of the original one

8 A well-preserved cast-iron direction post of the 1920s to the east of Kelso, complete with Roxburghshire County Council *annulus* and accurate black-and-white striped colour scheme. Even signposts can be assessed archaeologically; note how the numbering of the former 'A' road has been painted out because that road has been downgraded to a 'B' road instead

What is needed is a basic understanding of construction techniques to assess how the bridge or building, for example, was built. Then there is a need to understand the original form of the structure, its architecture and design. Finally, and most importantly, there is a need to understand its original function – whether it be a major engineering feat or a simple culvert – to assess how its original form was set out to perform that function, and how and why it has subsequently been changed. Much of this form of archaeology is common sense combined with objective observation.

Whilst these various types of archaeology may seem to be reasonably used on roads up until the turnpike era, it may seem to many people that the more recent past can safely rely on readily available documentary sources. After all, roads have generated swathes of generally reliable paperwork; even the Roman road builders were faced with a well-organised Imperial bureaucracy and whilst the amount of paperwork obviously decreased sharply in the so-called Dark Ages and only revived slowly in the later medieval period, it was certainly revived during the turnpike era and has continued to increase ever since. So why bother with archaeology at all for the past couple of centuries?

Surprisingly it is often the case that archaeological recording and analysis of even fairly recent road-related structures can shed light more accurately onto a past that had appeared to be well-documented. It was not always the case that the design of the engineer or architect was adhered to exactly in the field, and many other minor changes often occurred with no record at all. Records also have a habit of getting lost – and that is particularly pertinent when it comes to roads. As most of the records relating to them were either in the care of the local authorities or of the turnpike trusts, each reorganisation of the former and demise of the latter provided an opportunity for records to be thrown away or mislaid.

For example, on a small scale, few of the early records of Coalport Bridge, a less famous and slightly later neighbour downstream of the Iron Bridge across the Shropshire Severn, have survived and the bridge was clearly a very complex structure. It has only been through archaeological analysis that a better understanding has been achieved. The bridge is an intact structure of a main iron ribbed span between stone and brick abutments, dated 1818. An archaeological survey indicated that it has begun as a bridge of two timber trussed arches between stone abutments in 1780 which clearly had structural problems even before it was swept away in the Great Flood of 1795. It was rebuilt afterwards as a single span bridge with a wooden deck supported on iron ribs, and then, finally, rebuilt again in more or less its present form reusing some of the earlier ribs, some additional copies of them, and a cast-iron deck. There are traces of all of its phases in the masonry and in the ironwork, but only when the bridge was safely scaffolded in advance of recent repairs was a proper analysis possible.

On a larger scale, a recent pioneering study has been made of the whole of the Welsh section of Telford's early nineteenth-century Holyhead Road, from Chirk to Holyhead itself, under the auspices of CADW (Welsh Historic Monuments). This utilised the skills of a variety of experts and incorporated documentary research, archaeological study of the entire route, and a detailed analysis of the more complicated sections of engineering. It also involved understanding the relationship of the buildings along the route, the manner in which the road had been maintained and operated, and the fate of the road since it was first built. It clearly showed the benefit of using fairly straightforward non-destructive archaeological techniques in this way, and added a great deal to our knowledge of the road and the aspiration of its engineer and promoters. It also, incidentally, produced a very useful management tool for the future care of the historic elements along the route.

In the future, we cannot tell how latter day archaeologists will be confused by the road heritage, or how much of the paper records of today will survive. If it does not, there may be some confused archaeologists in the future trying to understand the odd logic of some of the most recent road schemes. Quite simply, not all of the expensively planned and expensively built parts of the modern road system have ever been used, and some parts have been radically changed in a very short space of time. A couple of examples will suffice to illustrate the point. Travellers starting out along the M1 from London may notice that the motorway starts on the North Circular Road at Junction 1 and then, in the short distance between Junctions 2 and 4, that there is no Junction 3. Junction 1 was meant to be the first junction on a motorway that should have started further south, in central London; that section was not built. In the original 1950s plan, a Junction 3 was planned to link up with the A1(T) but although started, was never finished. The impressive bridgework and slip roads were adapted for the service station – Scratchwood – built on much of the proposed site instead. In both cases, it was too late to renumber the other junctions – hence the oddities in the sequence.

Telford New Town, in Shropshire, was designed as a 'motorway' town on the M54. This runs across the northern edge of the town and dual carriageway 'primary roads' were planned to the west and east to link in with it. The Eastern Primary was started and finished in a slightly different form. Work also started on the earthworks of the Western Primary on either side of an expensively constructed triple-decker interchange with the M54. The junction, bridges, and earthworks were finished by the early 1980s but the road was never built. Instead, a much more convoluted single carriageway was built in the 1990s, ignoring the expensively built earthworks and meandering along this edge of Telford, joining the M54 at a roundabout; the original earthworks were remodelled and original junction works partly dismantled but mostly buried.

9 Ever-increasing vehicle sizes and numbers have placed much road transport heritage at risk. This photograph of around 1950 of a bus squeezing itself over the ancient 'New Bridge' across the Dart near Holne, on the eastern edge of Dartmoor, Devon, shows this is not a new phenomenon

Apart from some historic elements that have survived centuries of development – bridges, fords, inns etc. – much of the more visible road infrastructure that survives has been constructed in the last two centuries or so. Even in that time there have been dramatic and continual changes to the roads, their traffic and their infrastructure. Because of the sheer amount of material culture that does survive from the post-medieval period this book is, therefore, necessarily biased towards that period and some may feel that it is too biased to the very recent past – and in particular, to the twentieth century and the motor age. This may be true but no apology is felt necessary. Whilst the rarer ancient road-related monuments are usually protected by listing and conservation legislation, it is the more modern structures that are likely to disappear without record. Ever accelerating technological change brings about their premature obsolescence.

Whilst this is best illustrated by the fate of vehicles on the road – how many of the millions of Model 'T' Fords, Morris 1000s or Ford Cortinas survive? – it can also be seen in other aspects such as road signs and garages. The remains of the twentieth-century road infrastructure are in far more danger than those of the earlier past, a fact testified by the losses of several key sites in the past few years. Many losses are inevitable on a 'live' road network that needs to be constantly improved, and where the issues of safety should be paramount. Thus carriageways have to be constantly dug up and repaired, Roman road or not, and hard decisions have to be made about whether or not some structures can stand in the way of road widening. Others simply wear out and are beyond economic repair. Such was the fate of the Jackfield Free Bridge, a pioneering reinforced concrete bridge of 1909 crossing the River Severn in Shropshire.

Other losses are avoidable, but it often seems that, not only are the barbarians at the gate, they are inside and running things. The most controversial 'road loss' was the demolition of Thomas Wallis' Firestone Factory in 1980, pulled down by its new owners, Trafalgar House, just before it was to be listed. At least the loss of this fine art deco building, and particularly the way it was carried out, led to a public outcry and to changes in conservation legislation. Other potential losses have been less well trumpeted – the fate of Derby's fine 1920s bus station, still in the balance at the time of writing – being a case in point.

Those buildings were of a definite architectural quality, but most road transport related structures are not. Whilst their demolition is generally not to be mourned, it should at least be recorded for posterity. Car factories, for example, are seldom particularly attractive, although some are better than most. Even Coventry, a city that takes its motoring heritage seriously, and the home of the National Road Transport Museum, has recently seen the demolition of two important early twentieth-century sites – the Alvis factory and the Daimler office block. Whatever the reason for the loss of a building or structure, we owe it to posterity to at least record their passing. That 'preservation by record' needs to be to an appropriate level, and can range from a simple photograph and few lines to a complete archaeological analysis and detailed survey.

This is, then, a book of the archaeology of roads and their infrastructure – including both engineering and architecture. Because of the influence that roads have on so many aspects of society the scope is almost endless, as are the many different archaeological approaches that may need to be employed. This is, categorically, not a book on the history of roads. Instead, it is a book that concentrates on their archaeology – or, more accurately, on the archaeology of the road infrastructure. As such, it is a book that deals with the physical remains of roads and their associated structures. At the same time, it is, equally categorically, not a book on archaeological techniques. Given the many different techniques that can be used in studying the road infrastructure, such a book would have to be a comprehensive text book – which this is not.

Instead, this serves as a simple introduction to the various elements that make up the road infrastructure and could be the subject of archaeological and architectural study. In doing so, it also attempts to show that this infrastructure, whilst so varied, can also be seen as integral and interconnected parts of the continuous and ongoing development of road transport. Furthermore, it hopes to show the importance of understanding roads and their infrastructure holistically, rather than as individual and non-related elements.

CHAPTER 2

Outline history

The precursor of what we can safely call 'roads' are the countless numbers and types of prehistoric trackways and routeways, from short ones associated with transhumance to long-distance ones associated with hunting or trade. Whilst their existence and often their location is undoubted, they are generally impossible to date, especially as virtually none are 'structural' in any way that could be studied archaeologically. Their remains consist chiefly of holloways, often braided and intertwined. Given that the routes of many of the trackways were in use, continuously or not, for thousands of years, and that holloways are by their very nature erosive rather than additive, it is impossible to tell if they were first created 5,000 or 500 years ago.

The archaeological study of such trackways is, therefore, almost entirely the archaeology of association. The study of artefacts found in areas where they could not have originated helps to assess the degree of trade at a particular period in time and, if the origin of the artefacts can be identified, the existence of a route between the two becomes apparent and can be assessed in theory, if not in the field. Similarly, the relationship of prehistoric monuments and suggested trackways is also used to better understand the transport networks that must have existed to allow the construction of and continuous use of major sites such as Avebury or Stonehenge. From the available evidence, it is evident that long-distance and pan-European trade existed long before the Roman conquest of Britain.

However, archaeology by association can also be misleading. One of the greatest rethinks in our understanding of the prehistoric transport patterns has been the dismissal of the well-established theory that, because most of the prehistoric monuments and finds are related to upland and ridge routes, in contrast to the dearth of such monuments in the low lying areas, the main trackways were ridgeways high above supposedly hostile, well-wooded and

10 The prehistoric Ridgeway in Wiltshire, one of many such routes identified and once considered to be the main transport arteries of their day. Their present appearance (and width) bears no relationship at all to their original form. Recent archaeological study has shown that whilst they could be important routeways on the ridges, it is likely that lowland routes could be just as important, and we need to re-adjust our understanding of travel in this period

poorly drained areas. This idea was logically based on the careful analysis of the available archaeological evidence and cannot, as a result, be fairly criticised retrospectively.

There certainly were some important long-distance ridgeways and some sections were deliberately routed away from less favourable areas. However, modern archaeology has helped in reassessing the degree of archaeological survival within the lowland areas and shown that the monument and find scatters are far more evenly spread that previously thought. This in turn makes the existence of routeways along easy valley and lowland routes far more likely and a denser network of trackways than hitherto considered almost certain.

In addition, archaeology has demonstrated quite clearly that there was a flourishing and sophisticated society within Britain for at least 2,000 years prior to the Roman conquest. Any society capable of the construction of monuments such as Silbury Hill and Avebury in Wiltshire or the settlement of Skara Brae in Orkney would have been capable of road-related engineering should the need have arisen – and traces of the causewayed camps in parts of England and timber tracks in the Somerset Levels of the fourth century BC bear this out. The crucial factor was the need for such sophisticated engineering, given the transport requirements of the day.

All of the available evidence suggests that simple unsurfaced tracks sufficed for most long-distance travel. Certainly none of these would have come into the official and generally accepted modern archaeological meaning of what a 'road' is. The identified engineering was restricted to purely local use on paths and causeways linking homes and fields, or perhaps scattered islands in marshy areas.

The Roman roads are probably the most well-known and evocative of all British roads, and more books and articles have been written about them than on the roads of any other period. This is due in no small part to the fact that they can still be easily identified as monuments in the landscape or fossilised under modern main roads, and to the unquantifiable romantic visions that their remains can conjure up. They have attracted the attention of writers for centuries.

11 The West Kennet Avenue forms a 1.5-mile-long broad link between the Bronze Age stone circle of Avebury, Wiltshire, and 'The Sanctuary' on Overton Hill to the south. Considered to be associated with fertility rituals it was clearly a 'road' of sorts and demonstrates the ability to create such thoroughfares at the time, if they were needed

12 On the slope of Posterne Hill, just outside Marlborough, there are typical braided holloways that probably date back to the prehistoric period. They were formed by travellers finding the easiest ways up the hillside, wearing down a track in the process that was then acted upon by rainwater and further wear and tear. The young tree-cover over much of the hillside has begun to blur the overall impact of the holloways in the landscape

Geoffrey of Monmouth, as early as the twelfth century, thought that a mythical British king, Belinus, had ordered these great highways 'to be builded of stone and mortar that should cut through the entire length of the island'. By the turn of the twentieth century, the romance remained but a more academic approach to their study had developed – the two contrasting aspects admirably summed up by the poet and novelist Thomas Hardy:

> The Roman Road runs straight and bare
> As the pale parting-line in hair
> Across the heath. And thoughtful men
> Contrast its days of Now and Then
> And delve, and measure, and compare;
> Visioning on the vacant air
> Helmed legionaries, who proudly rear
> The Eagle, as they pace again
> The Roman Road.

Myths about Roman roads continue to abound despite being generally dismissed by modern archaeology. Roman roads were not built through a backward prehistoric land of primitive peoples, nor were they all built by the army in the early years of the Conquest, nor were they all arrow-straight without deviation whatever the terrain, and nor were they all beautifully paved with flagstones.

Roman road engineering was well established by the time of the Conquest in the mid-first century AD but, like so many other things, the basic concept of their road system was based on ideas formulated by earlier civilisations. The importance of good quality transport links to back up military operations, providing an umbilical link for supplies and to allow for unexpected reverses, had been recognised by the Persians. In the fourth century BC the Emperor Cyrus set up a special road building corps, made up of those not quite good enough for front-line fighting duties; instead, they had the perhaps more dangerous job of building or improving roads for the advancing army.

Although the British road network developed as a vital element in the transport infrastructure of the Roman colony, the initial roads were built to assist in its conquest. The first road would have been that from their main bridgehead at Richborough (*Rutupiae*) on the Kent coast heading westwards through the territories of the *Cantii* to London and a crossing over the Thames. This is now part of the Watling Street. Curiously, London (*Londinium*) was not the initial capital of the colony and there was no fort there; even though it subsequently formed the key hub of the developing road network, the main campaigns were directed from Colchester (*Camulodunum*), to the north-east in Essex, partly for political and tactical reasons.

From their southern base, three initial lines of advance have been identified and three arterial roads developed in their wake. These acquired their present names at a much later date. They were, in clockwise fashion, a campaign to the south-west to another Channel port at Chichester (*Noviomagus*) along what is now Stane Street, turning westwards along the coast with naval support as far as Exeter (*Isca Dumnoniorum*); a campaign to the north-west through the Midlands along what is now also called Watling Street, assumed to stop at a point on the much later Warwickshire/Leicestershire boundary called High Cross (*Venonae*), east of Hinckley; and a campaign to the north towards Lincoln (*Lindum*) on the route of what is now called Ermine Street.

Within a few years the whole of south-eastern England had been subdued and the Romans decided upon the establishment of a military zone along the border. In just the same way as they would later build a military road to the rear of their most famous border – Hadrian's Wall – a road was built along this one as well, though probably piecemeal rather than in one major campaign. This main road, later known as the Fosse Way, stretches in a long diagonal from the Devon coast in the south-west to the Humber estuary in the north-east. It is the only major Roman road that does not, ultimately, end in London.

As the campaign continued to conquer the rest of Britain, the road network was extended and, in the conquered areas, consolidated with more primary and secondary roads for mainly civilian use – and to assist in the exploitation of the British resources of food and minerals for the greater good of the Empire. As the impetus switched from military conquest and control to economic exploitation, the character of the new roads changed as well with less rigorous standards apparently employed and hundreds of miles of tracks and lanes, often reused pre-Roman ones, being incorporated into the expanding network.

At its peak, the Roman road network extended throughout what is now England, though roads in Cornwall and Devon seem to have been fairly few. There are roads in much of Wales and lowland Scotland; the system also penetrated beyond the Antonine Wall to the edge of the Scottish Highlands, in the Sidlaws to the north-east of Perth. A remarkable record, the *Antonine Itinerary* has survived which lists many of the main roads and towns in Britain. The total road mileage is not known, because most of the roads recorded to date have been the main ones, and thousands of miles of lesser roads and lanes await rediscovery.

So much has been written about Roman roads that it is worth only summarising the manner of their setting out in this section; aspects of their engineering are dealt with elsewhere in the book. The road planners appear not to have built a new system completely from scratch and almost certainly used some of the existing main trackways as a basis for their new roads. This was partly because of the already well-developed economic geography of their new colony and also because of the limited positions of fording sites and mountain passes.

Nevertheless, given the generally broad nature of such trackways, there was plenty of scope for realigning the much narrower constructed roads of the new order to Roman principles, and all of the completely new roads would, of course, have adhered to them as well. One of the new skills brought by the Romans, well established in the rest of the Empire, was that of surveying. Road surveyors were known as *gromatici* and their basic surveying instrument was the *groma* – a staff topped by four cross-arms at right-angles from the ends of which were hung plumb lines. This was a perfectly adequate tool for the setting out of the remarkably accurate and direct survey lines to which the Roman roads were built. The exact line between A and B was not necessarily built on for geographical reasons, but any diversions and secondary or tertiary surveying lines were based on that primary alignment.

Roman roads were generally built in straight sections, though such sections could vary from tens of metres to tens of miles; curves were unnecessarily complex to set out, and short consecutive lengths of straight lines could cope as well; nearly 1,000 years later, many Norman castle walls were built in the same manner. The fact that many of the changes of direction between straight sections of road occur near high ground has suggested that, logically, most of the survey points used were on high ground. Roman roads were generally designed for marching soldiers and pedestrians, so steep slopes were fairly normal; anyone walking up the Steep Hill in Lincoln towards the cathedral – part of the Roman Ermine Street – can testify to this.

Once the route had been decided on, the construction work could start. Initial work was undertaken by the military engineers, but later roads no doubt had civilian labour – willing or unwilling – as well. On some major roads, parallel marker ditches have been identified, fairly shallow and clearly not for drainage, to either side of the road line. These have been identified as being two main distances apart – 84ft (25.5m) and 62ft (20m) – and it has been suggested that they marked a 'road zone'. That could have been a legal boundary between the highway and the surrounding countryside and the two different widths could suggest different classification of roads. Because of their fairly small size, it is possible that many other sections of roads originally had such ditches but they have since been lost through ploughing.

Most roads were built on a raised embankment called the *agger*, and were well-drained and, if necessary, culverted with channels in stone or timber-lined. There were definite differences along the route in the build up of the agger and of the road surfaces on top of the agger, and there have been suggestions that these sometimes relate to different sections being built by different teams of military contractors. In many other cases, such differences relate to the available building materials, the varying ground conditions, and the terrain. Road widths vary tremendously, with the width of some known main road surfaces ranging from as little as 10ft (3.1m) to up to 30ft (9.2m). Aspects of road construction are dealt with elsewhere.

Once the roads were finished they were generally maintained by the civilian authorities and probably by taxes and forms of statute labour; even in Rome itself, the upkeep of the roads was, technically, the responsibility of those living in the houses alongside them. Archaeological excavations have shown that some roads went out of use fairly quickly, perhaps no longer needed for military purposes or because the civilian traffic expected by the road planners never materialised. In other cases, many layers of repairs have been encountered, resulting in the road surface being raised several feet above the original.

The end of the Roman road network was not sudden, and did not happen only after the final cutting of the Imperial ties in AD 410. There is evidence that some roads were already in decline before that time in the period of increasingly persistent raiding from overseas. When Romanised society finally began to break down, the maintenance of the road system inevitably suffered as well.

13 and *14* Roman roads were a key part of the conquest and control of Britain; even after the departure of the legions their often-tall *aggeres* dominated the landscape. Many roads are still in use either completely or, like Ermine Street, in sections. These two photographs of the road in Lincolnshire show a section now used by the busy B6403 near Ancaster and another that is just a track on Welbourn Heath – though its wide verges possibly indicate it was once used as a drove road

Traditional history used to be quite categorical in calling the troubled centuries between the departure of Roman rule and the later-Saxon revival the Dark Ages. The term was used to imply an uncivilised era of general barbarism and mass migration. The term is still apt, but this period is 'dark' not because of what was happening but because of our lack of understanding of it. However, modern archaeology is gradually shedding more light onto this important period.

For roads, as opposed to other aspects of the road transport infrastructure such as bridges or buildings, the archaeological evidence between the end of the Roman era and the beginnings of the turnpike at the end of the seventeenth century is very limited for just the same reasons as it is for the pre-Roman era. With little or no engineering required in road construction, there is no reliably directly related material culture to study. All of the archaeological evidence that can help in a better understanding of road transport during this period of a thousand years or so is yet more archaeology by association.

The amount of that evidence – through landscape study, settlement patterns, artefactual remains, historical analysis and documentary sources – increases massively in that period, but the specific dateable archaeological evidence for the roads themselves does not. Roads and tracks can be identified in the landscape that have evidently been in use for many centuries, and possibly in their time, had been extremely important. However, through archaeological study alone it is impossible to know when they were first used, for how long they were used, and when they were abandoned.

What does seem clear is the fairly sudden end to the cohesion of the Roman road network in England and Wales. Whilst Roman civilisation did not suddenly cease, the Romano-British society does appear to have fragmented due to the raiding parties or settlers of the various groups now lumped together under the term 'Saxons' – Angles and Saxons from northern Europe that affected most of southern Britain; the 'Picts' from Scotland that affected northern England; and the 'Scots' from Ireland affecting Wales and parts of north-western England.

As the province broke up into various regions and kingdoms of differing shapes and sizes, often fairly fluid in their boundaries and influence, there was no longer any need for a nationwide system of roads designed for an imperial power thousands of miles away. The great cities and towns that the roads had been built to link were now usually under the control of different groups, and later, of different kingdoms, and the post-Roman society was mainly agricultural, rather than mercantile, with no need of such towns. Instead, the transport requirements were met by paths and trackways between settlements and between settlements and their farms or pastures.

Most of the Roman towns were gradually abandoned, though work by the late Philip Barker at Wroxeter and others on settlements elsewhere has shown that, as usual, our given history can always be reassessed through archaeology. Nevertheless, apart from relatively short sections, most of the Roman roads appear to have fallen into partial or complete disuse; ironically the archaeological evidence for the deliberate blocking of the Ackling Dyke between Old Sarum and Dorchester is one of the best-known case studies for a definite abandonment of a Roman road, and that took place before the end of direct Roman rule.

They could, nevertheless, still serve an important purpose. Perhaps deliberately, most of the Dark Age and early Saxon villages and settlements were sited well away from Roman roads; it is noticeable that there were virtually no settlements in this period along the Fosse Way or the Watling Street, for example. It is possible that the roads were considered to be a threat, because they allowed rapid movement for potential aggressors. However, their prominent *aggeres* did make very useful and distinct boundary markers between the territories of the new settlements in their vicinity, and as these boundaries would often eventually become the basis of parish boundaries, it is perhaps not surprising that many miles of modern parish and county boundaries still follow the course of Roman roads – such as along most of the Watling Street in the English midlands.

By the later Saxon period there is documentary evidence for an improved road network to serve the needs of the emerging English state. In the later ninth century AD, Alfred, king of Wessex and accepted overlord of most of England not under Danish rule, set up 25 to 30 fortified towns, or *burhs*, at strategic places in his kingdom, all deliberately sited to be easily accessible by whatever means of transport was most suited – river or road. Some were linked in part by Roman roads and others by trackways. Later *burhs* were established by his descendants, particular Athelfleda, the 'Lady of the Mercians', as more of England reverted to native rule. Though evidence is fragmentary and occasionally confusing, roads of different degrees of importance were established to link these major towns and to be used for military purposes. At least four different types of roads have been identified. Two seem to have been primarily used for trade, whilst the other two seem to have had a military function.

A *port straet* or *port way* was a road linking the main markets, 'port' being an archaic word for a market town; the suffix *straet* could indicate that those roads were based on the surviving Roman lines. One of the most important commodities transported by road in the medieval period was salt. In England, this mainly came from two main producing areas, around Droitwich in Worcestershire and Nantwich in Cheshire. There are deeds relating to tolls for salt traffic from Droitwich surviving from as early as the tenth century implying a substantial trade; tolls were set at 1d per horse load and 1s per cart. At the time of the Domesday Survey in 1086, there were many salt pans and furnaces in these areas and they were clearly important centres for trackways by which the salt could be delivered. These *saltways* could be many miles long and are remembered in names such as Salterway, or Saltersford.

The two other types of roads mentioned in old charters of the period are the relatively common *herepaths* and the less common *cynges ferdstraets*. Herepaths – literally 'army paths' – appear to have been strategic roads for rapid movement of troops. Those that have been identified through the documentary evidence generally link not only towns, but also royal manors or ecclesiastical estates. They were presumably designed for the main armies of the king rather than for the local militia and the two *herefords* in modern Herefordshire – across the Wye in the county town and across the Teme at what is now Little Hereford – are associated with such a herepath. It seems likely that such roads had economical purposes as well, as would the lesser paths for local militias, the *cynges ferdstraets*.

Not being sources of income, roads or trackways are scarcely mentioned in medieval deeds, or even in the famous and comprehensive Domesday Survey drawn up in 1086. There are hints of transport, nevertheless, especially references to horses, in the late Saxon and early Norman period. A pack horse load was sometimes referred to as a *summa* (from the Latinised Greek word 'sagma', a saddle), and pack horses as *sumpter horses* from the same origin. The weight of these loads must have varied according to what they consisted of. A reference to a *summa* of salt in an entry in the Cheshire folio of the Domesday Survey unhelpfully states that each contained 15 *boilings*; fish, corn, malt and wheat are other commodities measured in this way. The term *rouncey* meant a cheap riding horse, and some manorial tenants had a duty of *avera* – carting the goods of their lords.

It is unclear who was responsible for road maintenance in the Saxon and medieval periods. It has been claimed that the upkeep of roads and bridges was one of elements of the *trinoda necessitas* required in land grants, and that manorial tenants were still responsible for their upkeep following the Norman Conquest in 1066. However, by the later medieval period the responsibility seems to have been taken on by the parish, certainly in England, and also occasionally by a local benefactor. In some circumstances, a monastic house would build or maintain roads, usually for their own benefit – to link outlying granges with the main house, for example.

After the Conquest, the Normans needed to control the often-rebellious Saxons in England and the even more recalcitrant Welsh princes, and must have relied on the road system for military purposes, but there is no evidence of deliberate planning or changes in their quality. There were, however, laws, including one decree of Henry I that stated that major highways should be wide enough for two wagons to pass in opposite directions and for sixteen knights to ride side by side. There were also punitive fines for obstructed such roads, up to the then massive amount of 100 shillings.

15 Bridges were the only significant pieces of civil engineering in the medieval period but show clearly what skills were then available, despite limited equipment. Bridges were also vulnerable to attack, and those associated with towns were often defended by gateways or towers. This is Warkworth Bridge in Northumberland, a late fourteenth century bridge over the Coquet with a gateway on the town bank

In the admittedly sparse relevant medieval literature up until the fifteenth century, there are few serious complaints about the condition of the country's roads. In 1066, the unfortunate Harold seems to have had no difficulty marching north to beat the Danes at Stamford Bridge and then rushing southwards again to defeat at the Battle of Hastings. In the late thirteenth century, Edward I only seems to have encountered difficulties in the tracks of north Wales, and in 1278 ordered the local magnate, Roger de Mortimer, to widen some of the key routes in advance of his military campaign. The English kings travelled constantly around their domain, complete with huge baggage trains and dozens of armed retainers but, with the unfortunate exception of the wagon train of treasure lost by King John in an ill-advised crossing of the Wash, these journeys seem to have been undertaken without any significant problems.

An early piece of legislation relating to roads occurs in the Statute of Winchester of 1285, in the reign of England's Edward I. As well as enshrining in law the right to trespass through neighbouring fields if a road was temporarily blocked, this also included a clause that, translated, stated that 'It is also commanded that highways from one market town to another market town shall be enlarged so that … there shall be no ditch, or tree, or bush where a man can lurk to do mischief within two hundred feet of either side of the highway'. If the local lord of the manor did not get the work done, and a murder or robbery was carried out, he would be liable to a fine; in addition, if his park boundary was close to the road, it had to be moved until it was at least 200ft (62m) from it.

This had nothing to do with the condition of the roads and gives few clues as to their traffic or their construction. It was simply an attempt to make the roads safe for travellers in often dangerous times. Brunetto Latti, the tutor of the Italian poet Dante, is said to have claimed, after travelling from London to Oxford at about this time, that the highways of England were infested with robbers – and that the local barons connived with them for a share of their booty.

Whilst there are some specific acts relating to individual bridges, such as an Act in the reign of Henry V in 1421 concerned with the repair of roads and bridges between Abingdon and Dorchester in Oxfordshire, the first surviving general Act related to the maintenance of the road infrastructure was the Statute of Bridges, passed in 1531. This simply stated that bridges were the responsibility of the county's Justices of the Peace if no one else could be proven to have liability.

During the medieval period, and well into the seventeenth century, there seems not to have been any consideration of the road as a structural or fixed entity. It was, instead, simply a linear zone for travelling along, a right of passage. Legally, it was 'a perpetual *right of passage* in the sovereign, for himself and his subjects, over another's land'. If the way, the 'beaten track', was blocked by an obstacle such as a tree or a bog, the traveller had the right to walk around it – even if that meant trespassing on adjacent properties and breaking down fences to do so. In 1610, Thomas Procter, in his pioneering book *Concerning the Mending of all the Highways*, complained of the 'great hurt and spoil of fences and grounds, with riding and going over the corn and such like, by shifting and seeking the best way'.

The often cited quote from the *Memoirs* of Colonel Birch relating to the way in which Sergeant Hoskins planned a coach trip in 1627 sums up the rights of travellers and the problems facing those farming along the road; he ordered his servants 'to study the coach-way; where to break hedges, and how to avoid deep and dangerous ways'. As such it was in the locals' best interests to try and keep the highways clear of obstructions to prevent damage to their crops. However, because of the poor condition of most roads, travellers inevitably did all they could to pick their way through by the best, or even merely a passable, route along the way. The width of the highway tended to become very wide indeed, especially on open heath land. Arthur Young remembered that in the early eighteenth century, carriages approaching Norwich could be a mile apart trying to find the best way.

Although wheeled chariots were used long before the Roman invasion of Britain, wheeled traffic on the roads was not that common until the latter part of the medieval period. The use of packhorses was far more widespread, and virtually the only way to transport goods overland in most of upland Britain – the Pennines and the south-west peninsular in England, most of Wales, and virtually all of Scotland. Variations of sleds and partly wheeled sleds were also used and wheeled wagons would have been very expensive to make and maintain in comparison to these other forms of transport. The importance of any form of water-borne travel – by sea or on navigable rivers – cannot be overlooked.

16 In most of Britain, long-distance road transport meant the use of packhorses, often dozens in a single 'train'. The packhorse remained important in many parts of Britain, particularly the upland areas, until well into the nineteenth century

There are references to wheeled carts (*carecta*), wagons (*chariota*) and coaches (*currus*) in medieval documents, usually those associated with the greater households. Most wheeled vehicles at that time seem to have been two-wheeled carts. Four-wheeled vehicles, sometimes referred to as *quadriga*, were less common. Coach travel was the reserve of the very wealthy, but in heavy, unsprung lumbering vehicles could hardly have been comfortable on the roads of the time despite the gold-cloth lined cushions in the coach used by Queen Isabella's ladies-in-waiting on a journey in 1311, or the fine tapestries and other hangings in Elizabeth de Burgh's coach in the 1350s. Even amongst the wealthy, coach travel was considered to be only fit for women; according to the mid-seventeenth century writer, John Aubrey, in the later sixteenth century it had still been 'held as a great disgrace for a young Cavalier to be seen riding in the street in a Coach, as it would now for such a one to be seen in the streetes in a Petticoate', but added 'So much in the fashion of the times nowe altered', implying that coach travel had become perfectly respectable by his time. That

17 Wagons only became common in the later-sixteenth century, and even then were mainly restricted to the lowland areas of Britain where the roads were capable of taking them. There was an ongoing debate over the width of the wheels of wagons and their impact on road surfaces until the 1820s; this loaded wagon has the wide wheels often dictated by decree – especially after the 1753 Wide Wheels Act

may have been in part due to Elizabeth I owning a coach, built by a Dutch coachman, in 1564. Shortly afterwards, John Stow had noted that great ladies 'made them coaches and rid them up and down the countries to the great admiration of all beholders'.

The growth of wheeled traffic, most of it in carts and wagons rather than coaches, was a direct result of the growth in trade in the sixteenth century. This certainly placed a greater strain on the road network and was one of the causes for what appears to have been a steep decline in the quality of British roads, which had probably been aggravated by the dissolution of the monasteries in the 1530s and the consequent loss of one of the few major organisations with the money and occasional will to maintain them.

Parochial responsibility over road maintenance in England and Wales was confirmed in the 1555 Statute for Mending Highways. The Act required the constables and churchwardens of each parish to call an annual meeting in Easter at which parishioners would elect a pair of unpaid people to act as 'surveyors and orderers'. They were to organise the necessary repairs and check on the state of all the roads and bridges in their area at least three times a year and to report to the Justices of the Peace.

Wealthier parishioners, those worth more than £50 a year and anyone owning a horse or a plough, had to provide the surveyors with a cart, horses or oxen to pull it, and two of their labourers. The poor had to work, unpaid, on the road repairs for four days a year or provide someone to do so in their place; this was later raised to six days a year in 1562. Anyone shirking his duty could be fined, and if the roads were not properly repaired, the parish could be 'indicted' and fined communally.

The system, theoretically, had some merit and worked up to a point. It did not, however, give any incentive to either the surveyors or the parishioners to actually carry out the work – other than the threat of fines. It also laid the onus of the repair of the roads firmly onto the parishioners, rather than the road users – although when these statutes were initially drawn up, that was not as unfair as it later became. The days set aside for road repairs tended to be treated as unofficial holidays and the surveyors either had to risk the wrath of their neighbours if they insisted on all of the chores being done, or the wrath of the Justices of the Peace if they did not.

According to William Harrison's *Description of Britain*, published in 1586, English roads through areas of 'claie or cledgie soile … are often verie deepe and troublesome in the winter halfe'. Despite the earlier edicts about clearing away the boundaries of the roads, their condition was made worse because 'trees and bushes growing by the streete sides, doo not a little keepe off the force of the sunne in summer for drieng up of the lanes'. Harrison also commented on the inefficiency of the parish system of maintenance and a recent trend to narrow the actual width of the rights of way – partly associated with the enclosure of the open field system in parts of England. He claimed that whereas 25 years earlier they had been generally around 50ft (15.5m) wide, that had since been reduced to anything between 12–26ft (3.7–8m), 'which is another cause also whereby the waies be the worse, and manie an honest man encombred in his iourneie'. This process, continued in subsequent centuries as more and more land was enclosed, also has much to do with the meandering course of so many of Britain's roads.

Economic changes led to increasing use of the roads throughout the seventeenth century as trade expanded and the first reliable road maps were produced by John Ogilby in 1675. This was accompanied by a small but significant rise in the numbers of wheeled vehicles, particularly for goods traffic. The net result was increased wear and tear on a medieval road system not really capable of dealing with it. With the increase in traffic, the statute labour system of parochial repair was shown to be totally inadequate and unfair in many areas.

In the remoter parishes where traffic was light, irregular infilling of pot-holes in the roads and the occasional clearance of roadside ditches could suffice to keep them in a reasonable condition and perfectly adequate for the local traffic. In contrast, where a major highway passed through a rural and fairly sparsely-populated parish, the amount of maintenance required to keep such a road in good condition was obviously much higher and became a significant burden on local resources.

In general, such parishes were understandably reluctant to do anymore than keep the main road in good enough repair for their own local use. They would naturally feel disinclined to improve a highway and then maintain it at a higher standard just for the benefit of those passing through the parish. As well as the different amounts of traffic, the character of the terrain and the nature of the geology would also have significant bearing on the relative costs of looking after roads – adding further problems for parishes in hilly terrain or where the soils were clayey and easily waterlogged.

Indulgences and tolls had been allowed to help fund the construction of bridges in the medieval period, but seldom for roads. There were a few exceptions; in Edward III's reign, a hermit called William Phelipe was apparently authorised to collect tolls in order to mend an ancient holloway from Highgate Hill to Smithfield, London. A few landowners had taken matters into their own hands as early as the medieval period and attempted to charge tolls as well. For example, in 1324 the Lady of Egrum was accused of charging people 'grievous ransoms and exactions' to use part of the King's highway in Nottinghamshire and an inquest was ordered.

Tolls to use roads in towns were more legally binding and tied up with other market tolls. An Act of Edward III in 1353 ordered the re-paving of the road between Temple Bar to Westminster; owners of houses on each side were ordered to pay for the footways on either side up to a ditch, whilst the main section of highway between the ditch was to be paid by a toll on all staple goods going to Westminster. A more general Act was passed in 1356 allowing the City of London to charge tolls to all goods brought into the city on vehicles or horseback to pay for the roads in the vicinity.

In 1663 an Act for Repairing the High-ways within the Counties of Hertford, Cambridge and Huntingdon was passed; it was a landmark piece of legislation, being the first to allow the collection of tolls from travellers – including 'horses, carts, coaches, waggons, droves and ganges of cattel' to pay for the upkeep of the road. One of the alternative main roads from London to York and Scotland passed through several rural parishes in these counties and the amount of traffic 'by reason of the great and many Loads which are weekly drawn in Waggons' had made it 'almost impassable, insomuch that it is become very dangerous to all His Majestie's Liege people that pass that way'.

The statute labour system alone was unable to repair or maintain the road and, with the tolls raised, the Justices of the Peace were allowed to appoint surveyors to repair the road using a mixture of statute and paid labour. Each county was allowed to collect tolls at a fixed point along the road, and these were to be at Wadesmill, Caxton and Stilton.

The success of this Act appears to have been mixed, and it was not until the end of the century that any other similar 'Justice Roads' were set up. However, part of the main road between London and Harwich in Essex and from Wymondham to Attleborough in Norfolk was 'tolled' following an Act of 1695; even so, when Celia Fiennes passed along the road to Wymondham in 1698, she complained that it 'was in many places full of holes, tho' it is secured by a barr at which passengers pay a penny a horse in order to the mending the way'. Just 13 such trusts were established in the half-century between 1663 and 1714, mainly financing repairs through loans guaranteed by projected income from the tolls.

A further major change came in another Act of 1706, passed to improve a section of the old Roman Watling Street between Stony Stratford in Buckinghamshire and Fornhill in Bedfordshire. This allowed the appointment of a trust of independent trustees that had powers to borrow money, appoint surveyors, and to levy tolls in order to maintain the road. It was the first of the proper 'turnpike trusts', and in the next half-century over 150 such trusts were established in England – although these were often fairly small and their distribution erratic.

Much depended on the interest shown in such matters by the local gentry and tradesmen and, of course, the road traffic itself. Many towns set up trusts in order to improve their links with the rest of the country, but where established forms of transport were adequate, little effort was made. For example, two similar towns in the western Midlands of England, Hereford and Shrewsbury, had very different attitudes in the early eighteenth century. By 1730 the Hereford Trust had nearly 120 miles of roads in its care, the longest route mileage of any. In contrast, only the main road from Shrewsbury to the south was turnpiked, and most heavy traffic went by the navigable River Severn.

The new type of road administration was seen by many as the sign of an improved future. Daniel Defoe, a noted traveller in the 1720s, wrote that the

18 Elegant carriages were the preserve of the very wealthy; others could use post-chaises (effectively hired carriages with the hired horses changed at inns or 'posts' along the way). This ink-wash drawing dates from the 1790s; note the depth of the river beneath the bridge; the ford is probably still in use

turnpikes 'are very great things, and very great things are done by them; and 'tis well worth recording, for the honour of the present age, that this work has been begun, and is in an extraordinary manner carry'd on, and perhaps may, in a great measure be completed within our memory'.

There was a rapid expansion of trusts in the second half of the eighteenth century, especially in the third quarter of the century when mortgages became a more common means of financing the necessary work; in that era of 'turnpike mania' around 500 new trusts were created in charge of around 15,000 miles of road. Trusts in this period were also established in much of Wales for the first time; several of these turnpiked roads – *ffordd fawr* – were completely new routes through the mountains. Thomas Pennant noted in 1776 in a steep pass in the Berwyns 'a fine road … then forming … one of the vast designs of the present age'. Lowland Scotland also saw several turnpike trusts established, but the Highlands continued to rely on native tracks and, in a limited way, to a very rare example of government intervention in the road network – the military roads begun by General Wade in between the two Jacobite risings of 1715 and 1745.

Those roads were designed and constructed on the same principles as the Roman roads had been in the latter part of the first century AD, and for most of the same reasons. The roads in Scotland were poor; statute labour had been introduced in an Act of 1669 similar to that in England and Wales and was as ineffective, though there had been some improvements after the unpopular Act of Union of 1707. As late as 1740 it was claimed that there was not a single road in Aberdeenshire – one of the more prosperous counties – capable of taking wheeled traffic. There were no roads in the Highlands at all, apart from near to the main towns; instead there were just the broad drove roads, for cattle, and narrow tracks through the mountains for pedestrians and horses. Wade's assistant, Edward Burt, wrote that 'the old ways consisted chiefly of stony Moors, Bogs, rugged, rapid Fords, Declivities of Hills, entangling woods and giddy Precipices'.

General George Wade had been sent to the Highlands in 1724 as Commander of the Hanoverian forces and reported on the tactical situation in that still volatile area. He concluded that 'The Highlands of Scotland are still more impracticable from the want of Roads, Bridges and from excessive Rains that almost continually fall in these parts …'. He was concerned that, whilst the local rebels could always find their way through mountain passes and paths, his regular troops could not. The upshot was the creation of a network of new military roads linking the main Crown forts in the Highlands, and on a few other strategic routes. These were built not for the economic benefit of the local population, but for their subjugation by the military – precisely the same reasons that the first Roman roads had been built in Britain nearly 1,700 years beforehand. The

19 The fine bridge across the Tay in Aberfeldy was designed by the architect William Adam and opened in 1733. Its grandeur was symbolic, as it was the culmination of the first phase of military roads in the Scottish Highlands built under the direction of General Wade to subdue the rebellious clans – the first act of deliberate road planning on such a scale since the Roman conquest

parallel was taken further because these new roads were built by the military as well and were a mixture of old routes taken over and improved, and completely new ones.

It is not clear to what extent Wade actually designed the roads, but his name has continued to be associated with them even though he was only directly responsible for the first 250 miles (400km) or so that were completed before he left Scotland in 1737. Most of the remaining 1,200 miles (1,900km) or so of roads were built by his chief surveyor, Major William Caulfield, who was in post until his death in 1767. They were the first roads to be built and maintained by central government since the Roman period. Ironically, the roads ready by the time of the 1745 rebellion proved very useful for the young pretender's rebel forces and gave them an initial tactical advantage over the depleted and ill-led Hanoverians.

Whilst they lacked the quality, both in their choice of route and engineering, of their Roman predecessors, these military roads were still far better than any other roads in Scotland – or in much of the rest of Britain – at the time. Thomas Pennant travelled through the Scottish Highlands in 1769 and wrote that he left Fort William 'and proceeded south along the military road … The roads are excellent; but from Fort-William to Kinloch-Leven, very injudiciously planned, often carried far about, and often so steep as to be scarce surmountable; whereas had the engineer followed the track used by the inhabitants those inconveniences would have been avoided'. Whilst some of the routes became the basis for later roads, many other sections, their original purpose no longer being relevant, have been abandoned just as their Roman antecedents were.

The military roads were built by the government for military reasons. Another major change in roads and lanes was the result of government legislation and the power of the wealthy local landowners. This was a direct result of massive social and economic change in the countryside brought about by the enclosure of the traditional commons and communally-farmed open fields. That process had begun long before the turnpike era but the amount of land enclosed increased dramatically between the late eighteenth and early nineteenth centuries – and not just in the more fertile areas; large tracts of uplands were also parcelled up with new walls and hedgerows.

The result of enclosures was often to make many of the well-established roads and paths redundant, and new ones needed to be created as part of the new pattern of individually owned fields. As these were seldom major highways, they were of no interest to the turnpike trusts and their maintenance fell, instead, onto the parish. These roads can usually be distinguished from the older and often winding lanes by the fact that they were laid out as part of a regular pattern reflecting the logical division of the land. Many have wide verges, sometimes to allow easy movement of stock, and long straight sections with occasional sharp bends. A large percentage of country lanes date to the enclosures, though many enclosure lanes have never been important enough or sufficiently well used to ever be properly surfaced and remain 'green roads'.

In Britain, there were additional minor 'manias' of turnpike road construction before and after the Napoleonic Wars but even by the late 1830s when the last of the turnpike trusts were formed, their total mileage, around 22,000 miles in all, was only about 17 percent of the total of 'proper' roads – excluding tracks and paths and other lesser by-ways. There were then over a thousand separate trusts and nearly 8,000 toll gates; non-turnpiked roads remained under parochial control. The percentage of turnpiked roads varied from county to county; in the early nineteenth century about a third of the roads in Middlesex were turnpiked, compared to about a tenth in neighbouring Essex. One of the more annoying aspects of the turnpike legislation was the fact the trusts could still call on the parishes for statute labour, which made this even more unpopular than it had been before.

In general, the turnpike trusts were set up for a limited period, usually of 21 years, with the idea that in that term the road would be brought up to a sufficient standard to be given back to the parishes. This seldom happened, even where a trust was efficient. Increasing traffic led to increasing wear and tear, and, in most cases, the trusts were under-financed and struggled. As a result, at the end of each term, their Act was usually renewed.

Most trusts were quite small, seldom with more than 25 miles or so under their control and generally far less. Inevitably, this led to a fragmented network of roads and to dramatic differences along the same main highway, depending on the efficiency and aspirations of the adjacent trusts along the route. A slightly different approach was undertaken in mid and south Wales where seven county trusts were set up to look after all of the main roads with their boundaries, the first being set up in Monmouthshire in 1755, the last in Cardiganshire 15 years later. In many ways these were the precursors of the county council control of a century later.

One of the hoped for improvements in the turnpiked trusts was a better, and more enthusiastic, surveyor in charge of the works instead of the reluctant unpaid appointee of the parish system. Sadly, this was seldom the case. In his *Treatise on Roads* of 1838, Sir Henry Parnell accurately noted that 'The business of road-making in this country has been confined almost entirely to the management of individuals wholly ignorant of the scientific principles on which it depends'. He was being diplomatic. In evidence to a Select Committee on highways in 1819, James MacAdam, John Loudon MacAdam's son and a surveyor himself, gave evidence that he knew other surveyors whose professions included an underwriter, a baker, a publican and a coal merchant. Several were infirm old men and one was bedridden and had not been out of his house for months.

This combination of disparate trusts and unqualified surveyors of different abilities are the main reasons for the very different comments by travellers in the eighteenth century on the quality of the turnpiked roads. For some, they appeared to be extremely good. A correspondent of the *Gentleman's Magazine* in 1792 claimed that 'The great improvements which, within the memory of man, have been made in the turnpike roads throughout this kingdom, would be incredible did we not actually percieve them …'. Another, in 1798, claimed that 'The public roads in England, though they occupy much of our chit chat and some of our abuse, are the admiration of foreigners'.

Indeed, several foreign visitors did seem to be impressed. Travelling in January 1776, the American Quaker Jabez Fisher was impressed by the way in which hundreds of people had cleared the snow from the turnpike between Bath and Bristol, and even more impressed the following day when he managed to travel the 108 miles to London in a day. Charles Moritz, the German, wrote in 1782 that 'The roads … are incomparable; I am astonished how they got them so firm and solid …'.

In contrast, the roads had virulent critics, like Arthur Young, who published his accounts of various *Tours* through Britain. Overall, most of the turnpiked roads on which he travelled he considered to be good, but a sizeable minority were not. In 1771 he wrote how he took the turnpike road from Newport Pagnel to Bedford, 'if I may venture to call such a cursed string of hills and holes by the name of *road*'; approaching Wigan, he did not have 'in the whole range of language, terms sufficiently expressive to describe this infernal road' with ruts up to 4ft deep; in general, he concluded that, as for the north of England, 'Until better management is produced, I would advise all travellers to consider this country as sea, and as soon think of driving into the ocean as venturing into such detestable roads'.

Nevertheless, it is certain that the road system was far better at the end of the eigtheenth century than it had been at the start, and that the economic well-being of the country had benefited greatly. The improvement of the road system is often overlooked in the appreciation of those elements needed to be in place to allow the so-called 'Industrial Revolution' of that century to take place. It is also, nevertheless, quite clear that the road system could have been far better if the finances had been available to match the engineering skills of the time. This is evident in the quality of those few roads built under government patronage, where funding was not an issue. Telford's early nineteenth-century works in Scotland and, more obviously, his rebuilding of the Holyhead Road through the difficult terrain of north Wales, show what could be done with adequate resources and contrasts with the piecemeal and cost-cutting enterprises of the small and generally under-funded private trusts.

The new or improved roads coped reasonably well with the increases in traffic and, to an extent, were direct reasons for that increase. Speed of travel also increased. Without the development of the turnpike system it would have been very difficult for the fast mail and stagecoaches to have succeeded from the late eighteenth century onwards. Stagecoaches had been introduced in the 1630s but were slow and lumbering and the roads totally unsuited to them.

By the Regency period – the brief golden age of coaching – journeys that had taken days now took hours and it was possible to travel from most of the main towns of England, south of York and east of Exeter, to London in less than a day and a half. The *Tallyho* coach between London and Birmingham averaged speeds of 15mph. As a general rule, the average journey time on the main roads was probably halved between 1770 and 1820. In 1754 the time taken to travel from Edinburgh to London was advertised as '10 days in summer; 12 days in winter', but by the 1830s could take just 42.5 hours.

Up until the start of the nineteenth century, most of the improvements to the road network had been due simply to better maintenance of the roads and better

20 A typical mid-eighteenth century scene (though one drawn up a century or so later) showing a coach passing through a toll-gate and the Bell Inn at Kilburn, then on the Watling Street well outside the boundaries of London

designs of road vehicles. Little innovation had been shown in the construction of the roads, or in greatly expanding the road network. A few new roads were built, but these were usually diversions from an original route to avoid a particularly steep hill or sharp bend or to produce a more even gradient. Few towns were then suitably busy enough to warrant a bypass, although in 1756 the New Road from Paddington to Islington and on into central London was a turnpike deliberately built to bypass congestion in Holborn.

Such new stretches were generally well engineered to take the easier and straighter routes, but occasionally they could be built through more difficult terrain if that meant a useful shortening of the distance. Thus, George Borrow, in his meanderings through Wales in 1854, regretted the choice he made when he took the old road - the *hen ffordd* - rather than the new turnpike – the *ffordd newydd* – by the toll gate just outside Ruthin; he realised later that he missed out on the new winding road through Nant Garth, one of the most scenic passes in the country.

Most turnpike trusts took on the main highways likely to be reasonably profitable and simply improved them. In this respect, the turnpike roads were very different to the canals being built in the later eighteenth century and the railways in the mid-nineteenth century. Similarly, no real effort was made to improve the quality of roads to such an extent that larger vehicles could travel on them at higher speeds. Instead, most of the toll arrangements and, indeed, government legislation in the eighteenth and nineteenth centuries, were directed at protecting the roads from their traffic, rather than making the roads serve the aspirations of that traffic.

One of the more obvious examples of this related to the issue of wheels. Contemporary road surveyors considered that narrow wheels cut into and damaged the road surface, especially when fitted to heavily laden wagons. For waggoners, narrow wheels coped better with the rough and rutted road surfaces and took less out of their horses. Instead of trying to produce a better road surface, laws were passed to limit the weight of wagons and to govern the width of their wheels. As early as 1662 there had been a law to ban wheels less than 4 inches wide, but it was ignored and effectively repealed. Then came an Act of 1753 to 'prevent the roads of the kingdom being ruined by the excessive weights and burdens loaded in and carried on wheeled transport with the small breadth and dimensions of the fellies of such waggons ...'. It stated that wheels on goods wagons had to be no less than 9 inches (23cm) wide.

This clearly did not work either and two years later, a follow up Act allowed wagons with 9 inch (23cm) wide wheels to be exempt from tolls for three years and permitted differential charges for wagons with different width wheels. As late as 1822 another Act banned all wagons with wheels less than 3 inches wide from turnpikes, but was quickly repealed because of the public hostility to it. There were also restrictions and excessive tolls on the common practice –again due to the condition of the roads – of adding studs to the wheel rims. This practice dated back to the medieval period; a cart with a studded iron tyre is shown on the early fourteenth-century Luttrell Psalter. Further restrictions were also made on the number of horses and on the weight of wagon loads in various measures throughout the heyday of the turnpikes.

Most turnpike trusts, then, charged wagons not only on their mileage but also on their weight and on the width of their wheels and numbers of horses or oxen. In one of the later turnpike acts, in 1835, the tolls for roads in Shropshire and mid-Wales included different charges for different width of wheels and were based on the number of horses pulling wagons or coaches. For wagons with wheels wider than 6 inches, the toll was 4d per horse; between 4.5 and 6 inches (11.5–15cm) that rose to 6d, and less than 4.5 inches, to 8d. In a foretaste of what was to come 'every Carriage moved or propelled or set or kept in Motion by

Steam or Machinery, or by any other Power or Agency than Animal Power', was charged at 2s 6d per wheel. By that time, the technique of surfacing the roads had recently been dramatically improved by the work of Telford and MacAdam – the less expensive system of the latter being by far the most commonly employed. This aspect is discussed elsewhere in the book.

Perhaps inevitably, although the turnpikes could improve matters for the rich traveller who could easily afford the tolls, the poor found it difficult to pay – or to find alternate routes around – the turnpikes. The very fact that tolls could be charged on ancient rights of way angered large numbers of both rich and poor. John Wesley, the founder of Methodism, spent most of his life travelling in the eighteenth century, and in 1770 wrote of 'the vile imposition of the turnpikes' on the poor. There was surprisingly little violence against the turnpikes, but there were two periods, virtually a century apart, in which they were subject to attack.

Riots in Somerset during the summer of 1749 led to the destruction of several toll-houses and gates, and in 1753 two or three members of a mob attacking toll gates around Leeds were shot dead. Between 1839 and 1844 there were more riots, mainly in south and central Wales, largely because of tolls charged on wagons carrying lime to improve fields and pasture. The first was at the Efailwen tollgate on the border between Carmarthenshire and Pembrokeshire in 1839, and there was then a gap until the gate at St Clears not far away was wrecked in 1842.

The attacks then multiplied. Gangs of men dressed up as 'the daughters of Rebecca'; this was a pun on a passage in the Book of Genesis in the Old Testament – 'the seed of Rebecca shall possess the gates of her enemies'. The 'daughters' terrorised toll-keepers, breaking down the gates and attacking toll-houses but usually did not physically attack anyone. They seem to have enjoyed widespread support from most sections of society, as many of their grievances were well-founded. However, many personal grudges seem to have been settled as well; the violence increased and the authorities over-reacted. Eventually, a newly appointed 75-year-old toll-keeper, Sarah Williams, was shot dead as her toll-house at Hendy, near Llanelli, was burnt down in 1843. The riots fizzled out, partly naturally, partly because of the introduction of troops to back the local magistrates, but mainly because of the Turnpikes (South Wales) Act of 1844 that finally addressed many of the issues regarding the tolls.

By this time the canals had taken much of the traffic off the roads, and the railways were being extended quite dramatically through most of Britain. A 'railway mania' seemed to be out of control in the 1840s, with investors eager to cash in on this new form of transport. Initially, there was scepticism from those involved in road transport, and then downright hostility – especially from those with most to lose, such as the stagecoach proprietors, the owners of coaching inns, and the waggoners. Inevitably, economic necessity did lead to some co-operation; until lines were extended, stagecoaches were re-routed to link up with the railways. This was particularly so in mid-Wales for example, where stagecoaches linked up with the railway junction at Shrewsbury until a second 'railway mania' led to a new batch of lines in the region in the early 1860s.

The battle between road and rail for the mid- and long-distance travellers and goods carriages was very short. The new railways provided a far cheaper and far faster and far more reliable service than even the best of the turnpikes ever could and soon spread across the country. Even the most remote parts of Scotland or Wales eventually had a railway within reasonable reach, and soon goods and people could be transported from one end of the country to the other in a day.

Although the turnpikes had benefited briefly from traffic generated during the construction of the railways, many soon became little more than feeders to the new lines and served purely local traffic. In one sense, the greater highways suffered most from the loss of their coaches and long-distance wagons. Walking through Anglesey in 1853, George Borrow found that 'the road was a melancholy one; my footsteps sounded hollow upon it. I seemed to be its only traveller'. Yet he was on Telford's great Holyhead Road, finished, at huge government expense, barely a generation earlier; it had been effectively ruined by the completion of the Chester and Holyhead Railway in 1850 and in the following year, passed into local authority care.

The sudden and dramatic drop in long-distance traffic on the roads led to huge problems for the many coaching inns along the main routes. Not only did travellers no longer stay at their premises, there was little or no call for 'posting', so that changes of horses were no longer needed and their stables became virtually redundant. Many inns closed as a result.

The effect on the turnpike trusts was predictably as bad. The rapid fall in toll revenue had a catastrophic effect on them. Most had been poorly funded when they were set up and much of their outgoings were to service their initial loans and mortgages. Trusts began to cut back on maintenance; suggestions were often made to narrow the carriageways and to use less expensive materials. Their financial plight meant that it became difficult to get anyone to bid for the 'farmed out' tolls and few trusts were anxious to renew their Acts when they expired.

As a result, turnpiked roads reverted mainly to parish control and the tolls were removed – though at least the surveyors had been paid since the Highways Act of 1835. Larger parishes could appoint highway boards instead and less populated parishes combine to form districts and appoint district surveyors. Various other new organisations were also created including 'Highways Districts' in 1862 and even Sanitary Authorities, either Rural or Urban, in 1872 and 1875. Counties got involved through the Justices of the Peace in 1878 and in 1888 the Local

Government Act placed main roads in the care of the new County Councils. In 1894 lesser roads were passed to the care of the new Rural District Councils and in 1895 the last of the turnpike toll gates closed – on the best road of that era, Telford's Holyhead Road at Gwalchmai on Anglesey.

Towards the end of the nineteenth century, a new and unexpected pressure for road improvement had also emerged. This was not from the proprietors of traction engines, or from the drivers of the pioneering motor cars, but from the growing numbers of cyclists. Although it is highly likely that carriage makers and others had experimented with two- or three-wheeled pedal toys of different types long beforehand, the true ancestor of the modern bicycle was probably the Comte de Sivrac's *Célérifère* first demonstrated in the grounds of the Palais Royal in Paris in 1791. This was a simple 'horse' consisting of a wooden frame with wheels at either end; the rider sat on a padded seat and propelled the machine along with his legs. As the wheels were in fixed axles, the only way to turn was to lean and the only way to stop was to dig the heels in. In the troubled times of the day in France the *célérifère* was a short-lived experimental toy that a change of name in 1793 to the *vélocifère* failed to revive.

After Europe was again at peace after the Napoleonic Wars, the idea was not only revived but dramatically improved by another minor aristocrat, the Baron von Drais de Sauerbrun of Mannheim – Master of Woods and Forests for the Duke of Baden. His simple alteration was to make the front wheel of the machine able to turn and steer the machine and in 1817 he was using his *draisienne* for his work in fairly hilly country where such roads as did exist were of poor quality. The machine caught on in much of Europe, including Britain, where it was known as the 'hobby horse' or 'dandy horse'; hundreds were made in England for the fashionable bucks of Regency society, and even three-wheeled versions were produced. It was never a particularly practical mode of transport and the craze eventually died down. Nevertheless, the idea of the bicycle had been demonstrated and its potential was realised by several people who experimented with improvements of differing, but mainly limited, success.

The first major innovation that was needed to make these machines a success was to provide some more efficient means of propulsion. Various forms of cranks were tried acting on the front or rear wheel and a Scot, Kirkpatrick Macmillan, devised a crank and treadle system at the end of the 1830s that had all of the principal elements of a rear-wheel driven bicycle, but little came of his work. Instead, the next major innovation in bicycle technology to be developed was the use of pedals and cranks to drive the front wheel directly. Whilst there are several competing claims for inventing this, the men that made it both workable and popular were Pierre Michaux, a Parisian already turning out and repairing old 'hobby horses', who thought of the idea, and his son, Ernest, who converted an old *vélocifère*. It was an instant success and the first useful bicycle – the *vélocipede* – had been made.

So successful was the idea that there was insufficient capacity to make enough for the huge demand in France, especially after the Michaux firm had exhibited their wares at the great Paris Exhibition of 1867. Also exhibiting at the show was Rowley Turner, a representative of the Coventry Sewing Machine Company, and he later took one of the *vélocipedes* back to his company and persuaded them to make them for the French market. By a stroke of luck for the Coventry firm, but disaster for the French, the outbreak of the Franco-Prussian War in 1870 and the subsequent rapid victory of the Prussians, led to dire problems for French industry.

The newly formed Coventry Machinists Company found a steadily growing home market for their new machines, nicknamed 'boneshakers'. Propagandists

21 Cycling became very popular in the 1880s, as this scene of 1888 shows; this is Ightham, Kent, well within reach of London by bicycle if the roads were up to it. The cycling lobby was an important element in road improvements prior to the development of the motor vehicle. Note the variety of machines on view

of the new machines urged the public not to treat it as a toy but, as written in Charles Spenser's 1870 manual, *The Bicycle: Its Use and Action*, 'to use it as a vehicle, as an ordinary means of transit from one place to another, over roads rougher or smoother as the case may be'. At that time, the roads were generally rougher rather than smoother. The 'boneshakers' evolved into faster and faster machines, and new innovations, including metal spoked wheels, ball-bearings, primitive springs, better saddles and solid rubber tyres all improved matters. Without gearing, the only way that this was achieved was to make the front wheel taller and taller until, by the mid-1870s, the iconic 'penny-farthing' had evolved. Also known as the 'high bicycle' or, more commonly and in retrospect bizarrely, as the 'Ordinary', its front wheels were several times the diameter of the diminutive rear wheel. Tricycle versions and quadricycle versions were also built and cycling continued to be popular amongst those that could afford it and had the time to do so.

The last major evolution in bicycle design was the modern safety bicycle. The first successful use of a pedal powered chain drive to the rear wheel of a bicycle was that developed by H.J. Lawson of the Tangent Bicycle Company in 1880. This still had different sized wheels. Then J.K. Starley produced several different versions of the same basic design, the first two with larger front wheels and then the third, in the late 1880s, with front and back wheels of the same diameter and a different type of 'diamond' frame. Apart from the lack of pneumatic tyres, which were not perfected until J.B. Dunlop patented them in 1898, Starley's 'Rover' bicycle is little different in its basics than those that would be built for the next century.

In the 1890s, the use of bicycles increased dramatically and for a while was a fashion for the aristocracy and wealthier classes. By the start of the twentieth century the working classes were gradually becoming able to afford the cheaper or second-hand machines leading to a very marked change in their general way of life and, especially, recreation. H.G. Wells was a keen cyclist and bicycles play important roles in some of his novels. The hero in *Wheels of Chance* probably echoed in retrospect the author's own delights on cycling on the roads when 'there were no automobiles and the cyclist had the lordliness, a sense of masterful adventure, that has gone from him altogether now'.

With the bicycle a serious means of transport in the last two decades of the nineteenth century, the only problem that faced them was the state of the roads. This varied enormously, with some sections well kept and others decidedly poor. In 1898 parts of the Great North Road in Lincolnshire was stony and had grass growing in the carriageway. Such was the influence of the cycling lobby that local authorities began to seriously consider the state of their roads and slowly began to improve them.

22 The bicycle also offered a sense of freedom of movement not previously enjoyed by most sections of society. It became seen as perfectly respectable for ladies having been taken up by High Society briefly in the 1890s. This middle-class lady is showing off her safety bicycle in about 1900. As second-hand cycles became available along with mass-produced machines, the working classes could afford them in the early twentieth century as well

The end of the nineteenth century, as the railways met their zenith, also saw the development of a new form of technology that would ultimately lead to a very radical change not only to road transport but to civilisation itself – the internal combustion engine. Its impact on the roads, as well as virtually all other aspects of civilisation, has been far more dramatic than most of the handful of early pioneer motorists could have ever thought in the early 1890s.

Self-propelled road vehicles have a long history, dating back to at least the eighteenth century. Sir Isaac Newtown had toyed with the idea of a steam carriage, but the first recognised vehicle to be built was by the French engineer Nicholas Cugnot. In the late 1760s he developed a rather cumbersome steam-powered tricycle gun 'drag' capable of just 2mph with barely a quarter of an hour's endurance but it, and further French experiments a little later, came to nothing.

In Britain, the development of steam-powered vehicles was partly discouraged by the state of the roads and available technology and partly by the mischievousness of one of the great pioneers of steam technology – James Watt. Although never seriously contemplating developing a steam carriage, he deliberately patented inventions that could enable such development to prevent others from doing so. He and his business partner, Mathew Boulton, discouraged the promising experiments of their faithful business associate and valued engine erector, the much underrated William Murdoch. He built a working model of a self-propelled steam-powered tricycle in about 1794 but was dissuaded by Boulton and Watt from producing a roadworthy full-sized version.

Whilst there were a few other attempts, it was left to the Cornish engineer Richard Trevithick to test a full-sized high-pressure steam-powered vehicle on Christmas Eve 1801, travelling, with eight brave souls on board, up Camborne Beacon. A slightly more sophisticated version was demonstrated in London in the following year, capable of 10 mph; like most of that engineer's unfortunate schemes, this did not lead to financial success, mainly because of a lack of investment and being ahead of his time.

In the 1820s there was a brief upsurge in experiments with steam-powered road vehicles, some of which were quite bizarre – including ones by David Gordon in which steam powered, through a series of cranks, three moving 'feet' on each side instead of wheels. Further advances were made largely due to the enthusiasm of a London-based but Cornish-born doctor who had seen some of Trevithick's work in his childhood, the elegantly named Goldsworthy Gurney, and of Walter Hancock.

Gurney later invented the freestanding 'Gurney stoves' that heated the churches and cathedrals of Victorian Britain. He originally toyed with the idea of a carriage 'on legs', then built a wheeled steam-powered coach which made a relatively successful *début* on a trip between London and Bath in the summer of

1829 and, finally, a smaller steam-powered 'tug' or 'drag' to pull a separate coach. On the 21 February 1831, Sir Charles Dance began a regular steam-powered coach service between Cheltenham and Gloucester using three Gurney 'drags' and specially built 16-seat 'omnibus' trailers. It ran until the 22 June, fairly successfully, but maintenance costs, increased tolls and deliberate obstruction by the turnpike company put an end to it.

Walter Hancock designed steam carriages for work in and around London and also ventured on several incident-packed trips to Brighton. A London & Brighton Steam Carriage Company came to nothing, but the London & Paddington Steam Carriage Company used Hancock's coach, *Enterprise*, for a short-lived regular service between Paddington and the Bank. Other Hancock carriages working in the 1830s included the *Automaton*, *Era* and the rather uncomfortably named *Autopsy*. He also built a four-seater *phaeton*, for his own private use. Despite their good safety record and relative reliability, various financial problems dogged the ventures and none succeeded.

A similar lack of success was enjoyed by the Steam Carriage Company of Scotland which, for a seven-month period in 1834, used steam carriages designed

23 Road locomotion had a long history before the first motor vehicles appeared. This is Thomas Hancock's steam coach, the *Era*, of 1833 which, temporarily named the *Erin* was demonstrated in Dublin and, on her return, was used on more demonstration trips in England and on a short-lived commercial service in London

by John Scott Russell between Glasgow and Paisley. This service had a tragic end when one of the carriages hit a pile of stones, allegedly placed deliberately on the road by the turnpike trust; a wheel broke and the boiler exploded, killing five people in the first fatal motoring accident on British roads.

Mechanical issues aside, these pioneers of steam carriages were defeated by two main things. The first was the hostility of the turnpike trusts. Though some impartial observers saw no problems with them, the clerk to the Middlesex & Essex Trusts complained that Hancock's vehicles 'frighten the horses to such an extent that I have often been requested to interfere …'. Other Trusts complained about the wear and tear on their roads. Some Trusts raised tolls for steam carriages to such an extent that they became uneconomic to run; for example, between Liverpool and Prescot in Lancashire, the toll for a coach-and-four was 4s whilst a 'steamer' was charged £2 8s. Even on some isolated mid-Wales turnpikes in the 1830s, when carriages were charged 4d per each horse, 'every Carriage moved or propelled or set or kept in Motion by Steam or Machinery, or by any other Power or Agency than Animal Power' was charged at 2s 6d per wheel.

The whole issue was then investigated by a Select Committee of the House of Commons in 1831. Accepting the view that steam carriages were certainly heavier than normal horse-drawn traffic, the Committee took the view that 'as they admit of greater breadth of tyre than other carriages, and as the roads are not acted on so injuriously as by the feet of horses … such carriages will cause less wear of roads than coaches drawn by horses.' Criticising the exorbitant charges made by the Trusts, and recommending restrictions on such tolls, the Committee concluded that steam-carriages were safe, did not cause a public nuisance, and 'that the substitution of inanimate for animal power … on common roads, is one of the most important improvements in the means of internal communication ever introduced'. Nevertheless, no legislation resulted from the Committee's findings and the high tolls remained,

The second main problem facing the development of the steam carriage was the very success of steam power on the rapidly developing railway system. That expanded dramatically from the 1830s onwards. With a highly efficient national railway network in place, the steam carriage on the road, like the stagecoach it had never managed to supplant, became effectively obsolete.

The use of steam power for virtually everything is almost symbolic of the Victorian Age, and not without reason. Steam power could be used for most mechanical processes, but usually required a substantial investment in fixed machinery. In agriculture, steam power had obvious uses as well, but it was only the largest of farms that could afford the cost of fixed steam engines to power threshing machines, saw mills and other processes within the farmstead.

Yet another pioneering idea by Trevithick, for a small portable steam engine that could be moved from farm to farm, resulted in at least two being made in 1812 but little else seems to have happened until the end of the 1830s. The Ipswich firm of J.R. and A. Ransome developed a portable steam engine and exhibited at the Royal Show in 1841 – and in the following year developed a rather clumsy self-propelled version which utilised the steam power but still needed a horse to steer it!

This was the direct ancestor of the traction engine that gradually evolved into a serious road-hauling vehicle from the late 1850s onwards. Despite their growing sophistication and size, many smaller 'portables' continued to be made and to be hauled around by horses. However, it became fairly obvious that the evolving traction engines had a greater role than simply taking themselves from site to site. Many towed the equipment needed in trailers behind them, and it was quickly appreciated that such 'road locomotives' could be used for general haulage in areas where the railways could not.

Whereas speed was not really an issue for traction engines, whether engaged in haulage or normal farm work, it had been for the steam carriages earlier in the

24 The traction engine represented the second, and more successful, development of steam locomotion from the 1860s onwards; steam locomotives continued to be used for less urgent and heavier loads well into the 1930s. House removals were a typical use, as shown in this early twentieth century photograph.

century. Developments in steam power and the fact that the more rural railways built in the last 'railway mania' of the 1860s had not really lived up to their investors' expectations, led to some people believing in the revival of road-going steam passenger vehicles.

One of the earliest of this new breed was built by the small Castle Foundry in Buckingham to the design of its manager Thomas Rickett, and based on their steam ploughs; it was a three-seater tricycle for the Marquess of Stafford in 1858. In 1860 a larger carriage was built by Rickett for the Earl of Caithness, which was taken on a highly publicised journey of nearly 150 miles through the difficult terrain (including a 1 in 7 ascent) between Inverness and Borrogill Castle (now the Castle of May) near Thurso, Caithness. Despite the publicity, few other steam 'cars' were built.

The potential of this innovation was limited by the repressive Highways Acts of the early 1860s. The Locomotive Act of 1861 had simply restricted the weight of road-going steam locomotives to 12 tons and their speed to 12mph. However, then came the infamous 'Red Flag' Act of 1869. Almost certainly the result of an unholy alliance between the railway companies, the virtually bankrupt turnpike trusts and elements of the landed gentry, it was passed, according to another potential pioneer of private steam carriages, Richard Tangye, by a 'bovine Parliament'. It reduced the permitted speed of road locomotives to just 4mph in the country and 2mph in towns and villages. It also decreed that each locomotive should have a crew of three – two on the vehicle (which was normal anyway) and a third walking 60 yards in advance who shall 'carry a Red Flag constantly displayed, and shall warn the Riders and Drivers of Horses …' whether on a busy highway, through town or on an isolated and empty mountain pass.

Another Act, in 1878, allowed local authorities to reduce the gap between the flag bearer and the vehicle to 20 yards, and also permitted the flag to be abandoned altogether under certain local conditions, but the red flag remained a potent symbol to the pioneers of road transport and was blamed by them of hindering Britain's role in the development of road vehicles.

The real impact on that development is open to debate. There were several attempts to try and built lighter self-propelled road-going vehicles, using a variety of power sources. Steam was popular, with fuels including coal, coke, methylated spirits and the new liquid – petroleum. Sir Thomas Parkyns built a reasonably successful steam-powered tricycle in 1881 but then was frequently fined for driving it at 5mph and finally gave up. Another pioneer, Magnus Volk, took a different line and developed an electric car capable of 10mph in 1887 and exported at least two to the Sultan of Turkey.

The real reasons for the lack of success of these ventures were not confined to restrictive speed limits but also included the condition of many roads, the efficiency of the rail network, and the cost and reliability of the new-fangled vehicles. The technology was there, albeit requiring a considerable degree of development, but the market was not.

The most significant developments in the internal combustion engine had taken place in France, following the first workable gas engine designed by Etienne Lenoir in 1860. The engine had potential and gas engines became fairly sophisticated towards the latter part of the century, used to power machinery and industrial processes. Lenoir adapted the engine to propel a road vehicle in 1862 but that was one of several similar experiments in France and Germany that failed to be commercially successful.

Even the early gas and then petrol-driven vehicles by the now famous pioneers such as Gottlieb Daimler and Wilhelm Maybach were crude and ineffective. The first of these vehicles to be sold, as opposed to being used purely by the builders, was a tricycle built by Carl Benz in Germany delivered to Emile Roger in Paris in 1887. A petrol-driven 'petro-cycle' was built by a London engineer, Edward Butler, in 1888. In the early 1890s the new-fangled motor car developed rapidly in both Germany and France, but hardly at all in Britain.

It is generally accepted that the first successful petrol-engine 'motor car' to be driven on British roads was a Peugeot driven around Guernsey in the summer of 1894 by a locally-born but Swiss-based Salvation Army office, Major A. Thom. The first to be imported to mainland Britain was a 4hp vehicle built by Panhard and Levassor of France and owned by the Hon. Evelyn Ellis in June 1895, an MP and a major shareholder in the Daimler engine company, who had used it in France for some time. Despite the draconian speed restrictions still in force, he managed to avoid prosecution. Evelyn Ellis visited his father, Lord Howard de Walden, and there is a story, possibly apocryphal, that the older man complained and said 'If you must bring that infernal thing here, kindly bring a little pan under it to catch the filthy oil drips', to which Evelyn replied, 'Certainly, father, if you'll bring a big pan for your carriage horses when you visit me!'.

A handful of others followed Ellis's example, and over 10,000 people attended a small exhibition of these new vehicles at Tunbridge Wells in October. In the following year, the first 'motor show' in England was held at the Imperial Institute in London. In that year, two other significant events took place. The first was the unfortunate demise of Mrs Bridget Driscoll, a 44-year-old housewife, who stepped off the pavement on her way from Croydon to the Crystal Palace on 17 August and was killed by a passing car – the first of many millions of car-related fatalities. The driver claimed to have been going under the 4mph speed limit.

The second event was the important Emancipation Act, passed in the summer but only implemented on 14 November. Confusing, poorly drafted and clearly

25 The first proper motor car to run in England was probably this 4hp vehicle built by Panhard and Levassor of France, owned by the Hon. Evelyn Ellis MP, in June 1895. It ended its relatively short career as a portable fire engine on his estate

ignorant of the technology of road vehicles, this did at least finally eliminate the need for crews of three and the 'red flag' for vehicles under 3 tons and replaced the 4mph speed limit with three others – a 12mph speed limit for vehicles under 1.5 tons, reduced to 8mph for heavier vehicles and just 5mph for those over 2 tons. The Act thus favoured the motor car over the traction engine.

A celebratory 'Emancipation Run' was organised for the next day, Sunday 15 November, by one of the more colourful and notorious of the early motoring promoters, Harry Lawson, between London and Brighton. A bizarre mixture of petrol, steam and electric powered motor cars set out – though by no means all finished; some ended the journey by train and in many ways the event was a bit of a fiasco. Nevertheless, this run is still celebrated every year.

In the next few years the numbers of motor vehicles began to grow, though it was still mainly a rich man's sport rather than anything else. One of the early books published on motoring, Alfred Harmsworth's *Motors and Motor Driving* of 1902 was in the Badminton Library series on 'British Sports and Pastimes', which included others on foxhunting, golf and fencing. In a chapter on the 'utility' of the motor car, most attention was given to it being used to transport 'beaters' on 'shoots', for transporting the wealthy to the hunt, getting to and from the station and 'when you are in your country house what an added joy to your daily life' the motor car brings by allowing better access to the neighbours. A short section on the motorbike (the first successful ones had been introduced at the end of the 1890s) saw them as 'an effective educational medium in connection with automobilism' to help those learn all about engines prior to becoming 'the owner of a larger vehicle'.

One of the contributors, John Scott-Montagu, MP (later Lord Montagu), a noted 'automobilist' of the day, acknowledged 'that the motor car has passed the limits of mere experiment, and that it has become a practical vehicle'. However, even he considered that 'we may still be far from the time when the horse-drawn vehicle will be a rarity upon country roads and London has begun to save fifty thousand pounds a year now spent on scavenging'. He was wrong. So was the writer in the *Scientific American* who thought that the motor car, especially in cities, 'would eliminate a greater part of the nervousness, distraction and strain of modern metropolitan life'.

In 1904 there were still only around 8,000 cars on Britain's roads, and this had doubled by the following year; by 1914 the figure had soared to over 132,000. In the same period, the number of goods vehicles had rocketed from 4,000 to 82,000 as both lorries and buses became more plentiful. By that time, the petrol engine had emerged as the most popular by far, with electric cars being too expensive and steam – once considered to be the future of the car – used almost exclusively for a small number of traction engines and steam lorries.

At this time it was also realised, in an early text book *Construction of Roads and Streets,* that whilst heavy lorries were 'doing infinitely more injury to roads and bridges than would be done by horse-drawn vehicles', that damage was 'comparatively insignificant compared with that due to pleasure motor cars which now frequent the highways in swarms, tearing at high speed through the mud in winter, and through the dust in summer'.

The new motor age would clearly require better roads, and at first most efforts were based on improving road surfaces with developments such as tarring and tarmacadam. There was also clearly a need for a different way of running the roads, based on national, rather than local, control. To this end following an Act of 1909, the Road Board was set up in 1910.

By the end of the First World War, privately registered vehicle numbers had fallen dramatically, to 78,000 cars and 41,000 lorries, but this was a direct

" SHE MOVED THE LEVER NEARLY TO FULL SPEED."

26 The motor car was quick to attract public attention and fiction writers. This illustration appeared in an 1898 short story notable for two things. Despite the general chauvinism of early motorists, the heroine of this story was Kitty, who saves the day when the brakes fail as the car 'whizzed round the corner on two wheels'. The car itself was electric – but in the oil-industry dominated century since, this potential form of propulsion has yet to be properly developed

27 The open road for the motorist in 1902 was not as pleasant for the bystanders having
to cope with the dust and fumes and noise; within a few years, the open road gradually
got more crowded, but at least improvements to road surfaces began to eliminate the dust
problem

Cabby (to Motor-driver, who is slightly disorganising the traffic). "WHY DON'T YER BRING YER OWN YARD TO TURN IN?"

28 The motor car was not initially a popular vehicle, especially with other road users and in already busy town centres, as shown in this *Punch* cartoon of 1910

result of hostilities. Thousands of vehicles of all types had been requisitioned by the military – around 1,300 London buses were used to transport men to the trenches in France and Flanders, and traction engines were used to haul artillery. In Britain, thousands of vehicles were simply taken off the road and stored until hostilities ceased.

In the immediate aftermath of the war there was an inevitable rapid increase in road vehicles – the novelist Virginia Woolf, visiting Newhaven in 1921, complained in her diary of the 'incessant cars like lice' – but motoring was no longer only the preserve of the very wealthy. The war had led to the training of many soldiers in driving and maintaining vehicles and many surplus military vehicles, particularly lorries, came back into the civilian use. Even before the war,

Henry Ford had introduced much cheaper mass-produced vehicles to the British market, and though motoring for the masses did not take off here as it did on the other side of the Atlantic, a small car did at least become a feasible aspiration for the middle classes between the world wars.

For the working classes, there was the motor bus, seen as a step up from the tram that, in its time, had revolutionised the mobility of the urban population. The motorised bus had been introduced before the war, mainly in towns. The hybrid lorry-cum-bus, the open-topped *char-à-banc*, had also appeared at that time, offering motorised transport for the masses. These enjoyed a period of popularity well into the 1920s until being superseded by the more versatile touring coaches. Lord Montagu bewailed the fact that their passengers were 'low-bred enough to disfigure the countryside'. It would be interesting to see his reaction to the hoardes that flock to his descendents' excellent motor museum at Beaulieu.

Vehicle ownership increased steadily between the world wars and was not confined to motor cars. There was a growth in the numbers of motorcycles, with or without side-cars, and of the relatively cheap hybrid part-motorbike part-car, the cyclocar. By 1920, car numbers had surged to 187,000 and lorries to 101,000, leading to a huge increase in lorry-borne road haulage largely at the expense of the railways.

A short slump followed, in 1922, but then due, in no small part, to the mass-produced no-frills family cars of Henry Ford's British rivals, William Morris and Herbert Austin, numbers continued to rise. By 1930 there were over one million registered cars on the roads and 361,000 lorries. Despite constant complaints about overcrowded roads, a Royal Commission, reporting in 1931, considered that, contrary to the road transport lobby's view, the roads in Britain were generally not too crowded, although there were 'hot-spots' on some key routes and that there was serious congestion in many towns. The Commission did not support the construction of new arterial routes, but did feel that bypasses were needed and 'in many cases absolutely essential' for major towns. By the outbreak of the Second World War in 1939, car numbers had reached two million and lorries, half a million. In addition, the number of motorbikes had grown from 36,000 in 1910 – the first year of records being kept for them – to a peak of 627,000 in 1930.

The development of road traffic inevitably led to major changes to the country, parts of which were completely physically transformed – especially around the major towns and cities. The railways had begun the development of suburbia, and the expansion of car ownership consolidated it. Garages became an important part of the middle-class house, petrol filling stations became common along most main and minor roads and in virtually all towns and villages, and ribbon development along major roads scarred much of the countryside even after an Act in 1935 specifically designed to curtail it. Another feature of the 1930s was

29 For most working-class people the first time they travelled on a motor vehicle would be on a motor-bus or motor *char-à-bancs*; these were particularly popular after World War I, and this photograph probably dates to about 1920. Note the solid wheels and the collapsible tarpaulin cover. By the 1930s the 'charas' had been replaced by more luxurious enclosed coaches

the creation of the bypass, taking major roads around urban areas and, at the same time, acting as an irresistible magnet for further developments of housing, factories and 'road houses'.

As well as the accelerated expansion of suburbia the motor car in particular also bought about other major social changes, less tangible but far more significant. These were particularly felt in the more rural areas. Whilst the railways had opened much of the countryside in the nineteenth century, the car did so to a much greater extent and accelerated, for better or worse, the decline of the old country ways. In his lyrical autobiographical book, *Cider with Rosie*, the writer Laurie Lee recognised the impact on his Cotswold valley in the 1920s of the 'brass-lamped motor car', the 'clamorous charabanc' and the 'solid-tyred bus' but realised too, in retrospect, that the process was not instant. The poet W.H. Auden, in *The Dog Beneath the Skin* in 1935 regretted the loss of the true rural population and their replacement by 'another population, with views about nature/Brought in charabanc and saloon along arterial roads'.

30 Between the World Wars the middle classes could afford their own motor-cars – such as this gentleman proudly at the wheel of his Jowett in the 1930s – but despite the mass-production methods introduced by the major car manufacturers and the dramatic reduction in prices, the poor economic situation meant that it would not be until the late 1950s that car ownership became more universal

As for the road and road users, already by the end of the 1920s some of the issues that still affect us at the start of the twenty-first century – congestion and bad road manners – were well developed. The much travelled H.V. Morton visited the Lake District in the summer of 1926 and 'joined the Windermere queue at Lancaster … Every one in the north of England seemed at this moment to have decided to visit …'. To the front, the queue was being held up by a young man in a cyclocar – 'a fifteen horse-power scarlet bath' – and the car behind was 'a neat saloon in the fair but reckless hands of a beautiful maiden, who, by edging in and nosing my suit-cases, seemed to be doing all she could to kill her father and mother.'

New road construction remained fairly limited between the wars despite traffic growth, though most roads were resurfaced with asphalt or tarmacadam. An arterial road programme, originally planned in 1912 but necessarily postponed until 1920, was begun in London and resulted in major new roads – the Great Chertsey Road, Great West Road, Western Avenue and the beginnings of the North Circular

Road. All were built wide enough to eventually be converted to dual carriageways, these have been blamed, rightly, for helping to concrete over Middlesex.

Away from the capital, one of the main spurs for new road schemes was not a long-term well-conceived national transport strategy, but a short-term response to the very real problems of mass unemployment, especially in the Depression years of the late 1920s and early 1930s. To help matters, major infrastructure schemes were started, included several new roads schemes. These included, for example, the Arterial Road in Blackburn, built between 1921 and 1928 with earthworks dug and built almost entirely by manual labour off 'the dole'; the much larger East Lancs Road between Manchester and Liverpool; in the Scottish Highlands, the new A9 road between Blair Atholl and Inverness in 1925–8; and between 1932–35, a new road through Glencoe and across the remote Rannoch Moor, replacing the road previously considered to be the worst road in Scotland. Nevertheless, by 1938, even the main roads were almost all single carriageway and there were just 27 miles of dual carriageway trunk roads.

31 Until the 1920s there had been few large scale engineering projects on the roads for nearly a century, mainly because of the dominance of the railways. Even then, most road schemes were not designed specifically for traffic improvement, but in order to alleviate chronic unemployment. The new road through Glencoe and across Rannoch Moor in the early 1930s was such a road, and despite very little traffic, was one of the finest in the country when finished

Not everyone was happy with the increasing speed of the motor car brought about by road improvements and legislation. One town planner writing in the early 1920s thought that main roads through villages and towns 'should be obstructed with trees, monuments, lamps, etc.' so that it was impossible for a car 'to thread its way through ... at more than a crawl'; if speed was needed, then a bypass should be built. He was in the minority.

The increase in traffic inevitably led to increases in injuries and deaths on the roads due mainly, back then as it is now, to poor driving and excessive speed. This was exacerbated by the state of roads designed mainly for a horse-drawn era, and the design of the motor vehicles. The new Labour government passed the Road Traffic Act of 1930 that attempted to improve matters. This got rid of the largely disregarded 20mph national speed limit (in place since 1903), introduced a 30mph in built up areas, authorised the introduction of a Highway Code, made third-party insurance compulsory, and introduced the first basic driving tests – though only for those who were physically disabled.

Although a 1930 guidebook claimed that 'the construction of new 'bypass' roads and the improvement of existing highways all over the country has made them much safer than formerly', road deaths in Britain had reached nearly 7,500 a year by 1934. This rose to 9,169 in 1941, though the figures were artificially inflated by the wartime conditions and, especially, to the restrictions on headlights for night driving because of the risk of bombing. There were then a little over two million motor vehicles (including motorbikes) in use; to put that figure into perspective, there are, in 2005, around 30 million vehicles on the road and the death toll – still far too high – is about 3,500 a year.

In the summer of 1939, the writer, L.T.C. Rolt, navigating the Trent and Mersey Canal near Burton-on-Trent where it ran alongside the A38, wrote that 'The knowledge that this busy highway was once the Roman Rykneld Street was small compensation for the din of the hurrying traffic, the glaring road-signs, ribbon-built bungalows and all the tawdry ugliness which the motor car has brought to the English road'. Even at that time, he, as many observers have in the many decades since, 'found myself marvelling at the mania of hurry that has infected our unhappy civilisation ... Cumbersome lorries were thrashing down the long, straight road with their engines running at peak revolution, little, mass-produced saloon cars clinging like terriers to their swinging trailers, dodging in and out in their attempts to pass, being evidently determined to maintain their 50mph, regardless of risk'. Only the speed has changed.

After the Second World War, Britain suffered from a period of austerity that included fuel shortages and rationing. This inevitably led to little expansion of the road infrastructure, despite ambitious plans. However, by the mid-1950s the worst was over and car ownership began to rise steeply. Vehicle numbers more

NEGOTIATING THE TOP BEND OF THE DEVIL'S ELBOW, GLENSHEE. THE HIGHEST PUBLIC ROAD IN BRITAIN, ALTITUDE 2000 FEET, STEEPEST GRADIENT 1 IN 3.

32 By the 1950s improvements in road surfaces and motor vehicles meant that even some of the most hostile terrain could be tackled. Several places claimed to be the highest public road in Britain, and the Glenshee Pass was a definite candidate; in places the gradient was 1 in 3. The bus attempting the 'Devil's Elbow', however, appears to have been cut-and-pasted into position

than doubled between 1955 and 1965. Despite major road improvements, the highways continued to become more and more congested to the detriment not only of motorists and business, but also of the towns and villages through which they passed.

The most dramatic development since the 1950s has been the development of the motorway network, the first nationwide government-sponsored road system since the Roman era. The first section of motorway in Britain was not opened until 1958, long after such roads had been well established in other parts of Europe and in North America. Nevertheless, the concept of a high speed arterial road dedicated solely to motor traffic had its origins almost at the very start of the motor age.

As early as 1900, Arthur Balfour, then the First Lord of the Treasury and a keen pioneering motorist, called for 'great highways constructed for rapid motor traffic and confined to motor traffic'. Hilaire Belloc, in his 1904 book *The Road* predicted high-speed motor roads with dual carriageways, flyovers and interchange junctions. Technically, the new Road Board set up in 1910 had the power to build completely new roads 'confined to motor traffic, and the speed limit [then 20 mph] will not apply on such a road'. For a variety of reasons, mainly financial, this was something that the Road Board did not achieve.

In 1906, Lord Montagu of Beaulieu had proposed such a road in outline between London and Brighton, and in 1920 suggested a route between London and Birmingham. This scheme 'to be reserved entirely to the new traffic and to be made specially for these new necessities' was extended into one from London to Liverpool and in 1923 a Bill was prepared to create the privately funded Northern & Western Motorway, a toll road 226 miles long. As there were no precedents for such a scheme, it was prepared under the auspices of the Light Railways Act of 1896! Its backers claimed that it was defeated by vested interests, but it seems simply not to have been economically viable at the time.

Despite much discussion and debate it was in continental Europe and the United States of America that the first motorway developments occurred. The idea of fully developed roundabouts, dual carriageways and 'clover-leaf' junctions had been set out by Eugene Henard in 1906 and the first proper road, restricted to motor traffic, was in Germany, started in Berlin in 1909. This was a dual carriageway for motor traffic only, over 6 miles long and almost finished before the outbreak of the First World War; the *Avus* finally opened in 1921, and was designed to be an occasional racetrack as well as a public road. By that time a short motorway of sorts had already been opened in Long Island, New York.

The first long motorway was built in Italy by a state-sponsored private company, the *Strada e Cave* (Roads and Tunnels) which later changed its name to the Autostrada Company. This was a single carriageway concrete motorway opened in 1924 between Milan and Varese in Lombardy; it was about 30 miles long and required a large number of over- and under-bridges, tunnels, and link roads. The Americans were, considering their development in mass motoring, rather tardy with the development of motorways. Their first motor-dedicated road was opened in 1925. However, these roads were not true motorways and initially lorries were not permitted to use them. The term 'parkway', incidentally, was derived from the fact that such roads could only be built by a private company through a loophole in US law; they were, technically, long, private parks for residential use – and the landscaped roads built by the Westchester County Park Commissioners were technically just for access to the houses.

The first of the major inter-urban German *autobahnen*, linking Cologne and Bonn, opened in 1929 but lacked a central reservation, unlike those built after 1933. In Germany, the United States and the third pioneering country in the field, Italy, most of these new super highways were built in the 1930s to relieve the chronic unemployment of the time. Other motorways were built in Canada and Holland prior to the Second World War, but Britain continued to lag far behind.

The nearest thing to a motorway in the inter-war years – and one that could have become one – was the East Lancs Road, built between 1929 and 1934 at a cost of around £3 million. It was the first inter-urban new road to be built in Britain in the motor age. Despite its name it actually linked Liverpool and Manchester, the two towns joined a century beforehand by the first modern railway. The road's full name was the Liverpool to East Lancashire Road, an idea formulated in 1912 and finally given serious consideration in the mid-1920s.

Labelled the A580, it was planned to have three separate carriageways and a wide band of land was purchased to accommodate them. The middle carriageway was to be a two lane highway and the outer carriageways were to be added later for slow moving traffic. Amongst its advanced engineering features were very shallow gradients (none more than 1 in 40), helped by cuttings and embankments, no sharp bends, and roundabouts at the main junctions; yet it also had a series of laybys, with water 'on tap', to cater for steam wagons. The road allowed for high speeds and there were initially many accidents, especially at the lesser junctions; the side carriageways were never built. The safest section was that at the Liverpool end, which was built as a dual carriageway; the rest remained mainly single carriageway until the 1970s but has, piecemeal, been converted to dual carriageway throughout.

In Britain, successive governments in the 1930s were reluctant to back the idea of new motorways and, in particular, of motorway toll roads – seeing those as a good excuse for highway authorities to save money on their own road repairs. However, by the end of the 1930s, organisations like the County Surveyors Society were strongly supporting the introduction of motorways, seeing them not only as a means of improving the traffic problems of the day, but, in retrospect ironically, as protecting the environment.

In *Proposals with Regards to Motorways* published in 1938, it was the Society's opinion that 'new roads and motorways, carefully designed in relation to the landscape and its preservation, whilst not causing injury to amenities are likely in time even to improve them. On the other hand, the widening of existing roads, with the attendant demolition of property, will in many cases offend against amenities'. In the same year the route for a toll motorway between Birmingham and London was surveyed but government attention was then elsewhere.

The Second World War delayed any road developments in Britain, and although the reforming Labour government elected in 1945 had many good ideas, the country had little or no money to develop them. The first priority for roads was to overcome the backlog of six years of limited maintenance and heavier than normal use. However, in 1946 the Minister of Transport, Alfred

Barnes, made clear his commitment to the 'comprehensive reconstruction of the principal national routes', which would include 'new roads reserved for motor traffic'. Although the powers to construct such motorways (or 'special roads') were authorised by the Special Roads Act of 1949, nothing was done because of lack of funds for many years. The Act had been needed to change the long-held traditional laws of the highways, which had always been open to all subjects and not confined to any particular class or type of traffic.

Finally, in 1956, work started on a stretch of the proposed new motorway planned to link the English Midlands to the Scottish border. This section was officially known as the Preston Bypass but was always designed to be a part of the M6. It opened in 1958, by which time work had started on the M1. That motorway – in the planning stages the London-Yorkshire Motorway – was started in 1958 by Sir Owen Williams & Partners and the first section opened in the following year; it was completed between London and Leeds in 1966.

The new motorway numbers roughly mirrored the original 'A' road system, but have since been adapted independently. Fairly strict safety guidelines were set out and issues such as ensuring that there are gentle gradients and gentle bends, avoiding long straight sections, detailed landscaping studies, new signage and so forth had to be dealt with in advance. Although the new motorways were initially not subject to a speed limit, they were designed with a maximum speed of 70mph in mind and that, eventually, was put in place.

Since then the number of motorways has increased dramatically and, occasionally, controversially. There are now over 2,000 miles of motorways in Britain. The latest section of motorway, the M6 (Toll) – a relief road around the north of the West Midlands conurbation – opened in 2004, became the first major road to be funded by private funds and paid for directly by the travelling public since the turnpikes. Controversial for many reasons, so far it has seen little of the heavy freight traffic diverted onto it from the older M6 section, due in no small part to the high and virtually unregulated tolls charged by the company. Despite that, the Labour government announced, in the summer of 2004, a proposal to add toll lanes to the M6 between Birmingham and Manchester amidst claims that it had succumbed, like other governments of all colours before it, to the powerful road-transport lobby.

The future of road transport has, as we know, been the subject of endless debate and argument for decades. Fossil fuel will eventually run out and despite the experiments with alternative means of propulsion over the last century or so there is still a very powerful oil lobby determined to keep their products in our fuel tanks. After all, it seems amazing that there were viable electric cars in the late 1890s and despite massive improvements in technology, these are still not economically viable alternatives to the petrol engine.

As cars become cheap, in relative terms, it is everyone's aspiration to own and run one. There is simply no spare capacity on the nation's main and urban roads and the only answer to this seems to be to create more capacity. The environmental impact on a local and a national scale is immense, and on the international scale extremely worrying – especially bearing in mind that, at present, there is a massive untapped market in the developing world of aspiring motorists. The simple fact is that the new roads quickly become as clogged as the old, and pollution increases.

PART II

ROAD ENGINEERING

CHAPTER 3

Earthworks

Earthworks are one of the key differences that distinguish a road from a track, yet even tracks with little or no engineering were still often quite important in the transport geography of certain more remote areas of Britain well into the nineteenth century. For example, in J.H. Burton's *History of Scotland*, published in 1876, the author wrote that, 'The old mountain track, as specimens of it still exist, is found by a traveller so slightly distinguished from the natural surface of the hill, that he cannot easily believe himself treading a path that had been a great thoroughfare for centuries, and is still used by the country people in passing from one strath to another ....'

Given the huge physical impact that the modern road system has made on the landscape, it could be argued that the prophet Isaiah's words in the Old Testament are on the way to coming to pass: 'Make straight in the desert a highway for our God. Every valley shall be exalted and every mountain and hill shall be made low; and the crooked shall be made straight and the rough places plain.' Whatever one's religious affinities, if any, the sad fact of modern life is that the particular god in question is the motor car.

The earthworks are the major engineering works associated with the roads, rather than their surfaces, and can be divided into two broad categories – accidental and engineered. Accidental features are those caused simply by the passage of pedestrian and vehicles and the action of the weather, rather than any deliberate intervention by man.

ACCIDENTAL ENGINEERING

Holloways

By far the most common accidental feature is the holloway. If enough people walk across a stretch of ground enough times over a long enough period, the gradual wear and tear of their footsteps will create a path. The path will gradually be denuded of any vegetation and, if it is left unsurfaced, a groove in the ground gradually forms. Rainwater will inevitably find its way into the formed hollow and, if there is any gradient at all, will flow. The water then begins to erode the hollow further and with continued pedestrian use and continued rainwater erosion, the hollow gets deeper and deeper. If the path continues in use for long enough, the surface can gradually fall well below the original ground levels to either side and the end result is a well-defined Holloway.

This process is accelerated if animals use the path and, especially, if it is used by wheeled vehicles. Animal hoof and wheel rim inevitably cause deeper cuts

33 A holloway in Yorkshire, showing how the effects of rainwater, slope, and traffic continue to cut it down into the landscape despite the tarmacadam surface. This particular holloway is probably not of any great antiquity but is already nearly 2m deep in places

into the soil: a horse or cow is heavier than a human and a loaded wagon could weigh several tons. The deeper the cut the more the base of the track or road is broken up and the more the rainwater affects it, exacerbating the deepening of the Holloway. The process is either slowed or halted when the path becomes disused or when a solid and better wearing surface is introduced.

In his famous book on the natural history of Selborne, Hampshire, published in 1788, Gilbert White wrote of a pair of holloways which 'by the traffic of ages, and the fretting of water' had been cut through the local bedrock and now looked 'more like water-courses than roads'. The speed at which a holloway can form depends on the nature of the soil, the gradient of the road and the amount and type of traffic using it. Steep roads, especially in areas of softer rock and soils, are particularly vulnerable, especially if they are narrow.

Many of the deep-set narrow lanes in parts of Devon, Derbyshire or Shropshire, sometimes 6ft (2m) or more below the fields, only date to the

34 This unsurfaced road in south-west Shropshire was effectively abandoned when a new turnpike road was built on the opposite side of the valley; the holloway formed in the fairly soft soil and would have continued to get deeper and deeper if traffic had continued to use it

35 When the roads in holloways were properly surfaced, especially by MacAdam-type surfaces in the early nineteenth century, or by tarmacadam ones a century or so later, the degree of erosion was considerably halted providing that surface was well-maintained. This holloway in Radnorshire forms part of the route of the former 'Great Road' from Presteigne to Rhayader in mid-Wales – a route probably in use since the medieval period, but replaced by a more easily graded turnpike in 1767

enclosures of the early nineteenth century. An unsurfaced 'enclosure road' could quite quickly turn into a holloway and, apart from the boundary fence or wall on either side, could seem as if its been there for thousands of years. This is partly because all of the traffic is restricted to the area between the walls, rather than being allowed to spread out sideways as was often the case prior to the enclosures. Other holloways, even within fence or wall, could have been in use for hundreds, if not thousands, of years and can sometimes be over 15ft (4.7m) deep.

For all of these reasons, dating holloways is notoriously difficult and largely depends on their archaeological and historical context rather than their physical dimensions or profile. Even then, just because a series of holloways appears to be related to a prehistoric field system or a Romano-British settlement, it does not necessarily mean that they are all contemporary. Nevertheless, close study of the associated archaeology should produce a reasonable assessment of their origin, age, purpose and development. In addition, the geographical and historical contexts can also be important when studying longer distance routes.

Up until the later medieval period, and the beginnings of enclosures on a larger scale, the manner in which roads were used could lead to the development of 'braided holloways' – an awkward but apt term. It will be remembered that the right of way was then not restricted to a narrow line, but was much more liberally interpreted. Once a particularly line had become too deep or too rutted, temporarily or permanently, travellers simply bypassed it and, gradually, the 'road' could spread out for tens, if not hundreds, of yards. As a result, given the right conditions, a whole series of roughly parallel holloways could develop. This is often best seen on a hillside where it formed part of an important routeway.

Occasionally, a place or field name may help in assessing the date of a holloway – or at least give an idea of when it was in use and thus indicate that it must be older than that date. Perhaps the best-known name of this type is Holloway in London, a name first recorded in the fifteenth century. In Derbyshire there is, to the south of Matlock, a small hamlet called Holloway, first recorded in the thirteenth century, and there several other similar names around the country. The many 'Dark Lanes' could be related to holloways as well.

MAN-MADE EARTHWORKS

The Romans were the first to bring road engineering on any scale to Britain when they arrived in the mid-first century AD. It is likely that the main campaigns of new Roman road construction had largely ceased by the early second century AD and most other road building was on a much more limited scale. Whilst there were limited and small-scale road building projects in the medieval period,

36 Most of the Roman road between Old Sarum and Dorchester has been unused since the early fifth century and as a result, despite the efforts of quarrying by eighteenth-century turnpike road proprietors, it is one of the most impressive of Roman aggers in the country. It has acquired the name Ackling Dyke; this section is in the north-western corner of Hampshire, close to the Dorset border

the next major campaign of road building in which earthworks were to play a substantial part was not until the very end of the heyday of the turnpike roads early in the nineteenth century – and then only on those projects where funds were not a problem.

The most notable examples are the government-sponsored highways, and especially those engineered by Thomas Telford. He tried to achieve a much lower and more regular gradient than other road builders and was able to obtain the resources to pay for the additional earthworks and to alter routes to achieve further improvements. For example, on the Anglesey section of the Holyhead Road he chose a virtually new route and in 24 miles reduced the total vertical distances travelled (up or down) from 3,540ft (1097m) to 2,257ft (700m) – and the new route was 2 miles shorter.

Any further engineering advances of this scale were not to be. With the rapid decline of the road system following the development of the railways from the middle of that century, further significant investment in such earthworks were unwarranted until the development of the motor car at the start of the twentieth century. Even then, it was only really between the world wars that significant purpose-built new roads with steady gradients achieved through large-scale engineering works were started. At the time, these were seen as being deliberately over-engineered for the traffic of the day.

Some experts, such as Stanley Adshead writing as early as 1923, thought that 'too little consideration has been given to their design and too much attention directed to the question of the unemployed labour absorbed in their construction', adding that 'Cutting and embanking appear to have been works sought after rather than avoided' so that the new roads are 'graded more in the nature of railway tracks than of tracks for vehicles'. In the modern high-speed motorway, the amount of earthworks required and the amount of earth moved around as a consequence is out of all scale with anything that preceded it.

Embankments

The most common form of earthwork is the embankment, a logical means of placing the level of the road surface above that of the ground to either side and, in doing so, to allow the surface to be reasonably well drained. This presumably has its origins in the more marshy areas, where a reasonably dry path became desirable. Simply digging up soil from the sides of the path and piling up its centre would have raised the level of the path and created drainage ditches at the same time.

One of the key features of a Roman road, and one that survives to a lesser or greater degree in the landscape, is the agger. This is the raised embankment above the natural ground level upon which the actual road surface is formed. Almost invariably, the agger is considerably wider than the road itself. In its simplest form, the agger was built up by quarrying materials from either or both sides of the proposed road – sometimes the traces of miniature quarries or 'scoop ditches' can still be found in the vicinity of the road line. In some cases, the archaeological evidence suggests that suitable materials had to brought in from longer distances. The earth and rock would be augmented by material from the digging of the continuous ditches on either side of the agger, formed to provide good quality drainage.

The materials used for the construction of the agger varied greatly, and were usually dependent on the available local materials. Some are built simply of earth, occasionally stiffened with turves; others are of rammed chalk mixed with flint. The better materials included carefully layers of large stones set within rammed earth built up to the required level. Over particularly marshy areas, timber piles were sometimes used to provide a more solid basis on which the agger could be built.

37 The sheer size of the agger of Ermine Street to the north of Ancaster, Lincolnshire, is visible in this photograph, though how much is due to successive resurfacing of a road that has continued in use until the present day is uncertain

The width and height of the agger recognised on British roads varies considerably, depending partly on the available local materials and the importance of the road. On some roads, the agger can be nearly 50ft (15m) wide and over 6ft (2m) high, whilst on others it can be considerably narrower and less than 3ft (0.5m) high. It is likely that the sides of the agger were originally fairly steep, but centuries of gradual erosion and soil slip have meant that most that have been studied archaeologically have fairly shallow sloped sides instead.

The agger was seldom used to help relieve a particularly steep gradient, but generally followed the contours of the land. In some cases, in terraceways and zigzags, the agger became an integral element in the engineering and it is difficult to disengage the one from the other. However, in general there is a great difference between the construction and function of this type of embankment and, for comparison, a nineteenth-century railway embankment in which all effort is made to create a fairly level surface for the tracks.

As when dealing with Roman roads in general, it should be remembered that only the more important roads had an agger of any significant height; lesser roads may well have had much lower agger or none at all – especially on the many minor lanes and pathways linking farms and settlements. In addition, military roads in the more remote areas, such as the north-west of England, tended to be less 'conventional' in their construction and design, due to the terrain and the purposes for which these roads were built.

The utility of the expensively constructed agger in providing a well-drained base for the road surface on top of it is unquestionable, and the quality of the engineering is more than evident in the way such features still survive in the landscape nearly 2,000 years later despite the effects of ploughing and deliberate quarrying of materials – especially that in the eighteenth century for use in the new turnpiked roads.

Nevertheless, in many sections the size of the agger seems out of proportion to the engineering and drainage requirements. This is particularly the case when roads were built over well-drained high ground, where an expensively raised embankment is hardly necessary for good drainage; the suggestion by many experts is that this was a deliberate means of propaganda to demonstrate the power of the new order to the conquered tribes through which these roads were built. Nowhere is this more powerfully expressed than in the great agger of the Ackling Dyke marching purposefully southwards from Hampshire into Dorset. With an improved understanding of the native population distribution, this is no longer a universally held belief and, unfortunately, is not one that can be proved or disproved on the archaeological record alone. One simpler solution is that by keeping the road high above the surrounding ground, it gave those on it a better view of potential danger and a better defensive position if attacked.

One other type of embankment on the Roman road system is the type that would have been required on the approaches to major bridge crossings. Most of these bridges would have been built fairly high above the rivers they crossed to cope with the seasonal differences in water levels and the inevitable floods. As they would have taken wheeled traffic, the approaches to their main decks would not have been steep or stepped but fairly gradual. This would have resulted in the need for a built-up embankment either side, usually, but not always, higher than the normal level of an agger.

Although a far more detailed archaeological study of river crossings is needed, the apparent paucity of such approach embankments does seem to provide support the widely-held belief that, in Britain, fords were commonly used on even the major roads in the Roman period. There are, nevertheless, plenty of examples, varying from some in hilly ground where the agger itself seems to stop abruptly at the point where the bridge abutment would have been, to more gently sloping approaches just identifiable in the modern landscape.

Embankments do not usually have the kudos of other engineering features, such as bridges or tunnels, but whilst their construction was relatively straight-forward they could also represent very significant achievements. To a great extent, the success of the more ambitious embankments on the later turnpike roads owned much to the experience gained by the canal engineers; they needed to create level routes for obvious reasons.

Up to the end of the eighteenth century most of the material for road embankments seems to have been derived from the immediate fringes of the roadside wherever possible. The concept of cut-and-fill – in which the materials excavated in the cuttings could be transported further down the line to be used in the formation of the embankments – became important in canal and, in particular, railway construction in the nineteenth century. Isolated and small-scale use of this technique has been identified on some Roman roads – such as where the spoil from a cutting at the top of a hill on the route of the Ackling Dyke in Dorset was probably used for the adjacent sections of agger on the slopes of each side of the rise.

Similar uses of the technique can be seen on turnpikes of many centuries later, built in the late eighteenth and early nineteenth centuries, again where a cutting has been made to ease the gradient at the top of a hill and the material from it taken for use in easing the gradient from the base of the slope by use of a sloping embankment. Generally, this was a fairly empirical science until the end of the eighteenth century, but the advent of canals and the need for a more scientific approach influenced road engineers as well. By the early nineteenth century, Thomas Telford, who also built canals, produced cut-and-fill calculations for the difficult upland sections of the Holyhead Road and in his specifications often set out strict instructions as how this was to be done.

Telford was responsible for some of the finest engineering monuments in the country. His important embankments are generally overlooked but were vital elements in his work. The world-renowned Pontcysyllte aqueduct on the Ellesmere Canal would have been useless without the massive southern approach embankment, for example. On the Holyhead Road project Telford had the resources to build massive rising embankments at nearby Chirk, easing the gradients across the Cerriog valley, and rising to the top in a curving zigzag.

Even with advances in both the theory of cut-and-fill and the ability to carry it out in the twentieth century, it has not always proved possible to produce as much material from the cuttings as is required in the virtually continuous embankments. For example, when the East Lancs Road was built in the early 1930s, 150 million tons of material from the excavations could be used for the embankments, but that was only half the amount required; for two years a fleet

38 As part of his rebuilding of the Holyhead road in the early nineteenth century, Telford replaced the existing route across the Cerriog valley at Chirk with an impressive embankment, though its scale is now cloaked by tree-cover. This is the foot of the embankment, just on the English side of the border with Wales

of 200 lorries were kept busy transporting colliery waste and ash from sites all over south Lancashire and the surrounding area to the embanked sections of the route to make up the shortfall.

Terraceways

Where sheep walk around the flank of a hill their tracks, over time, form a flat, if narrow, surface – partly cut into the slope on one side and unevenly built up on the other; a natural *terraceway*, or *bench*, is formed. If man had to walk on the side of a slope, it made sense to create this feature artificially, and the task was fairly simple. By digging into the slope on the higher side of the path and depositing the soil on the lower side, a level terraced path resulted that could either be left as it was or surfaced in some way. In one sense, the terraceway is part cutting and part embankment, in varying proportions depending on the terrain and the aspirations of the engineer. Its construction could perhaps be described as 'slice-and-build'.

Identifying pre-historic terraceways in the British landscape is very difficult, but the Roman engineers certainly used them for their roads in upland areas. In comparison with some of the more ambitious Roman terraceways built on the Continent, often cut dramatically into the bare rock, those in Britain were fairly modest in scale, yet still represented significant feats of engineering and surveying.

The terraceways could be level, especially when the road is cut into the flank of a steep hillside, or carefully graded. Usually they had a drainage ditch on the inward, or upper, side of the slope to take the rainwater flowing off the hillside before it got onto the road. One of the more spectacular graded Roman terraceways is the partly rock-cut one taking High Street down the valley of Hagg Gill to the north of Troutbeck; at times the gradient is 1 in 5, but this difficultly-made road through the Cumbrian fells was mainly for the military.

The more ambitious the terraceway, the greater the degree of engineering required, both in cutting away on the higher side of the road and in building out on the lower side. Depending on the nature of the land through which such a roadway is made, there came a point at which merely building up a part-embankment on the lower side could no longer suffice and a revetment wall was needed instead.

One of the more dramatic terraceways of the turnpike era was that cut into the cliffs by Penmaenmawr, on the north Wales coastal route to the west of Conwy. In the early seventeenth century the 'Kinges Highway', and 'the only passage that the Kinges Poste hath to ride to and from Ireland' was a rough track 'scarce a yard and a quarter or a yard' wide still apparently maintained by a hermit. A new road was made on terraceway in 1720 at the instance of the Lord Lieutenant of Ireland, the Duke of Ormond. In 1774 Dr Johnson passed along this way and noted approvingly that the road was 'a way lately made, very easy and very safe. It was cut smooth, and enclosed between parallel walls; the outer of which secures the passenger from the precipice, which is deep and dreadful … The old road was higher, and must have been very formidable.'

Perhaps not as dramatic for those travelling on it, in sheer engineering cost and skill, the long and continuous terraceways built by Thomas Telford in the early nineteenth century were quite remarkable. On the Welsh section of the Holyhead Road, there are two particularly impressive sections of terraceway, both with their own distinct character and both clearly with their own specific engineering requirements. In each case Telford followed the approximate line of an earlier and far less ambitious road.

Heading westwards from Corwen, the road left the relatively easy Dee valley and at Glyn-diffwys had to cope with the narrow gorge of the Afon Cerrw in order to maintain its steady gradient. To achieve this, the sinuous cliff side on the north of the river had to be cut into and a tall revetment wall built to support the terraceway; in parts, this was up to nearly 30ft (9m) high and the narrow, sharp, bends were a major headache to motorists on the A5 until a short bypass was built in a cutting through the hillside in the 1990s. The wooded gorge is, nevertheless, beautiful and Telford even provided a couple of laybys for travellers to enjoy the view.

The other terraceway is set in the rather bleaker, but equally impressive, Nant Francon pass in Snowdonia, to the south of Bethesda. Two earlier turnpikes, one on either side of the pass, had been built since the 1790s, but Telford decided that neither had steady enough gradients and built his anew, partly on the route of one built in 1802–05. This was a relatively straight graded terraceway, roughly 3 miles long, with an even gradient. It was revetted by a tall stone wall partly built on top of or generally built high above the revetment of the earlier terraceway of its predecessor. Unlike the terraceway at Glyn-diffwys it is still in use today.

Most terraceways are less dramatic, such as the sinuous route up the Hope Valley in south-west Shropshire built in the 1830s. Indeed, most will be virtually ignored by those using them as they are quite a common, and logical, formation for roads of all types and sizes through hilly or undulating countryside.

Zigzags

When walking up particularly steep slopes, man or beast will usually not climb in a straight line but will zigzag in order to ease the gradient. In prehistoric times, such *zigzag* routes were almost certainly fossilised through use and in mountainous areas such as Nepal or parts of China, some of these zigzags seem to rise endlessly upwards and may have been in use for thousands of years.

Opposite above: 39 One of the most dramatic terraceways built before the mid-twentieth century was certainly this one, again by Telford, on the Holyhead road. With a steady gradient of about 1 in 22 over a considerable distance through the Nant Ffracon, it towered over an earlier turnpike road sneered at by Telford, and is still in use by the heavy traffic of today on the A5

Opposite below: 40 This is part of the route of the earlier turnpike built between 1802 and 1805 through Nant Ffracon, from which the base of Telford's terraceway wall can be seen on the left. Even so the older road had its own terraceway and a cutting, representing considerable investment and engineering skills. As it had only operated for a short time before being replaced, much of it is well preserved and unaltered

Such zigzags are simply combinations of graded terraceways. Whilst in the confused series of holloways and tracks found on the steep slopes leading up to suggested ridgeway routes there may be elements of zigzags that have been in use for centuries, their actual dates are generally impossible to assess and they will seldom have any engineering features of note. The earliest and most significant engineered zigzags in Britain are, like the terraceways, Roman.

Despite the myth that the Romans built their roads straight up and over hills, their road engineers were pragmatic people and often had to resort to zigzags even on main highways. Often these can be identified on a map, where the straight course of the road could clearly not have continued down a very steep slope without causing great inconvenience to travellers but where, instead, a zigzag had been required – usually just a short diversion from the main arrow-straight surveyed line of the road.

A good example of this on a main road is at Birdlip, on the edge of the Cotswolds escarpment overlooking the Severn valley, where the Ermine Street from Cirencester to Gloucester was taken down the slope in a zigzag; even now lorries find the ascent of the modern motor road nearby difficult. In the north-west of England the Romans built roads for the military in the Cumbrian mountains and these required large numbers of quite steep zigzags, particularly on their roads leading up from Eskdale through the Hardknott Pass – still a challenge to the motor car – and, further east, up to what is now called High Street, a place no motor car would want to go.

With a few exceptions, mostly difficult to date, the next phase of expensively engineered zigzags occurred in the next major phase of military road building in Britain, 1,700 years after the Romans conquered England. These were on some of those roads begun by General Wade in the north of Scotland. The mountainous terrain of the Highlands naturally led to the need for terraceways and zigzags, several of which were quite dramatic and still survive relatively intact. The most dramatic zigzags are those on either side of the Corrieyairack Pass on the route between Fort Augustus and Melgarve. The southern set is particularly impressive and was originally made up of eighteen short stone-revetted sections rising from the top of Allt Yairack. Now part of a mere footpath, these are still difficult for the modern and well-booted hiker and the road itself is one of the least altered of all the Wade roads. Incidentally, despite seeming to be modern, the term zigzag would have been in common usage by the time that these roads were built.

Causeways

The differences between an embankment and a causeway are often subtle and the words are sometimes interchangeable. It is noticeable that earlier antiquaries often referred to the embankment of a Roman road, the agger, as causeways and some sections of Roman road are still referred to as such. In Wales, the word for causeway in *sarn* and many Roman roads are called *sarn Helen* after that mythical road maker.

To confuse matters further, from at least the medieval period, the name had another meaning related to the paved surface of a horse or pedestrian track, dealt with in another section of this book under the subtitle 'Causeys'. Without getting dragged into a fairly pointless semantic debate, for the purposes of this work a causeway is seen as an embankment with a significant degree of structural intervention and support, as opposed to an embankment made up mainly of earth and rock piled up and allowed to settle.

The earliest identified causeways in Britain are probably the so-called 'causewayed camps' of the Neolithic period, though the causeways were only related to access in and around these settlements or market centres. The distinction between causeways and the wooden raised tracks identified in parts of England are blurred but those are dealt with elsewhere in the book.

Roman engineering was clearly capable of building causeways when necessary, and some of those in the low-lying parts of the Fens could have been of Roman origin. To the south of Lincoln, the remains of a concrete-based causeway well over a mile long carrying the Ermine Street across the valley of the River Witham, many feet below present ground levels, have been identified. Such major engineering works would have been more difficult to organise and finance in the five centuries or so after the departure of the Romans, but it does seem that there were numerous causeways built in the Saxon period. For example, a causeway supported by rows of oak timbers between the Essex mainland and Mersea Island in the Thames estuary has been dated through tree-ring analysis to the end of the seventh century AD. A causeway at Brandon, Suffolk, in which the earthen embankment was stiffened by wooden posts and possibly topped by a timber road, was probably of the same date. A causeway was also built in Saxon Oxford to a major crossing of the Thames.

In the medieval period, more causeways have been documented and the basic structure of some survive despite many campaigns of repair. A large proportion of these were funded by the great monasteries. Sometimes, these were vital links to their great houses or the markets under their care. For example, in 1697 Celia Fiennes approached the Isle of Ely on 'a flatt on a gravel Causey' maintained by the Bishop, one of the vital links in this low-lying area still prone to being under water.

Sometimes a causeway would be built in association with a new bridge or a new market town. The Abbot of Ramsey developed his own medieval 'new town' in Huntingdonshire on the River Ouse next to an existing village in the early twelfth century; that was at the site of a ford, but the new town of St Ives was given a bridge-crossing a little downstream, reached by a long causeway on the south side that is still in use. Also in the twelfth century, a short causeway built by the Bishop of Lichfield across a marshy area between city and the cathedral precincts dramatically improved communications in this part of Staffordshire. It also led to the diversion of the main highway from London to the north-west of England through Lichfield – to the obvious benefit of the city, and of the Bishop.

Another form of causeway was that linking an off-shore island to the mainland, and some of these could and still can only be used at low tides – such as those to Mount St Michael in Cornwall and to the castle of Eilean Donan in the Scottish Highlands. Longer causeways across flat low-lying valleys would often need to incorporate bridges to cross watercourses, and the approach across the flood plain of the River Severn into Gloucester would have been impossible without its long causeway, probably built in the medieval period (41). Subsequent changes to the river course and redevelopment of the area have virtually obliterated all traces of it. In the Fens, a medieval causeway near Skirbeck incorporated about thirty bridges. Occasionally there are specific Acts relating to the repair of causeways, such as one 1711 Act concerning the Great Yarmouth to Caister Causeway but, in legal terms, the definitions of a causeway was often difficult to refine.

Telford, especially when given fairly limitless government resources, was a great exponent of large and ambitious earthworks and two of his largest causeways survive in use. The most dramatic is the Fleet Mound carrying the modern A9 road across Loch Fleet, a few miles to the south of Golspie, Sutherland. It was part of the major road improvement scheme north of Inverness. Prior to that, traffic was taken by ferry across the narrow mouth of the loch at the hamlet of Littleferry, and Telford had originally planned simply to improve the ferry termini on each side. A causeway was then decided upon, further upstream, and the road was diverted accordingly. The Mound took two years to build and was opened in 1816. It acts as a tidal barrier as well as taking the road, and had a stone-bridged section of four arches, later increased by two, at the northern end. Between 1900 and 1960 the Mound was also used by the Dornoch Light Railway.

On the Holyhead Road, Telford's solution to the crossing of the last obstacle on the route was typically ambitious; Holyhead, the port and final destination of the road, is on an island separated from the rest of Anglesey by a tidal channel. Telford ignored the earlier bridge crossing and instead decided on a man-made causeway 1,300ft (403m) long across the Stanley Sands at Beddmynach Bay. This was given a deliberately shallow cross-section, to limit the impact of sea erosion.

1 The image of the lonely prehistoric traveller taking to tracks over the moors away from the dangerous wooded valleys is one that is difficult to shake off. Whilst traders would have used tracks not dissimilar to this one in the Pennines, there is increasing archaeological evidence that there were other routes through the valleys as well

2 Ackling Dyke, the name given to the Roman road between Old Sarum in Wiltshire and Dorchester in Dorset, has been virtually disused since the end of the Roman era and is one of the least altered examples of a particularly fine agger marching uncompromisingly across the landscape. This section crosses a corner of Hampshire

3 It is difficult to believe that this shallow rutted track, overgrown with trees, a few miles to the west of Marlborough, Wiltshire, used to be part of the main road between London and Bristol in the medieval and early post-medieval periods. However, the present line of its replacement, the A4, is only a few yards away and parallel to it

4 The tarmacadamed road in the foreground is on the line of one of General Wade's early eighteenth-century military roads, in the village of Amulree in Strath Braan. The modern road to Crieff turns to the left but the original line of the road can be seen clearly rising directly up the hillside on its more direct route to Glen Almond

5 A typical enclosure road in the Yorkshire Pennines, formed when the moors were divided up into separate ownership. Many of these roads would have been similar to this up until the early twentieth century. Major changes came as a result of a road being deemed worthy of proper surfacing, to accommodate motor traffic. This one was not

6 All over the country, short sections of road have been left isolated after road improvements to straighten out particularly dangerous sections. These can find their way into private ownership, become laybys or, as in this case, access roads to houses formerly on the side of the main road. This is on the former Roman military zone road, the Fosse Way, near to the source of the Thames in Gloucestershire

7 An unsurfaced and little-used country lane can quickly revert back to nature, like this one to the west of Eastington, Gloucestershire. Sometimes there are other obstructions too

9 Even in the early morning, until a few years ago, the ferry terminals of South and North Kessock near Inverness would have been busy with traffic waiting to cross the Beauly Firth; the completion of the nearby bridge carrying the A9 (several years after the approach road to it) in the 1980s led to the ferry becoming redundant, but the sloping piers survive

10 At low water, the stone piers of the wooden bridge that once crossed the River Teme at Dinham, below Ludlow Castle, Shropshire, can still be seen from the graceful replacement stone bridge alongside

Opposite below: 8 Stepping stones have seldom been the subject of detailed archaeological study, but would have been quite common ways of crossing streams, especially at fording points. These well-worn ones are across the River Esk at Egton Bridge in the North Yorkshire Moors; carefully crafted, they even have pointed cutwaters

11 Many medieval bridges throughout Britain, such as this small one in the village of Horrorbridge on the edge of Dartmoor, Devon, still have to cope with the needs of modern traffic

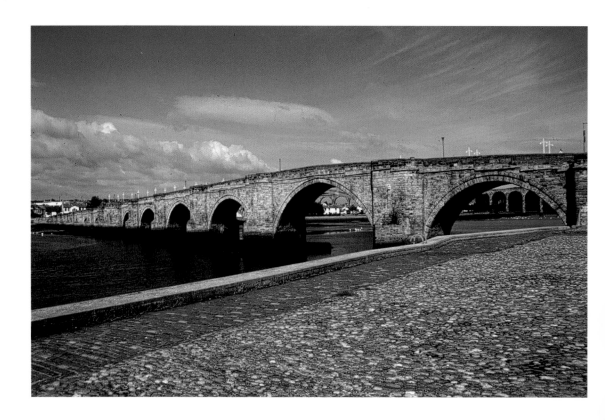

13 Scotland has few medieval bridges but does have some of the finest Georgian ones in Britain, including this particularly fine one at Kelso in the Borders built by John Rennie between 1800 and 1803. He used many of the basic *motifs* for his later Waterloo Bridge across the Thames in London.

14 Road viaducts before the mid-twentieth century were fairly rare; this is George Manner's viaduct at Limpley Stoke on the Black Dog Turnpike. It was opened in 1834, and is still very busy today

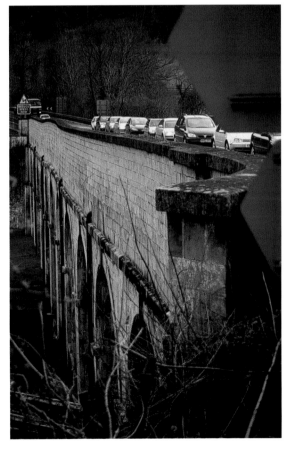

Opposite below: 12 Bridges across the Tweed, for centuries a zone of battle between England and Scotland, were not only at risk of damage from the elements but also from opposing armies – both in defence and attack. Several were built across the estuary at Berwick-on-Tweed and demolished before this one was completed in the early seventeenth century; local road traffic now uses a rather fine early twentieth-century concrete bridge built upstream, and the A1 crosses on a new bypass bridge several miles upstream

15 Well-designed and well-maintained concrete bridges can have a charm of their own in the right setting. This bridge carries the rebuilt early 1930s road over Rannoch Moor across the River Etive

16 The restored chapel on the medieval bridge across the Nene in St Ives, Huntingdonshire, is one of the most attractive of the handful that survive in Britain. The building of the bridge, incidentally, was associated with the construction of a new market town slightly downstream of an existing village, and it required a substantial causewayed approach on the opposite bank

Opposite above: 17 A causeway not designed specifically for travellers, but attractive in its own right, forms the approach to the impossibly picturesque castle, Eilean Donan, at the junction of Lochs Duich and Alsh in the Scottish Highlands

Opposite below: 18 A different type of causeway – and really a *causey* – was once typical of packhorse routes in the southern Pennines. This well-preserved section of slabbed packhorse path is near to Penistone, Yorkshire

19 The south portal of the Reigate Tunnel, Surrey, opened in 1824 and is now confined to pedestrians

20 The George, an ancient pilgrim's inn in Winchcombe, Gloucestershire, finally closed as a hostelry at the end of the 1980s and was converted into apartments. An archaeological study unravelled its fascinating history and also found that many of the later ranges to the rear were built of stone and timber quarried from the abbey after its closure

21 A typical view of Blackpool would be incomplete without its tower and its trams. It was the only town in England to retain them and they have since become one of its attractions. Elsewhere, modern versions of the tram are slowly making an appearance in larger cities

22 No book that deals with the roads of the twentieth century can ignore the contribution made by the two main motoring organisations, the AA and the RAC. Originally pressure groups, for most motorists they became safety nets in case of breakdown. Their telephone boxes have been superseded but a few survive such as this AA one at Devil's Bridge in mid-Wales

23 A collection of typical milestones and markers of the late eighteenth to mid-nineteenth centuries: a) a simple stone one in Cardiganshire, b) stone with an iron plate in Wiltshire, c) an unusual all-iron example in Somerset, d) a more typical cast-iron one in Yorkshire, e) a different sort of iron one in north Staffordshire, f) a typical mid-nineteenth-century example in Herefordshire

Opposite: 24 A miscellany of signposts and traffic signs: a) a typical south Pennine stoop, b) a finger post in Norfolk, c) a finger post in Somerset, one of the counties that virtually ignored orders to replace them in the 1960s, d) a finger post in Dorset with experimental grid reference, e) an increasingly rare direction sign of around 1960 still in use, f) a 50-year-old warning sign, minus its triangle, also still in service

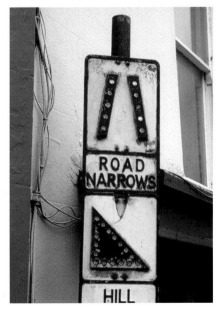

25 The danger of jumping to conclusions (i): there is a Roman road leading up this valley to the north of Ingleton in the Yorkshire Dales – but it isn't this one. This turnpike with its long straight sections was built on the opposite side of the valley to the Roman road, which is on the extreme left of this view

26 The danger of jumping to conclusions (ii): this straight section of embankment running across the meadow looks very much like the agger of a Roman road. In fact, it is part of the earthworks of the Bishop's Castle Railway that closed as early as 1936.

27 The recently restored former Daimler Garage and car park on Herbrand Street, London, a rather fine building opened in 1931 and still curiously modern-looking

28 The fate of this toll-house, to the south of Kington in Powys, is uncertain. It has been as ruinous as this for at least 20 years but was recently put up for sale. Quite how it can be restored and adapted for a new purpose is unclear – but such work will have to be quite radical

29 Occasionally, a building will survive the ravages of time, developers and vandals. This garage has probably not been used for nearly half a century but most of its fixtures and fittings survive intact. Suffice to say it is somewhere in the Welsh Marches

30 The road archaeology of the future. This is the expensively built triple-decker junction built to link the M54 motorway in Telford with a proposed new dual-carriageway around the western edge of the new town. That was never built so since this photograph was taken in 1987 the junction has been partially demolished and infilled, along with the earthworks of the dual carriageway. A much simpler junction and smaller lane are now in its place

41 The causeway leading to the west side of Gloucester across the flood plain of the Severn, as drawn by the Buck brothers in 1734

It had at its core, soil, rock and sand; this was capped by a thick layer of clay up to 5ft (1.5m) deep which was, in turn, capped by rubblestone around 2ft (0.6m) deep that was extended along the bed of the sands to either side of the embankment for additional protection. Both the clay and rubblestone layers were continued upwards to form flanking walls protecting the roadway. In addition, a new cut was made in the rocks to channel the tidal flows. It also took nearly two years to build and was ready by the end of 1824. Later, the embankment was widened to take the railway that would so damage the traffic on the Holyhead Road, and further changes have been made to cater for modern road traffic as well. The core of the original Stanley Embankment, however, survives.

Cuttings

In contrast to embankments of various forms, cuttings were rarities on British roads until the early nineteenth century and not particularly common until the new motorways and main roads were being built in the second half of the twentieth century. Whilst an embankment or a terraceway was a useful way in obtaining a well-drained road formation, a cutting was only really useful in providing a short cut through hilly ground or reducing particularly steep gradients. As such they were of more use for wheeled traffic and only then if gentle gradients and speed were considered to be important; these requirements did not become important in Britain until the advent of fast carriage traffic towards the end of the eighteenth century.

Inevitably, road cuttings were known in the ancient world long before they were dug in Britain and the Romans made use of them particularly in the rockier parts of Italy where construction was relatively straightforward. There are few specific references to cuttings in ancient texts, and most are fairly vague on detail. Plutarch, writing in around AD 100, credited the current emperor, Trajan, with building roads 'cutting through the mountains and eliminating the curves'.

In Britain there are very few identifiable Roman cuttings of any magnitude. One on the Ackling Dyke in Dorset has already been mentioned. One of the deepest is on the difficult road across the watershed between the rivers Duddon and Esk close to the Roman fort of *Mediobogdum* – now appropriately known as Hardknott. This rock-cut cutting at the foot of Raven Crag is about 16ft (5m) deep in parts and up to 16ft (5m) wide. In a few other places there is a different form of Roman cutting, where the often quite thick peat or topsoil was deliberately cut away to reveal a solid rock strata that was then used as the base for the road metalling. The most dramatic use of this technique to be identified so far is near Melrose, in the Borders region on the road from Carlisle to Newstead. Several lesser cuttings have been identified elsewhere on the Roman road network, some probably to expose the bedrock, others to relieve a gradient, and some probably the result mainly of wear and tear and thus really variants of holloways.

Fairly few road cuttings of any size were constructed between the early part of the Roman period and the early nineteenth century, simply because there was no real need for them. Even in the eighteenth century, most of the turnpike trusts were more concerned with upgrading existing routes than creating significant deviations or completely new and better-engineered roads. However, in that brief period of a quarter of a century just before the development of steam railways, several new and impressive road cuttings were dug.

Cuttings through hard rock were far easier to make than those through softer soils. Normally, the sides of such rock cuttings could be left almost vertical with little fear of subsequent collapse to block the road or injure those travelling on it. Thus it was that the earliest turnpike cuttings tended to be in those areas where rock cuttings were possible – for example, through the sandstones along the

42 A typical late eighteenth-century cutting on a turnpike road in the Severn valley between Stourport and Bewdley

Severn valley. There are quite impressive cuttings, for example, at Harley Bank, Shropshire, where the Shrewsbury to Ludlow road climbs the Wenlock Edge, and on the road between Bewdley and Stourport, Worcestershire. Other rock-cut cuttings were needed on the approaches to road tunnels, such as the one in Reigate, Surrey.

In softer rocks and shales the 'angle of repose' – the steepest gradient at which soils would not continue to slip under normal circumstances – is much less than in hard rock. This inevitably meant that either the cutting had to be revetted by masonry walls, or that they were given shallow sloping sides. Obviously, shallow-sided cuttings would require a wider band of land than steeper sided ones and thus incur more cost to the turnpike trust in obtaining it. Such cuttings were also more difficult to form and maintain. Revetted cuttings had the advantage of not requiring additional land but did demand added initial structural costs. If, in such circumstances, trusts saw no real need for cuttings, they simply did not create them.

Where money was no object, the situation changed. In the early nineteenth century, the Earls of Shrewsbury developed their former lodge at Alton, in the moorlands of north Staffordshire, into one of the largest and grandest gardens in England. The main grounds of Alton Towers, now the country's major theme park, are approached by miles of long and sinuous drives, deliberately over-engineered to make use of the carefully crafted Romantic views and to obtain very gentle gradients. In places, these run through cuttings carefully lined with stone revetment walls – and one of these was later used by the park's miniature railway. The Earls also introduced terraceways, a false bridge that was really a dam, and even a flyover.

By far the largest road cuttings have been the result of major government projects from the mid-twentieth century onwards. They occur especially on the motorways and bypasses where huge cuttings have been carved through hills with, in Britain, particularly deep ones at Stokenchurch on the M40 and on the A34 bypass around Newbury.

CHAPTER 4

Tunnels

There is a tradition, difficult to prove, that the first major road tunnel was built on the orders of Queen Semiramis of Assyria, also credited by some with the Hanging Gardens of Babylon. She is said to have had a tunnel built under the Euphrates to link her palace with the Temple of Jupiter on the opposite bank in around 2200 BC; no archaeological evidence has so far come to light. In the Middle East there was plenty of early expertise in tunnelling, but this was associated with very impressive irrigation schemes rather than road transport.

It is thought that one of the earliest surviving road tunnels was a short one built at Furlo, Italy, in the Etruscan period, around 400 BC. Creating a safe short cut in the gorge of the River Candigliano it is just 26ft (8m) long but probably took two years to make; it was probably formed by burning timbers against the cliffs to heat up the rock, then rapidly cooling it with water and causing it to crack. Much later, it was bypassed by a second tunnel over 125ft (38m) long, built on the orders of the Emperor Vespasian c.AD 70, which took thousands of slaves six years to build; amazingly, it is still in use.

There is evidence for the construction of two much more ambitious road tunnels in Naples, built around 40 BC by the Roman engineer and architect Lucius Cocceius Auctus to relieve traffic congestion. One was at Cumae, 3,280ft (1,000m) long, and the other, at Puteoli, was 2,296ft (700m) long. After passing through the tunnel at Cumae in the first century AD, Seneca complained that 'Nothing is as long as that prison, nothing as dim as those torches', adding that the dust was unbearable.

Tunnelling was not unknown in Britain, even before the arrival of the Romans, but was associated purely with mining up until the eighteenth century; there was simply no need for road tunnels. The first transport related tunnels in this country were, excluding those in the mines used by primitive underground sledges or tramways, associated with the canals. Unlike roads, canals were difficult to take up and over hills without using locks, expensive both in construction and water usage. By the time that canals needed to cross over the higher watersheds, a summit level tunnel was often the logical solution. Before the end of the eighteenth century, huge tunnels several miles long, like those at Harecastle in north Staffordshire and Sapperton in Gloucestershire, had been completed at great expense, having taken several years to build.

In general, until well into the twentieth century road tunnels were not seen to be worth their expense of construction and maintenance as most road traffic could cope with steep gradients and go up and over hills. Speed was not that important a factor, except on some of the key mail routes. Where some ambitious thinkers thought tunnels could be of use was under busy and wide waterways where bridges would impede shipping.

An engineer called Ralph Dodd began to build an extraordinarily ambitious road tunnel under the Thames estuary between Gravesend, Kent, and Tilbury, Essex, in 1798. The initial shaft on the Kent shore was built and a starter tunnel begun, but the works flooded and were abandoned. His plans for another tunnel, under the Mersey at Runcorn, in 1800 never got off the drawing board. However, Dodd was no fool and would later build the country's second longest, but tallest, canal tunnel at Strood, Kent, on the commercially unsuccessful Thames & Medway Canal; this was later adapted for, and is still used by, main line trains.

The next two attempts to build major road tunnels in Britain were spectacular failures, and both were the work of a Cornish mining engineer called Robert Vazie, nicknamed 'the Mole'. In 1802 he planned a tunnel under the Thames between Rotherhithe and Limehouse, London. The specially formed Thames Archway Company was authorised to build it in 1805 and a shaft was dug at the Rotherhithe end but work stalled. In 1807 Vazie was replaced by his more famous fellow Cornishman, Richard Trevithick; a timber-lined 'starter' or 'header' tunnel, just 5ft (1.6m) high and about 3ft (1m) wide, had reached about 1,000ft (317m) along the line before being flooded and abandoned.

Undeterred, in 1809 Vazie was empowered by Act of Parliament to raise the huge sum of £60,000 to build a tunnel 750ft (237m) long through Highgate Hill to the north of London to eliminate the steep gradient of the main road out of the capital. In April 1812, after about two-thirds had been bored, the tunnel collapsed due to poor workmanship. A deep cutting was substituted, spanned by a bridge taking an existing lane over it, designed by John Nash (replaced in 1897); thus Archway Road was opened in 1813. The unintended flyover was known sarcastically thereafter as the 'Highgate Tunnel'.

The first significant and successful road tunnel in Britain was a short one, beneath the Castle Mount in Reigate, Surrey. It was built as a private venture by a local aristocrat, Lord Somers, in 1823–24. For a fee, it provided a short cut for road traffic through the town. The tunnel, with its elaborately arcaded and battlemented brick portals and arcaded side walls, is approached through steep-sided rock-cut approaches and is about 180ft (55m) long on a slightly rising gradient. It is still used by pedestrians.

Two short road tunnels of the early 1830s survive in Dorset and one still takes main 'A' road traffic. Both were built by the Bridport Turnpike Trust, though are quite far apart; one is at Thistle Hill just outside Charmouth and the other at Horn Hill to the north of Beaminster. The main road was diverted around the Thistle Hill tunnel in a cutting in the 1980s, but the Horn Hill tunnel is still in use. It was built by an engineer, M. Lang, in 1831–32 and was largely paid for by a local man, Giles Russel; it has a fairly flat three-centred arch and a profile quite different from contemporary railway tunnels. The tunnel has stone portals but is brick lined, although the lining has been sprayed with a modern cement surface as part of some recent repairs.

By the time the two Dorset tunnels had opened, work had been started, and abandoned, on another attempt to build a tunnel under the Thames in London. An émigré French engineer, Marc Brunel, had patented a special tunnelling 'shield' in 1818 intended for an ambitious tunnel scheme under the River Neva in St Petersburg, Russia. That idea was abandoned but in 1823 the shield, and its inventor, came to the notice of the doomed and desperate Thames Archway Company. Their idea of a tunnel below the river was revived. An Act of Parliament was obtained and work began under Brunel's supervision on a new tunnel, from Rotherhithe to Wapping. Despite the safety features of the 'shield', the work was fraught with problems and disasters and men lost their lives. Several times the tunnel workings were flooded and had to be restarted.

In 1826 Marc's son, Isambard Kingdom Brunel, then just 20 years old, took over as resident engineer from his sick father, but was not officially given that title until the following year. In 1828 the money ran out; work was suspended and not restarted until 1835 with considerable grants from the government. It opened as a twin-bore tunnel in March 1843. Each bore had a horseshoe section and was 14ft (4.3m) wide and 16ft (4.8m) tall; the total tunnel length was 1,200ft (366m). Unfortunately the vehicular traffic it was originally designed to take did not materialise because the approach ramps in the terminal shafts – each 50ft (15m) in diameter – at either end were never built.

Instead the tunnel was used for pedestrians only, though for most people it became a tourist attraction rather than a major thoroughfare, with music, a coffee room, stalls selling trinkets and souvenirs and a 'Steam Cosmorama' in the middle turning out views for a penny. Even this could not make the tunnel pay its way and in 1865 it was purchased by the new East London Railway. They extended

43 Marc Brunel's tunnel under the Thames, finished off by his son, Isambard, was one of the engineering wonders of the age and attracted world-wide attention; this engraving is German. Finally opened in 1843, it was difficult to build and was sadly never a commercial success. Nevertheless, it is still in use, albeit by 'tube' trains

the tunnel at either end and converted it into a rail tunnel that opened in 1869; it remains a vital part of the capital's underground railway system. Brunel's pump house of 1842 on the Rotherhithe bank is now a small museum, and most of the tunnel structure survives intact. Travellers on the East London line will notice the central arcade as they pass under the Thames and see the portals of the twin bores at Wapping station – and the lift and steps there are housed in the original cylindrical brick-lined 'drum' in which the spiral ramps were never built.

Whilst Brunel's Thames tunnel was a road tunnel converted for a railway, the next tunnel to be built under the Thames was a railway tunnel converted for pedestrian use. Built in 1869 by P.W. Barlow, the boring of the Tower Subway was the first successful use of a 'Greathead' tunnelling shield, a much improved version of Marc Brunel's original idea. It was also the first tunnel to be lined in cast-iron with grouting behind. Although nearly 1,350ft (411m) long it was only

6ft 8 inches (2.1m) tall inside. Intended to be used by cable-hauled trams, it was quickly converted into a pedestrian tunnel and was then made redundant by the opening of Tower Bridge in 1896; the tunnel now carries water mains and other services.

Later road tunnels under the Thames had less dramatic and more successful stories. The Blackwall Tunnel was the next to be built, between that suburb and Greenwich on the south bank, by London County Council. Just over 4,400ft (1340m) long overall, it was built by Sir Alexander Binnie between 1891 and 1897, using a 'Greathead' shield and compressed air – to hold back the water – during construction. It is lined with a mixture of cast-iron ribs and concrete faced with glazed white tiles, similar to the station sections of the city's 'tube' railways. Even by the start of the 1930s over a million vehicles a year were using the tunnel and a second tunnel was added alongside in the 1960s; both now take the traffic of the busy A102. At the southern entrance is the rather fine Tunnel House, an elaborate art nouveau building by Thomas Blashill.

Further upstream, the Rotherhithe Tunnel to Shadwell was built at a cost of over £2 million pounds, also by the London County Council. Opened in 1908, and around 4,800ft (1460m) long overall with a diameter a little under 3ft (10m), it was designed by Sir Maurice Fitzmaurice and is now used by the A101. An unusual surface reminder of this tunnel is the circular air vent in King Edward's Memorial Park, Wapping, a functional but attractive building of brick and stone and art nouveau ironwork in the windows. Its main role was not to vent the fumes from the new fangled motor cars in the tunnel – then a rarity – but mainly to get rid of the smells from the piles of horse dung! Two more pedestrian tunnels, both fitted with electric lifts and staircases, were built under the river. One was from Greenwich to the Isle of Dogs by Sir Alexander Binnie, opened in 1902, and the other from Woolwich to North Woolwich, by Sir Maurice Fitzmaurice, opened in 1912 to ease overcrowding on the Woolwich Free Ferry.

One of the most famous road tunnels of its day was that built under the Mersey estuary between Liverpool and Birkenhead, and is over 2 miles (3.2km) long. The Queensway was the joint work of engineers Sir Basil Mott and John A. Brodie. It was begun in 1925, but took nine years to build. Over 1.2 million tons of rock and soil were excavated and over half a million pounds (250,000kg) of gelignite were used. The main single tunnel is circular in section and is of cast-iron ribs sprayed with concrete and bitumen emulsion; the total length of the main tunnel and dock branches was 2.75 miles (4.4km). The roadway is of reinforced concrete supported on pillars and when the tunnel opened in 1934, its four carriageways were paved with cast-iron slabs, divided by white lines and the newly developed 'cat's eyes'; it was lit throughout with

INTERIOR OF MERSEY TUNNEL, UNDER THE RIVER MERSEY,
LIVERPOOL & BIRKENHEAD.

44 This Valentine's postcard shows an artist's view of the first Mersey Tunnel, the Queensway, opened in 1934. It was probably printed at the same time. The amount of traffic and the lack of a central reservation make the tunnel seem a rather dangerous place. Note the electric light, iron road surface and cats' eyes

electricity. As in all tunnels, most of the real engineering expertise is hidden and the main superstructures were relatively simple elements of the whole. These surface buildings, which included the important ventilation towers and generator blocks, were designed by the architect Herbert Rowse in a vaguely French *moderne* style with a hint of ancient Egypt. A second double-tube tunnel under the estuary was fully completed in 1974.

Before the Mersey tunnel had opened, another much shorter tunnel of under 650ft (200m) had been carved through the cliffs of north Wales at Penmaenmawr to the west of Conwy on the Chester to Holyhead route; lit by electricity throughout, it was built in 1932 as part of road improvements finished in 1935. The tunnel portals were designed by the Secretary of the Royal Fine Art Commission, H. Chalton Bradshaw, and the Coats of Arms were carved by Mr Gilbert Ledward. The portals were built of limestone from the Bryn Euryn quarries near Colwyn and the concrete-lined tunnel had an elliptical arch. Other major road tunnels were being planned in the later 1930s,

THE PENMAENBACH TUNNEL, PENMAENMAWR, EAST ENTRANCE.

45 The fine portals of the Penmaenmawr Tunnel to the west of Conwy were designed by
H. Chalton Bradshaw. Although the tunnel was finished in 1932, the road scheme was not ready
until 1935, which may be when this photograph was taken

including one under the Thames near Dartford and another under the Tyne
near Jarrow. Postponed because of the Second World War and subsequent post-
war austerity, these two tunnels were finally opened to road traffic in 1963 and
1967 respectively; smaller pedestrian and cycle tunnels had opened under the
Tyne in 1951.

More recent major tunnels under river estuaries have included one under the
Conwy estuary on the Chester-Holyhead coastal route, opened in 1991 to take
the A55 away from the middle of historic Conwy. This was the first significant
use of the 'immersed tube tunnel' technique in Britain and was followed by
one under the Medway between Strood and Gillingham opened in 1996. In
simple terms, the tunnel is built in prefabricated sections of tube, floated out
on the water to the correct position, sunk into a pre-prepared cutting in the
river bed, joined to the sections at either end of it, and then covered over. The
series of individual sections thus form the complete tunnel and no dangerous
subterranean boring work is required.

This technique had been pioneered mainly in the United States early in the twentieth century. Ironically, the earliest attempts had been in England a century beforehand, by none other than the ill-starred Thames Archway Company. Desperate to complete their tunnel from Rotherhithe, they experimented with the idea of building brick-lined cylinders on land, taking them out on barges into the Thames, and sinking them in place to form segments of tunnel that could then be joined together. Trials in 1810 and 1811 proved that the system would work, but it proved too expensive for the virtually bankrupt company and the technique was abandoned a century before its time.

In the late twentieth century, other tunnels have been built that are not 'traditional' in boring through high ground or underneath rivers. Most are shallow tunnels built using the 'cut-and-cover' method, in which a cutting is dug and then roofed over. Indeed, many such tunnels, such as that taking the A1(M) under a shopping centre in Hertfordshire, the inner ring roads in major cities such as Birmingham, those on parts of the motorway system, and one taking the main approach road under the runway at Heathrow Airport, are really just very wide bridges.

Perhaps the most unusual, and certainly the narrowest, road tunnel presently in use is in the delightful hills of north Staffordshire; it takes a minor lane in the Manifold valley through a hilly spur. The Swainsley tunnel was built for the narrow-gauge Manifold Light Railway, engineered by E.R. Calthrop and opened in 1904. Despite the picturesque scenery, the line was not a success and it closed in 1934. With great foresight, the local county council converted most of the route into a cycleway and footpath, but the tunnel was, instead, converted into a single-track road tunnel.

CHAPTER 5

Road surfaces

Unsurprisingly, there are very few remnants of any surfacing of prehistoric tracks in Britain. In the ancient civilisations of the East, sophisticated road surfaces were developed thousands of years ago. For example, the 20ft (6m) wide road between Antioch and Aleppo in Syria had a fine, smooth pavement of hewn limestone raised above the adjacent ground level, and was just one of several great highways of the age.

In contemporary prehistoric Britain it is likely that, for the most part, hard-wearing surfaces were simply not needed for the limited and mainly pedestrian traffic of the day and that, apart from possible infilling of swampier areas of tracks with rocks or brushwood, tracks were simply left in the natural, ever eroding, state.

Certainly by the fourth millennium BC the lack of surfacing of most tracks was not because of a lack of sophisticated engineering, merely the lack of need. Where natural obstacles did have to be overcome, considerable ingenuity could be displayed. This can be seen in areas where the environmental conditions have preserved 'soft' materials, such as the Somerset Levels. Whilst not strictly 'roads' as such, whole series of trackways linking settlements and fields on the solid 'islands' in the marshes have been identified.

The earliest of these, dating to around 4000 BC, consisted of tracks made up of bundles of brushwood simply laid on top of the marshy area and held in place by pegs. Other versions were more sophisticated, using planks or split logs pegged to a sub-frame. In Somerset the most famous of these is the 'Sweet Track', over a mile long across a reedy swamp, which has been accurately dated through tree-ring analysis to 3806 BC.

In the late nineteenth century a log path was discovered in Lindow Moss in Cheshire, where, a century later, the body of 'Pete Marsh', the famous Lindow Man, was found. A similar trackway was discovered during archaeological excavations in advance of the extension of Manchester Airport in the 1990s and, far to the south, another timber trackway, dated to around 1500 BC was rediscovered at Beckton on the north bank of the Thames in East London assumed to have led to some type of 'hide' used in hunting. In the Humber Wetlands Survey, two separate tracks made up of woven 'hurdles' of hazel and alder pegged in place by stakes were identified and given a date of about 1400 BC.

Another recent discovery has shown that some pre-Roman tracks may have been surfaced in a more sophisticated manner than hitherto thought. The Oxford Archaeology Unit excavated what appeared to be a metalled road at Yarnton, near Oxford in the mid-1990s. It was deliberately surfaced with carefully laid limestone and small quartzite pebbles and was wide enough to allow carts to pass each other; it seemed to be a causeway – or perhaps a ford – across a channel of the Thames and was considered to be of early Bronze Age date. These surviving traces of Neolithic and Bronze Age road engineering in specific areas of the country were certainly not unique and there would presumably have been similar sophistication shown in other parts of the country – where needed.

As yet, the archaeological evidence remains that it was from the Roman Conquest of Britain in the mid-first century AD that the biggest improvement in roads and their surfaces took place. There are still certain myths about Roman road construction that survive despite archaeological evidence to the contrary, and it is still sometimes claimed that all Roman roads were built in the same manner. This is palpably not true, even for the more important roads that have generally been the subject of most archaeological attention.

The agger, or embankment on which most of the main roads were built would have provided a well-drained platform for the road surface. From the available evidence in Britain, the surface, almost but not invariably much narrower than the agger, was generally made up of several carefully laid and consolidated layers of stone, usually derived from the line of the route. These layers vary greatly in their thickness but one common feature is the fact that the surface was deliberately given a pronounced camber to facilitate drainage.

In many roads the initial layer on top of the agger is made up of larger stones, with successively smaller stones in the layers above, but this construction method is by no means universal. High Street, perhaps appropriately enough, one of the highest Roman roads, in the Cumbrian fells, has a base of rough stone, a middle layer of peat, and then a wearing surface of gravel. In general, the top, or wearing, layer of the roads was of fine gravel, if available, though where such material was either not available or where other suitable materials were more abundant they were used instead. For example, flints were sometimes used in the south-east of England and in some areas where ironworks were established, especially in the

Weald, slag waste was used instead and provided a fine smooth surface – the most apposite metalling of all.

Given that only the main Roman roads have been studied in any depth, it is not really known how or to what extent the lesser roads and tracks were properly surfaced. On some of the minor Roman roads that have been studied, the agger was often omitted and the surfaces consisted merely of a single compacted layers of stones and gravel laid on and into a levelled sub-stratum of clay or soil; in general, these lesser roads still had well-designed drains. In very wet areas different measures had to be taken; on Stone Street, Somerset, a raft of woven timber 'corduroy' and posts was used as the base for a surface of concrete. Kerb stones were used on some roads to retain the surface layers, and other stretches may have had kerb stones that have since been robbed out for reuse.

The rarest surface of all was that of paved slabs, though these were common enough in most of the rest of the empire, and especially in its Italian heartland. Well worked and carefully laid paved slab surfaces have been identified in fords believed to be Roman in origin, but on the surface, the most famous section of paved Roman road is still the subject of continuing archaeological debate. This is the portion of the trans-Pennine route over the Blackstone edge, between Lancashire and Yorkshire. On the western slope is a well-preserved section of

46 There are only a few places in Britain where the surface levels of a Roman road are visible; this is the so-called Wade's Causeway across Wheeldale, though there is considerable debate as to whether or not the stone flags on the surface were originally covered in gravel

neatly paved road that climbs steeply and uncompromisingly upwards to the top, and a medieval marker pillar – the Aiggin Stone. John Taylor, the Water Poet, took this road in 1639 and recorded that 'I went downe the lofty mountaine called Blackstone Edge, I thought my selfe with my boy and horses had been in the land of Breakneck, it was so steep and tedious, yet I recovered …'.

Where visible, the road surface is of carefully laid paving slabs between stone curbs and its most remarkable feature is a central shallow slot for which various theories have been put forward. One, that it was for drainage, is clearly not plausible as it is in the middle of the road and the road is cambered in the normal manner. The other main theory is that it was designed for a central brake pole to help slow down wagons descending the hill. Other academics believe that the road is not Roman at all, but medieval, possibly associated with a quarry at the top. Yet another possibility is that the road was indeed Roman, but with all of its central trough stones originally spine stones (seen in only a handful of other places in Britain but not unusual elsewhere in the Empire); that road was then used by medieval traffic from a quarry still plainly visible at the top of the hill. That quarry, of course, could have been where the paving slabs came from and thus have been Roman. To confuse matters further, there is a paved 'zigzag' diversion half way up the hill, perhaps for wheeled traffic but of uncertain date. Not surprisingly, the debate continues, and the road continues to amaze visitors. Similarly, there have been debates about the surface of another well-preserved Roman road across Wheeldale Moor to the south of Goathland, Yorkshire; it has a stone slabbed surface of sorts and preserved culverts, but some experts consider that it was originally gravelled.

Archaeological evidence has shown that Roman roads were constantly repaired and maintained until the end of the Roman era; the only exceptions were those roads that went out of use, mainly for strategic reasons or because they had been largely supplanted by a different route. Then, after the end of Roman rule, the roads were allowed to decline and their surfaces allowed to erode away or be quarried – though the worst period for the loss of surface metalling of these roads was during the construction of adjacent turnpikes in the eighteenth century. Miniature 'quarry pits' of that period can be identified in many of the surviving Roman roads.

Whilst there is some erratic evidence of metalled surfaces within towns and settlements in the centuries between the end of Roman rule and the Saxon period, so far no evidence has emerged for the maintenance of the roads between them – and the historical evidence in any event suggests that the main road network was effectively abandoned. Most of the lines of communications appear to have been no more than well-worn tracks little different than those of pre-Roman Britain and, as outlined earlier, the archaeological evidence for deliberate road engineering up until the end of the Saxon period is virtually non-existent.

47 The most remarkably preserved Roman road is also one of the most baffling. Climbing up to the top of Blackstone Edge on the Lancashire/Yorkshire border is this fully-paved road with its unique central trough – perhaps worn away by brake poles to prevent descending wagons running away. The trough's true purpose has yet to be established

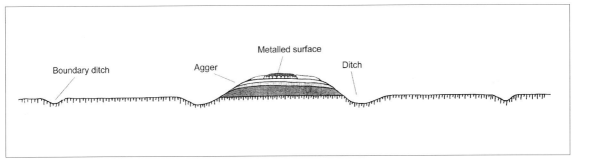

48 A simplified cross-section of one of the more important Roman roads. Differences in size, status and available materials throughout Britain mean that there really is no such thing as a 'typical' construction

Indeed, there is very little evidence of road engineering, and especially of road surfacing, up until the end of the medieval period, apart from the paving within the major cities, occasional *ad hoc* attempts at metalling, and some evidence for roadside drains and a few culverts. The lack of archaeological evidence is partly due to the lack of any attempt or need for scientific and logical surfacing of roads in this period, and partly due to the fact that most traces would have been removed or obscured by later road surfaces if a route was successful enough to warrant being upgraded. There have also been very few excavations of medieval roads away from the towns. Some traces of attempts to cope with particularly boggy areas have been found, mainly in towns, such as the use of interwoven logs and hurdles in various different designs, sometimes known as *corduroy roads*; one was discovered across the former King's Ditch in Hereford, for example.

Most of the substantive archaeological evidence for road surfaces has been largely confined to excavations within towns and cities and is generally associated with street paving rather than long distance travel. Deeds related to the paving of many towns have survived; such paving was usually of cobbling, with little attempt initially at anything but the most primitive drainage systems of open gulleys usually in the centre of the street. Matters became more sophisticated in certain areas of certain towns in the eighteenth century, especially in the 'better' parts of London and other major towns, and the fashionable resorts such as Bath. One development that must have been very welcome by those travelling in carriages was the introduction in some places of *wheelers* – long flat stones in pairs, not dissimilar to railway lines through the cobbles – on which the wheels of the carriages could run smoothly.

Away from the towns, the roads and tracks appear to have been mainly unsurfaced, apart from *ad hoc* infilling of holes with stones and, presumably, on bridges and perhaps on the approach embankments to them. That situation was largely unchanged by the seventeenth century. A fairly reliable commentator on the state of British roads in the early years of that century was the much-travelled John Taylor – the self-styled Water Poet. He wrote in a mixture of prose and poor poetry, but with some humour.

On his way from London to Scotland in 1617 he passed through Cheshire where 'The clammy clay sometimes my heeles would trip/One foote went forward,/th'other backe would slip.' Once in Scotland, to the north-east of Perth he found the way to be 'so uneven, stonie, and full of bogges, quagmires, and long heath, that a dogge with three legs will outrunne a horse with foure …'. The streets in towns proved to be better kept. In 1622 Taylor obviously had a good time in Leicester, where the 'streets are so well paved, and kept so clean from dunghills, filth, or soyle, that in the wettest or fowlest weather, a man may go all over the towne in a paire of slippers, and never wet his feet.' However, his

49 Paving in towns, known from the medieval period onwards, was usually no more than well-laid cobbles. These continued to be used, with some refinements, into the early-nineteenth century. Long paired lines of specially worked stones, *wheelers*, could be used to help the smooth running of carriages, especially in the more upmarket areas such as these in Abbey Square, Chester

objectivity may be called into question as, many years later, he said much the same thing about Barnstaple in Devon.

In some areas of the country, especially in the southern Pennines in England, pedestrians and those on horseback were saved the troubles of the muddy roads where the wagons went. Packhorses were the best means of transporting goods in hilly areas and special paths were often created for them on important routes, made up of a line of flagstones. These were known as *causeys* – a name not to be confused with, but clearly related to, *causeways* – and in many instances the names were interchangeable. However, in this sense the word causey meant a paved path.

Sometimes the line of these paving stones was in the centre of a lane on which there was no wheeled traffic but, if there was such traffic, placed on one side of the road instead. In such cases, as the causeys tended to bear up better to the weight of their traffic whilst the lane alongside did not, almost inevitably the causey ended up being at a much higher level as the road gradually became a deeper and deeper holloway.

The origins of causeys are unknown, but some may have existed in the medieval period. They were clearly a common and accepted part of travelling by the late seventeenth century; Celia Fiennes, on a journey to Wigan in southern Lancashire passed 'mostly in lanes and some hollow waye' that were so bad that they were forced to climb 'upon the high Causey' alongside many times.

Dating individual causeys is difficult, and in many cases the flagstones will have been replaced on one or more occasions. The depth of the any adjacent holloway is no guide, as it is seldom related to the date of the causey. Similarly, there are some causeys that were set into the bottoms of already well-established holloways. A surprising number of causeys of various kinds survive, perhaps because many of the packhorse routes were eventually replaced by better roads for wheeled traffic from the later eighteenth century onwards. Two of the best examples are the Long Causeway and the Cat Hill causeways, both to the west of Sheffield.

Despite the development of the turnpikes, roads in Britain, though gradually improving, were still fairly poor well into the eighteenth century. Arthur Young, in Lancashire in 1770, measured ruts in the road 4ft deep and noted that 'The only mending it receives is tumbling in some loose stones which serve no other purpose than jolting the carriage in the most intolerable manner'.

Up until the early nineteenth century the normal way of trying to repair a road was to pile up the soil in the middle to create an exaggerated camber, with the generally forlorn hope that this would enable the rainwater to drain off into side ditches. There seems to have been a belief that the greater the camber the greater the efficiency of the surface drainage. Despite the growth of turnpikes, most of the roads in the country were still parish roads, repaired by statute labour and usually under the direction of surveyors who had little or no idea of what they were doing. Many of the turnpikes were no better, and surveyors were often appointed for their contacts rather than for their skills.

A Parliamentary Committee in 1809 reported that it was still standard practice on most roads to use the central convex camber. When the road had got to such a state that repairs were unavoidable, they were still usually left until after the harvests; then a labourer or group of labourers were hired by the surveyor and told to fill in the holes and rebuild the camber and 'to be sure that he threw up the road high enough, and made the stones of the old causeway, or foot pavement, go as far as they could'.

Once the camber had been made, it was sparsely scattered with gravel. This usually had to be done before Michaelmas, so that by the time the magistrates passed by on their way to the quarter sessions, they would have no choice but to admit that the road was then in a reasonable condition; the parish could, therefore, not be indicted for non-repair. Almost straight away the road would deteriorate and within a short time begin to get worse than it had been before the repairs. Wagons and coaches could not cope with the 'barrelling' of the road and had to drive on the top and in the centre; the unconsolidated camber was quickly eroded, and within a year or two the road was virtually impassable.

The poor quality of road surfaces had nothing to do with a lack of available technical knowledge; either surveyors simply never bothered to read or implement methods promulgated from the mid-eighteenth century onwards, or they never had sufficient resources available to do so. As early as 1675 Thomas Mace of Trinity College, Cambridge, had urged for careful building and maintenance of road surfaces, partly in rhyme:

> First let the wayes be regularly brought
> To artificial form, and truly wrought;
> So that we can suppose them firmly mended,
> And in all parts the work well ended,
> That not a stone's amiss; but all compleat
> All lying smooth, round, firm, and wondrous neat.

In the winter of 1737, Robert Phillips read before the Royal Society *A Dissertation Concerning the Present State of the High-Roads of England … Wherein is Proposed a New Method of Repairing and Maintaining Them*; it was later published as a pamphlet. In it he advocated several of the improvements that would be taken up by road engineers later in the eighteenth and early in the nineteenth century, including the need to carefully grade and wash stone and the care needed to produce a properly consolidated surface. In particular he complained of 'the practise of laying down large heaps of unprepared gravel to be gradually consolidated into a harder mass'.

The military roads in the Scottish Highland built between 1725 and the late 1760s had generally been better made than the average turnpike road, being government funded. They had relied on an initial scraping away of the top soil; a

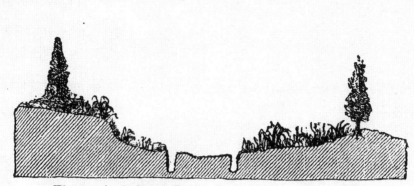

Fig. 2.—An Indicted Road.—Its first state.   Year 1809.

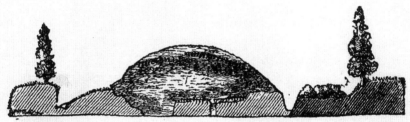

Fig. 3.—The Indicted Road thrown up, to take off the Indictment,
under the direction of a Parish Surveyor.   Its second state.

Fig. 4.—The same Road, in its third year after repair, or its last and worst state.

50 The typical repair of a parish road according to the report of a parliamentary commission in 1809, showing just how bad some roads could get. This also applied to many of the turnpiked roads as well

solid base of larger rocks was then laid between crude kerbs, a second cambered layer of smaller stones on top of that, and a top layer of gravel. These well-drained roads were, in theory, fairly well designed, though mainly for soldiers on the march and artillery rather than for carriages and wagons.

Whilst a few of the turnpike trusts built good roads or rebuilt existing ones to a good standard, most did not and so had little use for high cost engineering or new forms of efficient surfacing. This was due in no small part to the lack of quality in their surveyors. One of the greatest exceptions to that was a Yorkshireman, John Metcalf. Despite being blind from childhood, he had an eventful life; as a young man he even joined a volunteer regiment to fight the Jacobites in the 1745 uprising. Twenty years later he won the contract to set out and make a 3 mile long road from Harrogate, surveying the route himself. Quite how he managed this is not really known, but so successful was the route and the quality of the road that he would eventually survey and construct around 180 miles of roads in Yorkshire. His road building technique was simply based on the best methods then available, typically a solid cambered base course of stones, often supported on a raft of heather or ling, with a layer of smaller stones above and good drains on both sides.

In the early nineteenth century, the subject of road surfaces in Britain attracted a considerable degree of interest. Despite several other men's experiments and theories, it was the work of two men, both from the south-west of Scotland but with very different backgrounds and very different philosophies, that resulted in the formation of some of the very best roads in the world at that time. One thing that they did have in common was an awareness of the need for good drainage and both incorporated efficient drainage systems – culverts, ditches etc. – into their designs.

Thomas Telford was one of the greatest engineers of all time and only a road builder by default, having been commissioned by the government to improve the roads in Scotland and then the main London to Holyhead road. The ideas that he used for his road surfaces were very similar to those of a French road maker, Pierre Trésuguet, developed half a century beforehand. In the mid-eighteenth century, France had its own *Ecole des Ponts et Chausées* and in theory its road technology was far in advance of the rest of Europe. However, its roads also relied heavily on statute labour – *la corvée* – which was even more unpopular and even less well run than the parish system in Britain. Even after *la corvée* was abolished in 1764, French roads tended to be well built but poorly maintained and even Trésuguet's roads could not cope with that.

In his system the top of the road embankment was cut away and scarped to a camber. At either side large 'curb' stones were laid that would hold the rest of the road surface in place. Onto the base, a row of large stones, generally on edge, was laid and roughly beaten to an even surface; a second layer of smaller stones was laid on top of the first and hammered in by hand. Finally, a top course of small hard-wearing broken stones – specified as being the size of walnuts - was spread by shovels to form the wearing course; the camber was relatively modest.

One of the main problems with Trésuguet's system was cost. For Telford, working mainly on government projects, that was not an issue and his system was very similar to the Frenchman's. Unlike Trésuguet, Telford did not require a camber to the stripped natural ground level beneath the formation stones and, instead, relied on the grading of those stones – getting gradually taller in the middle – to achieve the camber required. Telford also allowed for specific local issues to be accommodated, such as using turves of brushwood beneath the base course where the land was particularly marshy, and also the use of puddled clay if needed. Above the base course was a layer of hard broken stone up to 6 inches (15cm) deep, usually of granite or one of the better limestones, and on the surface, a thin binding course of gravel up to 2 inches (5cm) deep. Apart from constant maintenance of the top layer, the design was extremely strong and if the road was well-built in the first place, capable of many years of work before major repairs were needed.

John Loudon MacAdam was born in Ayr, of minor gentry stock; he had an interesting business career in Scotland and the United States before moving to England in middle age. He claimed later that he spent many years travelling

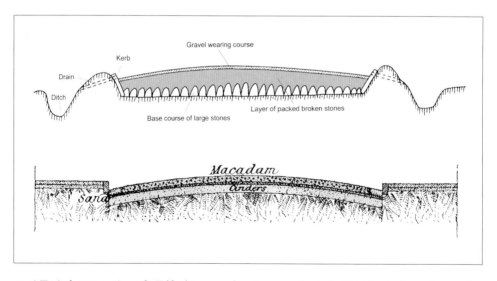

51 a) Typical cross section of a Telford-type road, quite expensive to build b) In the later nineteenth century, debased forms of MacAdam's type of road developed, such as this one, published in a contemporary road-making manual. He simply would not have counterbalanced the cinder base and sand beneath the upper surface

the roads of Britain and assessing the best means of maintaining them for no pecuniary award. In 1811 he was a witness to a government Select Committee and his views were printed as an Appendix to the Committee's report.

Unlike Telford's, his proposals were very simple, and based in part on a couple of well-made roads he had travelled over. He realised that the road legislation to date – mainly related to wheel widths and vehicle weights – was the wrong way round; instead of trying to make the traffic meet the state of the roads, the state of the roads should meet the demands of the traffic. He considered that roads could be simply made and that this was merely a matter of the better use of the available resources. Specifically, the roadstone was being laid in too irregular a manner and the size of stones was generally too large and too varied.

His basic recommendation was for all roadstone to be broken up – by hand and by people sitting down – into jagged pieces less than an inch wide. The road base was to be 'laid as flat as possible, if it is not hollow in the middle it is sufficient; the less it is rounded, the better …'; on roads 16ft (4.9m) wide the middle of the road would only be 3 inches (7.5 cm) higher than the verges. In direct contrast to Telford's system, no solid base was to be used and instead the surface layers would be laid directly onto the ground. Indeed, MacAdam insisted that, as a base from which to build up a road, he 'should prefer a soft one to a hard one' and even a bog, 'if it was not such a bog as would not allow a man to walk over it'. His argument was that 'when a road is placed upon a hard substance, such as a rock, the road wears much sooner than when placed on a soft substrata'. The first layer of stones, up to 6 inches (15cm) deep, was to be laid and allowed to be exposed to the weight of traffic for a short period before a second layer was added to it.

The basic theory was that the weight of the traffic would consolidate the stones and if these were properly clean, devoid of earth, sand or clay, they would interlock as a flexible but hard-wearing and smooth-running surface. For turnpike trust surveyors, its main advantages over the Telford system were financial; the roadstone could usually be the existing and inefficiently laid road stone, cleaned, broken down to the requisite size and relaid; the resultant lowering of maintenance costs would more than pay for the wages of the stone-breakers.

MacAdam was 60 years of age before he actually put these principles into practice, after being appointed as surveyor of Bristol turnpikes in 1816. Unlike Telford, he was never an engineer of great works and always considered himself to be, in this last phase of his career, a road surveyor – but became the most successful one in the country in the short period left of the heyday of the turnpikes. So successful was MacAdam that his name was quickly applied to those roads built using his system – which became the most common throughout Britain and even in France – though inevitably, the quality of construction was not always as good as it could have been.

The combination of two separate innovations from the 1830s onwards, into a period of general decline in the road system as a whole, led to the development of a surface system known as 'water-bound macadam' that lasted into the early years of the twentieth century. One of these was the apparent success of watering road surfaces regularly with horse-drawn water carts to clean off residual gravel and other litter whilst also helping to bed in the type of loose and insubstantial materials – earth and dust – specifically banned by MacAdam. The second was rolling the roads with special machinery rather than relying on the weight of the traffic. In a sense, the introduction of road rolling helped to alleviate the potential problems that would otherwise have come about by turning away from the simple purity of MacAdam's system.

There are hints of possible attempts at road rolling in the seventeenth century, but the first scientific theories were, not surprisingly, developed in France in the late eighteenth century. In 1787 M. de Cessart, recommended use of a cast iron roller for new roads. Nothing seems to have been done – other than small scale work on private country house drives – until the start of the 1830s when horse rollers were first recorded in use in France and Prussia. In 1843, Colonel John Burgoyne, chairman of the Board of Works in Ireland, wrote a paper outlining the advantages of road rolling.

He had noted that when new roads were made, people were reluctant to use them until their rough surfaces had been consolidated by the traffic, using instead 'the worst and most hilly old roads'; he also indicated the economic benefits of road rolling, and this was again the main argument to sway the turnpike trustees. The logical development from horse-drawn to steam-hauled rollers, and then integrated steamrollers – essentially traction engines with rollers instead of wheels – was again initiated in France, arguably the first patent being that of Louis Lemoine of Bordeaux in 1859. The first steamrollers in Britain were not used until the end of the 1860s.

With constant maintenance, original Macadamised road surfaces or the water-bound variants could generally cope quite well with the wheeled traffic of the nineteenth century. The development of the motor vehicle at the end of the century and the accelerating growth in vehicle numbers and speeds from the start of the twentieth led to the need for a radical change in road surfaces. This was not because of the weight of motor vehicles, but because of their tyres – and their speed. Up until the patenting of pneumatic tyres, tyres had either been metal rims on wooden wheels for carriages and wagons, evolving into solid rubber ones for bicycles and the first motor cars. These had little detrimental effect on the better road surfaces of the day. However, the effect on the surfaces of the new pneumatic tyres was dramatic and damaging.

The new tyres had a tendency to adhere to the road surface and to 'suck' up loose stone chippings out of water-bound road surfaces, and this was exacerbated by speed

– even at the 20mph speed limit imposed in the early part of the twentieth century. This not only broke the road surface up and made it more prone to accelerated erosion from rain and frost, but it also led to the creation of clouds of dust as each vehicle passed by. This inevitably made the early motorists extremely unpopular, making life uncomfortable for pedestrians, increasing the costs of expenditure on the highways and literally reduced the prices of roadside properties on particularly busy routes. So serious was this matter taken that a Royal Commission was set up in 1906 to look into the matter and the RAC formed a 'dust committee'. In 1907 the Roads Improvements Association ran a special competition on a road near Reading to try and obtain solutions to the ever-growing problem.

All of the investigations led to the conclusions that new roads should to be surfaced with asphalt or concrete and that older water-bound macadam roads needed to be treated with tar or bitumen. In the early twentieth century there were two main ways of using tar in road surfaces, both of which had been tried in the previous century in a very small way. The easiest and cheapest was surface tarring, which could be applied to both old and new roads. This was initially done by hand, and the tar was heated in special 'kettles' heated by wood fires along the road side. The tar could be just smooth, or, to improve its wearing capabilities, sand or grit could be spread on its surface whilst it dried. Specialist tar-painting and tar-spraying machines were developed that sped up and improved the process.

The second way was to mix stone aggregate and hot tar in a similar way to concrete; indeed, this was still known both as 'tar-macadam' – being, incorrectly, seen as an improvement of MacAdam's basic system – and 'tar-concrete' up until the First World War period. Once mixed, the material was laid onto a well-compressed cambered base and rolled; a top course of material with aggregate made up of much smaller stones was then added and rolled. In 1901 the Nottinghamshire County Surveyor, E.P. Hooley, apparently noticed that tar accidentally spilled onto a road surfaced with slag formed a hard-wearing and impervious crust. Although not the first to realise this, he did develop machinery to mix a type of tarmacadam using slag instead of stone as the aggregate and patented it as TarMacadam (Purnell Hooley's Patent). The original company set up to market it was later renamed Tarmac Limited.

Kent was one of the pioneering counties when it came to the adoption of tar for road surfaces. The county had commissioned an independent report from D. Joscelyne, produced in 1903, that concluded 'motor power has come to stay' and that water-bound macadam simply could not cope. In the summer of the same year the county tarred a section of road near Farningham and by 1914 had more tarred roads than any other county in Britain.

Tarmacadam, in its various forms, was not the only new material being tried on the roads at this time. The first use of asphalt, a naturally occurring

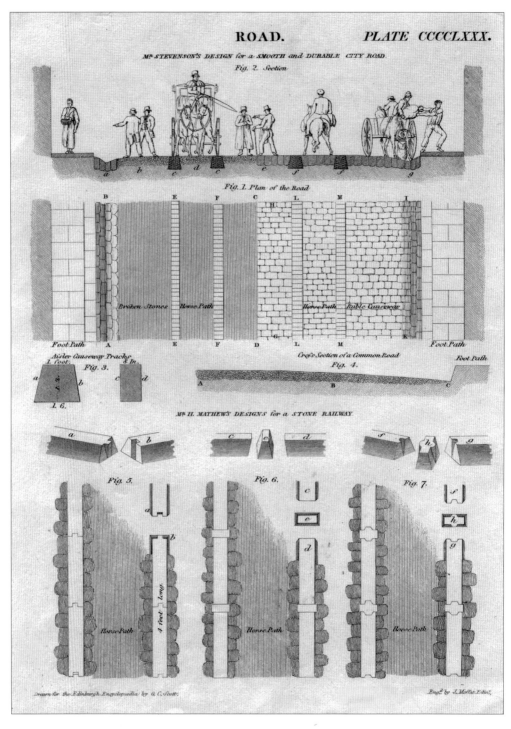

52 There were many attempts to promote better forms of surfacing for roads in towns and cities, such as these two variations on the same theme for use in towns by a Mr Stephenson

compound of bitumen and limestone, was in Paris in the 1850s. It was heated, crushed and then powdered before being laid. It could also be made artificially from a mixture of bitumen, stone, pitch and sand and formed a hard-wearing material for paths. The first recorded use in Britain was on Threadneedle Street in London, laid by the Val de Travers Asphalte Paving Company in May 1869. Normally, the asphalt was laid on a cambered sub-base of concrete and was, in effect, merely the wearing course of the road or pavement. A huge number of variants on the basic theme have evolved since.

Advances in design and technology led to great improvements in concrete and inevitably, to the construction of all-concrete roads – with no wearing coat of different materials – especially designed to take heavy motor traffic. Where new roads were built, concrete, usually reinforced on busy roads but not on lesser ones or estate roads, was the most obvious choice from the 1920s onwards.

53 An advert for the British Concrete Road Limited, showing the basic concept behind the laying of a reinforced concrete road in the late 1920s

Typical of these in the early 1930s were the first Gloucester bypass, the Kent Coast Road, the Newcastle to Tynemouth road and, longest of all, the East Lancs Road opened in 1934.

In general the use of all-concrete roads became less common in the later part of the twentieth century, mainly because of the problems of the surfaces – despite some motorways being built 'on the cheap' in the late 1970s and early 1980s with this type of concrete carriageway. In general, a wearing course of variants of tarmacadam on top of roads with a concrete base has proven to be the most desirable and most of the all-concrete highways have been upgraded in this manner.

Away from the main roads there were many other different types of surfaces in use in Britain, especially in town streets. Given their complete absence for nearly half a century, perhaps one of the more surprising surfaces used from the nineteenth century well into the middle of the twentieth were varieties of wood block. Ignoring temporary plank roads, the first serious use of wood for pavements and roadways evolved in the early nineteenth century. These were usually short lengths of regularly cut blocks of wood set vertically onto a bed of beaten sand or concrete, their edges generally coated in bitumen to form a solid and impermeable surface.

The shape of the blocks varied. Both hexagonal and square blocks were tried in New York in the mid-1830s. In 1838, David Stead laid an experimental pavement of hexagonal blocks of Norwegian fir onto a bed of concrete outside the Royal Infirmary in Manchester, but attempts to lay similar pavements in London failed due to poor workmanship. Variations of interlocking blocks were patented, the most successful being Carey's Wood Pavement of 1839. More sophisticated

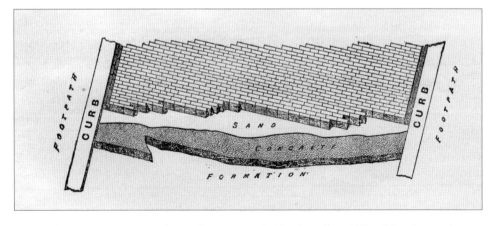

54 Wooden paving was quite widespread in towns and cities from the middle of the nineteenth century and some were still in use up until after the World War II

forms evolved, and hard woods – particularly those from Australia, such as jarra, blackbutt and red gum – proved to be the most hard-wearing, though soft woods could be impregnated with preservatives as well. Although other forms of street paving were more reliable and needed less maintenance, some English towns still had wood block streets until the early 1950s.

In contrast to wood block pavements, the other main surface of town streets in the nineteenth century has proven to be far more hard-wearing. In 1824, Thomas Telford recommended the replacement of cobbles with granite setts laid on solid foundations. Originally the setts, square in profile and set close together with or without bitumen or pitch between, were about 6 inches square, but gradually the size was reduced to about 3 inches square – being more efficient in the wearing patterns and also kinder to pedestrian and horses. Gradually the use of cruder cobbling died out, though some towns still had streets paved in this manner at the start of the twentieth century. Ironically, streets paved in setts – either lain onto rammed earth, sand, or very commonly, concrete – are now usually called 'cobbled streets'. Most were either completely relayed in the twentieth century but, in many instances, the setts survive, covered with concrete, tarmacadam or asphalt.

Painted lines

Indirectly related to the introduction of solid and hard-wearing road surfaces designed for motor traffic are the lines painted on them. The idea of using painted lines on the road surfaces to aid and control traffic was obviously difficult to develop until the road surfaces were of a sufficiently smooth and durable quality, and that did not really happen until the early twentieth century. However, as early as 1843 the idea of using a central dividing line using white stones and lamps had been put forward. The painted central line was first used in the United States in 1911, and in Britain, single white lines were painted onto the more dangerous bends near Ashford, Kent, on the main London to Folkestone road and more were added elsewhere during the First World War.

The Ministry of Transport issued a circular advocating the use of white lines in 1926, but only in 'areas where special guidance is called for', so only short sections of lines were used. By 1931, however, 5 miles of the busy Great West Road leading out of London were made safer by the use of the central white dividing line. Also in the 1930s, white lines were used to mark the ends of minor roads at junctions with major ones, and in 1935, the first major section of 'hatched' central line was laid on some main roads in Devon.

Solid and dashed white lines continued to be laid until the late 1950s without any distinction in law regarding overtaking. In 1957 many European countries agreed to the idea of making overtaking on solid white lines illegal and double

55 By the mid-nineteenth century, stone setts had become a popular surface for town streets in particular, due in no small measure to the improvements brought about by the railways, allowing the costs of buying and transporting them to be radically reduced. These setts survive under later 'tarmac' in a Sheffield back street

white lines – with either both solid or one solid and one dashed – were then tried in Britain, at first experimentally; regulations issued two years later made their use obligatory where conditions warranted.

In 1934 the first reflecting road studs, or cat's eyes were installed in Britain. Famously the invention of a Yorkshireman, Percy Shaw, they were first installed near Bradford a few weeks after a different type of stud, the Follsain Gloworm invented by Jean Neuhaus, had been installed in Market Harborough in Leicestershire. However, it was Shaw's version that was simpler, cheaper and more effective during extensive Ministry of Transport testing in the late 1930s. There are now estimated to be over 7 million cat's eyes in use in Britain, not only on lane dividers but also at junctions and elsewhere.

PART III

RIVER CROSSINGS

To avoid often long and tortuous detours, roads had to tackle the obstacles posed by water – either small streams, fast-running rivers, or broader estuaries and sea-lochs. Over time, different ways have been found to do so, based on need, available funds and technology.

Travellers in Britain can seldom travel far without the need for their route to cross a stream or a river. For the modern motorist on modern well-made roads, most streams and small rivers pass unnoticed, and on the larger trunk roads and motorways, whole valleys are crossed on viaducts – works of engineering excellence, if seldom of architectural merit, that are completely unappreciated by those speeding over them.

CHAPTER 6

Fords

In the pre-motor age, even small streams could be a significant barrier to road traffic. The smaller stream could simply be stepped over, as we still step over those on the footpaths of the countryside, but even then the pressure of traffic could erode the banks and lead to marshy conditions on either side.

In the prehistoric period, prior to the development of the engineering skills necessary for proper bridges, a ford would have to suffice – and would still have to suffice well into the medieval period and beyond if a bridge was considered too expensive or otherwise inappropriate. Often a ford would continue to be used even when a bridge was built nearby, generally by animals or farm traffic and especially if tolls were being charged on the bridge.

On wider crossings, the choice of a ford site generally depended on a natural shallow crossing of the stream or river, usually in the form of a gravel bank. The identification and use of such sites could lead to the development of early settlements and hundreds of villages and towns throughout Britain owe their existence to their location by a ford. Some grew up as trading centres and others from forts or fortified settlements deliberately sited to control such important points in the transport network.

Often the names of such places indicate their origins – Ford, Hereford, Bradford, Bedford, Oxford, Chalford, Ludford, Wallingford, and Welford to name just a few derived from the Old English *ford*. In the north of England, the word *wath*, derived from the Norse, has resulted in several settlements called simply, Wath, as well as others such as Wath-upon-Dearne. The Wash is probably similarly derived, and it is known that it was fordable in the medieval period. Watford, in Hertfordshire, is a potentially confusing combination of the two – being written *Wathford* in the medieval period; the normal meaning given, however, is the 'ford of the hunters'.

56 Fords were one of the most common ways of crossing streams and rivers and there are a surprising number still in use today. This one is in Pontesbury, Shropshire. It is in fact a double ford; for a short distance the lane in the foreground is the ford and, on the other side of the footbridge, another lane fords the stream; both join the curving lane beyond

In Wales, English speakers may be confused by the place name element *ffordd*. This is not a direct equivalent of the English 'fords', but generally means a 'way' – usually interpreted as a road or track, although a 'way' across a stream by a ford cannot be completely ruled out. In Welsh, the more precise word for a ford is *rhyd*, resulting in names such as Rhydwyn, Rhyd Gwy, Rhydycroesau, and Rhydyfelin. Benbecula, in the Western Isles of Scotland, is thought to be derived from the Scots Gaelic, *Beinn a'bhfaodhla* – the 'mountain of the fords'; across in Ireland, the more usual Gaelic word for a ford is *ath*, hence names such as Athlone and Athy. As a rough estimate, in mainland Britain there about three times as many place names associated with fords as there are with bridges.

Sometimes there is also a degree of historical 'phasing' in the place name. Thus English names such as Fordingbridge, Fordbridge, West Bridgeford, Stamford Bridge and, in Wales, Pontrhydmeredydd ('the bridge at Meredydd's ford') all indicate places where a bridge has taken its name from a ford that it presumably supplemented or replaced.

57 The arrangements at this river crossing at Wycoller, in Lancashire, would have been typical up until the nineteenth century in these parts. Wheeled traffic uses the ford whilst packhorses and pedestrians used a narrow bridge nearby. The two-arched bridge is probably late medieval in date

In their natural form, streams and rivers tend generally to meander and 'braid' and are generally shallower, but wider, than they became after generations of farmers improved the drainage systems of their fields. Those actions tended to confine the streams and rivers between more established banks, but also led to the deepening of their channels; it also made them less easy to ford.

Prehistoric man certainly used fords on his travels, though it is impossible to know to what extent he may have improved the crossing places. However, as travel became more important, fords became important as well and remained so well into the medieval period. They also became, in some cases, important meeting places and boundary markers.

For example, the ford across the River Severn just to the north of Montgomery was a traditional meeting place for parlays between the Welsh and the English. To the Welsh this was Rhydwhiman, the 'swift ford'; to the less romantic Anglo-Normans, it was, instead, the '*vadum aquæ de Mungumery*', simply 'the ford at Montgomery'. This ford, which thankfully has retained its Welsh name, also became the western end of a section of the boundary between the ecclesiastical dioceses of Hereford and St Asaph that followed the river downstream until a second major ford at Shrawardine, Shropshire.

The earliest tangible evidence of maintained fords in Britain is, inevitably, Roman. Roman roads were not seasonal tracks but designed to be used all year round and in all climatic conditions. As such, their river crossings had to be capable of being used all year round too, and that included all the fords.

Despite their expertise with bridge building, the archaeological evidence in Britain suggests that the ford – or *vadum* – was by far the most common means of a Roman road crossing a river. Fords, being natural features, did not necessarily line up with the linear routes chosen by the Roman engineers, so that the roads would usually have to be diverted off their main alignment to the river crossing. However, the Romans were also capable, where it suited them or if no natural fording point was available nearby, of creating man-made fords on the preferred route.

Evidence of Roman fords has been found occasionally, such as one near Benenden in Kent in the mid-twentieth century, and another across the Tees at Barnard Castle, County Durham, identified in the late nineteenth century. A substantial paved ford or causeway across the River Trent at Littleborough, near Lincoln, of squared stones held in place by wooden piles and horizontal cills, was removed in 1820 to improve navigation and was considered to be Roman. On an important branch off the Ermine Street to the north-west of Lincoln, it was recorded as being 18ft (5.7m) wide and the stakes were up to 12ft (3.8m) tall and made of oak. Until recently the largest substantially intact ford convincingly identified as being Roman was at Kempston, Bedfordshire, though this has been damaged by floods.

However, a recent discovery in north Yorkshire could have identified another well-preserved paved Roman ford, which would now be the longest as well. Investigators working for English Heritage identified a broad paved ford directly underneath Kilgram Bridge, near Masham. As the bridge is considered to date to the twelfth or early thirteenth century, the ford clearly pre-dates it. The quality of construction and certain structural elements – such as 'Lewis-holes' in stones bonded together by water-hardened mortar – that are of Roman origin but which did not reappear in Britain until well after the date of the bridge, all indicate that the ford is indeed Roman. The large sandstone slabs are held in place by iron straps on the edges, known as *opus revinctum*, and the river water has preserved much of the timber piles and planking that prevented the whole structure being swept away.

Given the known quality of their road engineering, it is likely that many such paved fords existed on the Roman road network, although others, where the river beds were suitable, could have been simpler. In the 1,600 years or more since the

Roman infrastructure was slowly abandoned, the scouring of rivers and streams, and inevitable floods, will have eroded much of the evidence away. Hundreds of fords of all sizes and types certainly existed on the Roman road network. The obvious clues to locate their remains are where a known Roman road crossed a river or large stream and where there is no evidence of a contemporary Roman bridge or bridge abutments.

Sometimes a place name may also offer a clue as well. Stratford, and its variants – Stretford, Strefford, Streetford etc. – could be derived from the 'ford on the street'. The word 'street' as already outlined, was commonly derived from the Old English *stræt*, generally referring to a Roman road. Similarly, names such as Stamford, Stanford, or Stainforth, could be derived from the Old English *stăn ford*, the 'stone ford', again possibly indicating a Roman origin because of the engineering skills suggested by the name.

The fate of Roman fords after their departure no doubt varied as much as did their roads. There was a general lack of maintenance and whilst some would have continued in use, others would either have been abandoned because the route was no longer in use, or the ford was damaged beyond repair by the river. Fords, nevertheless, clearly continued to be important elements in the landscape and for travellers. As the continued lack of maintenance inevitably led to the collapse of most, if not all, the Roman road bridges, fords became virtually the only form of river crossing in the so-called 'Dark Ages'.

Fords varied in their length and depth and reliability. Those close to estuaries could be very deep and treacherous, such as the crossing of the tidal Wash where the entire baggage train of King John was lost and where, in the eighteenth century, a guide equipped with a long pole took travellers across the Nene estuary – the pole being used to sound the depth, to make sure that the sand was firm, and to take a bearing on the far bank. This type of 'ford' could be seen more as a tidal crossing, similar to those across Morecambe Bay or Levens Sands on the edge of the English Lake District; both of these were, in the medieval period, served by guides from the local monasteries.

Most fords, however, were and are associated with streams and rivers. Unless traffic was exceptionally light, even a natural ford would need to be enhanced by man. Approaches needed to be made on either side of the crossing, usually with gentle slopes for wheeled traffic. The bed of the ford had to be retained to protect it from being swept away in floods, sometimes by introducing curbs on either side of the natural gravels, but often by surfacing in laid cobbles or stones blocks on top of the natural gravels. A smooth surface became particularly important with the growth of wheeled traffic.

On major crossings at least, fords were slowly supplanted by bridges, both for the safety and comfort of the traveller. Fords could be dangerous; in 1718 the

58 The ford across the Derwent at Holme, near Bakewell, Derbyshire, with the seventeenth-century packhorse bridge alongside

Justices for Derbyshire agreed to build a packhorse bridge at Alport ford, because 'Carriers with loaden horses and passengers cannot pass the said ford without great danger of being cast away'. Many bridges would have been like the one at Alport, narrow structures built for horses and pedestrians whilst carts and cattle continued to use the ford alongside. Sometimes, even if the bridge was wide enough for wheeled traffic, people continued to use the ford – either because of the bridge tolls or because of legal restrictions.

Leland, the early sixteenth-century traveller, recorded that at Deritend, near Birmingham, he 'went thrwghe the forde by the bridge'. Defoe, writing almost two centuries later, admired the 'very fine stone bridge' at Bideford, Devon, built across the Torridge estuary in the early fourteenth century, but added 'the passage over it is so narrow, and they are so chary of it, that few carriages go over it; but as the water ebbs quite out of the river every low water, the carts and wagons go over the sand with great ease and safety'. At Pontypridd, Glamorgan, the steep hump of William Edward's elegant bridge of 1750 across the Taff meant that the adjacent ford remained in use until the middle of the following century.

Sometimes, the upkeep of a bridge-side ford was deemed necessary to prevent wear and tear on the bridge itself. In 1495, for example, it was decreed that the Stoke Bridge in Ipswich, a new wooden bridge, could only be used by carts if the water level was too high in the ford alongside it.

When a ford was completely replaced by a bridge, the new bridge would often be sited on the same alignment. This made sense, given that most fords were sited on natural gravel banks in the river suited for bridge foundations. However, the construction of the bridge at Kilgram directly on top of a ford's pavement is extremely unusual. In most cases, a major new bridge would be sited above or below the ford crossing. This would lead to the need to divert the approach roads on either side of it and the effect of this in rural areas depended on the distance between the old and new crossings. In an urban context, the effect could be more far-reaching and could affect the entire urban morphology. Alternatively, the needs of the town could affect the location of the new bridge.

In Ludlow, Shropshire, the ancient ford crossing of the River Teme taking the main north–south route along the Welsh Marches was at Ludford, a small riverside settlement probably in existence in the late Saxon period. After the Norman conquest a new planned and defended town in the shadow of a huge castle was laid out on the higher ground to the north and eventually a new bridge was built upstream of the old ford at the foot of what became Broad Street. This was commented upon by Leland, in the early sixteenth century, who wrote that before the new bridge had been built, 'Men passyd afore by a forde a lytle benethe the bridge'.

Hereford's Saxon street pattern appears to have been dislocated when a bridge was built some distance upstream from the ancient *hereford* (the 'army ford') that gave the city its name. This could have had more to do with the demands of the bishop, whose palace was sited close to the old ford and the road leading down to it; however, the building of the new bridge in the medieval period led to a new street pattern in the south-western corner of the city and a new suburb on the opposite bank.

Despite the growth in the number of bridges, fords continued to be used though their numbers declined. As the weight of wheeled traffic increased, culminating in the development of motor vehicles, the fords that remained had to be capable of taking much greater wear and tear than had previously been the case. As a result, all but those fords on lesser tracks and lanes were, by the mid-twentieth century, generally well paved with cobbles, the same surface as the road itself or, more commonly, by concrete. Virtually all have a pedestrian bridge or stepping stones, and posts to mark the depth of the water – though changes to water tables and in drainage systems has led to many fords becoming dry in all but the wettest of weather.

CHAPTER 7

Ferries

Where a river, or an estuary, or a lake or an arm of the sea was too wide for a bridge and too deep for a ford, the only solution was – and in many places still is – a ferry. The word 'ferry' in English means both the crossing point and the vessel used and stems from an Old English word *ferien* meaning 'to carry'. Ferries and ferrymen were obviously important in early civilisations. The most famous in Western culture was that across the Styx, the ancient Greeks mythical river that circled Hades; the ferryman, Charon, was paid to take the souls of the dead across the water.

There is no evidence of any fixed ferry routes in Britain prior to the arrival of the Romans in the mid-first century AD, but it seems highly likely that some may have existed, albeit on an *ad hoc* basis. The alignment of certain main Roman roads shows that these also relied on what must have been regular ferry services – the two longer crossings being across the Humber and Severn estuaries.

The Ermine Street stops abruptly on either side of the Humber estuary but considering its importance as a main highway, there must have been a ferry on the route between the modern villages of Winteringham and Brough (*Petuaria*) on the south and north banks respectively. The exact location of the broader and trickier crossing of the Severn estuary is less evident, but Sea Mills on the banks of the Avon downstream of Bristol, and possibly a site on the Usk near Caerwent have been suggested, rather than termini on the banks of the estuary itself.

Although evidence is not forthcoming, it seems likely that these major crossings were run by the military, but the organisation of other ferry crossings of the time is simply unknown. Similarly, the status and numbers of ferries up until the later medieval period is unclear. Evidently many had been established long before an Act was passed regulating ferries on the River Severn in 1534.

One of the earliest recorded ferries of note was that across the Firth of Forth to the north-west of Edinburgh linking Lothian and Fife. This was where Margaret of England, wife of Malcolm III of Scotland, crossed the firth in the second half of the eleventh century on her journeys from the capital to the shrine of St Andrew's. Margaret was later canonised and by 1183 the ferry crossing was known as the *Passagium S. Marg. Regine*; at the end of the thirteenth century the settlement at the south end of the crossing was known as Queensferry. The route, constantly updated, continued in use until the opening of the Forth Road Bridge in 1964.

Many other medieval ferries had religious origins and were often the responsibility of religious houses, part of their general portfolio of looking after the needs of pilgrims and other travellers. Horseferry Road in London takes its name from an ancient horse ferry across the Thames at Lambeth; the Archbishop of Canterbury had the toll rights. Other typical examples are those of the Woodside Ferry across the Mersey between Liverpool and Birkenhead, operated by the priors of Birkenhead, probably well established before the drawing up of a charter of Edward III in 1330, and the Arlingham Passage ferry across the Severn estuary operated by hermits who had their own chapel of Twrog near Beachley, for the spiritual comfort of their passengers prior to a potentially difficult crossing.

Long before the Reformation most ferries were, nevertheless, in secular hands, either by a specific charter – often now lost – or by prescription, indicating early but unknown origins. Some ferries could be very profitable, especially on the major routes, whilst the hundreds of smaller ferries were probably not. By common law, all ferry-keepers were bound to have their ferries ready for use throughout the day or night and to charge a reasonable toll. Sometimes a specific charter for a ferry outlined the rights and responsibilities; in the 1591 lease of the Cremyll Ferry across the Hamoaze near Plymouth, the 'great passinge boats' were to be kept going by 'sufficient men, boats, and oars for the passage of people … att all tymes convenyent and att prices accustomed and lawfull'.

Ferry crossings could be dangerous, even on inland rivers, though the major tidal crossings were the ones that travellers feared most. The Earl of Clarendon wrote from Beaumaris on New Year's Day 1686 to the Earl of Rochester and told him how his party had crossed the Menai Straights in 'little round sea boats … [that] will not hold above three horses at a time, so that we were very long coming over the river. But God be thanked, we are here'. Celia Fiennes, travelling a few years later, used the Cremyll ferry, 'a very hazardous passage', and despite five men rowing the vessel, joined by some her own servants, it took them an hour to cross less than a mile; 'blessed be God I came safely over', she ended her diary entry. Ferries could and did sink and passengers, and ferrymen, sometimes drowned. One of the worst recorded ferry disasters in inland waters was the loss of the Dornoch ferry in 1809 when around 100 people lost their lives.

Where possible, and where money was available, ferries would be replaced by bridges. The replacement of a ferry by a bridge was not always welcome. In the early eighteenth century, Defoe was 'very much applauding … [the] … generous action…' of Lord FitzWilliam of Castor in the Fens when he replaced a dangerous ferry across the Nene with a bridge; however, he continued 'my applause was much abated, when coming to pass the bridge (being in a coach) we could not be allow'd to go over it, without paying 2s 6d of which I shall say only this, That I think 'tis the only half crown toll that is in Britain'. No doubt the residents on Skye and the surrounding parts of north-western Scotland had a similar view of the controversial privately built toll-bridge across Loch Alsh towards the end of the twentieth century; the Conservative government that allowed it to be built rather went against the spirit of competition when it decreed that the ancient and highly efficient ferry between Kyle of Lochalsh and Kyleakin could not even remain open to compete for the traffic.

59 Strome Ferry became an important crossing when the road through Strathcarron to Inverness was built in the early nineteenth century and switched from the north to the south bank of Loch Carron at this point. This 1930s photograph shows why it became a bottleneck in the motor age – just two small cars could be manhandled on to a 'turntable' on its deck; although upgraded later, the ferry was made redundant when a new 10 mile stretch of road was opened along the south bank in 1970

With its large number of wide estuaries and, particularly in the Highlands, dozens of inhabited islands, Scotland has always relied heavily on its ferries. The main ones were upgraded in the early motor car era, but even so, H. V. Morton was not the only traveller to bemoan the fact that 'Ferries are an unfortunate feature of motoring in Scotland' as he crossed the Tay estuary on the Newport–Dundee ferry in 1928, 'sandwiched between a van horse of uncertain temper and a young woman … whose small two-seater tried, with clumsy affection, to sit on my offside mudguards'.

Large numbers of ferries have been abandoned over the years, and particularly from the late nineteenth century onwards. The construction of bridges, the development of railways and, especially, of better roads, all contributed in different and not always direct ways. For example, there were several ferries across the navigable Severn related to the manner in which the towpath changed from one bank to another. The railways brought about the end of the river trade and that led to the end of many of the ferries; these can now be identified by the way that public footpaths stop inconveniently on one side of the river and recommence on the other. Another factor was the speed of movement offered by the motor car, even if that meant a longer roundabout journey.

The development of motor traffic usually meant that surviving ferries and their facilities needed to be upgraded, and decisions had to made by the operators whether or not this was worth the investment. In the early years of motoring, ferry crossings could take a long time because of difficulties of loading the vehicles. In 1904 the RAC warned motorists of the dangers of some crossings. Its *Handbook* warned that at the Beverley to Sutton ferry in Yorkshire 'the approaches are very dangerous when the cobbles are wet, as the incline is very steep and there is no hold for the wheels'; the arrangements between Gravesend and Tilbury were 'very inconvenient'; the Upstreet to Preston ferry in Kent was 'very unsuitable for cars'; and the ferry between Totaig and Dornie in Ross & Cromarty was 'Quite impossible for motor cars, but available for motor bicycles'. Many crossings were considered to be far too expensive in this period as well.

In 1919 a Ferries Act was passed for England and Wales, followed by another in Scotland in 1937. Both allowed local authorities the powers to acquire privately operated ferries deemed to be part of the highway system and many local authorities did. A Ministry of Transport committee recommended in 1948 that all ferries should be considered to be part of the highway, and that all tolls on them should eventually be dropped. The committee also recommended that ferries that were little used could be abandoned. At this time there were still 44 vehicular ferries considered to be integral parts of the highway system.

The increasing demands for speedier travel and increasing congestion at the busier ferry crossings led to more ferries being replaced by bridges in the later

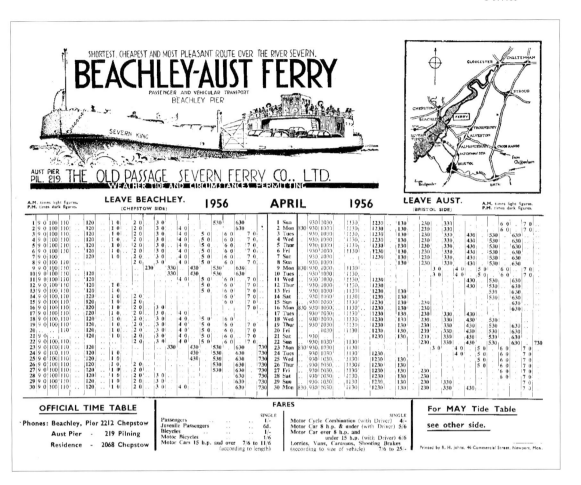

60 A 1956 ferry timetable for the Aust-Beachley ferry across the Severn estuary, which includes a sketch of one of the ferries at work; this was scrapped after the opening of the Severn Bridge though another, the Severn Princess, has survived and is in the process of being restored

twentieth century. On the east coast of Scotland, the broad firths of Forth and Tay were bridged in the 1960s, and since then there have been other major bridges in Scotland replacing well-established ferry crossings across the Beauly Firth to the north of Inverness; Loch Alsh between Kyle of Lochalsh and Skye; and Loch Leven at Ballachulish. Nevertheless, ferries are still important parts of the road transport system in some parts of the Highlands and Islands, where missing the last ferry in the evening can lead to, at best, a long detour and, at worse, an unexpected overnight stay.

There were several different types of ferries, even excluding the larger car-ferries that ply the seas – across the English Channel, for example, or the

Skagerrak. The two main types across rivers or estuaries are those that are vessels completely unrestricted and those that are in some manner fixed.

The first type is certainly the oldest, and simplest, derived just from a boat rowed or punted or, on longer crossings, sailed from one bank to the other. The second, fixed type of ferry probably evolved naturally. In its simplest form, a long rope would be strung from one side of the river to the other, probably supported on poles on each bank. To operate the ferry, it was just a matter of hauling on to the rope to pull the vessel over the water. As a precaution, it would have become sensible to secure the ferry to the main rope with another length of rope ending in a 'running eye'. Where the flow of water was sufficiently swift, a secured ferry could be manoeuvred without the need of being hauled; simply angling the vessel diagonally against the current would enable it to move across the river – a manoeuvre still known as a 'ferry glide' to canoeists.

In many cases it would have been rather inconvenient to have a rope swung across a river, either because the crossing was too wide or because the rope would interfere with other vessels. The logical thing then was to drop the rope to the bottom of the river instead. As rope under water is not conducive to longevity, the alternative was a chain and several chain ferries were established in the mid-nineteenth century. The basic principal was the same in all of them, though they varied enormously in size. The chain, fixed in place on each bank and usually tensioned by counterweights, was linked to the 'winding' apparatus on the vessel which, when turned, picked up the chain and hauled the vessel along it – the chain dropping back to the bed of the river as the ferry past. Another term for chain ferries was the 'floating bridge', incidentally.

Some minor chain ferries were hand operated, and a handful of these still operate – including one across the Avon at Stratford-on-Avon, and one to an island in the Thames in west London. Horse-power was tried on the first chain ferry across the Dart estuary, Devon, in 1831; the poor horse had to walk round and round in circles in a rotunda or 'gin' in the centre of the boat.

For the larger chain ferries carrying vehicles, more power was needed – and the logical source of such power was steam. By the start of the 1830s, the engineer James Meadows Rendel set up a steam-powered chain ferry across one of the different routes across the Dart – the High Ferry – and was then commissioned to design a more important one across the ancient Torpoint ferry crossing of the Hamoaze in Plymouth, which was nearly 1,000m wide. He also introduced moveable prows, or drawbridges, at the ends of the ferry vessels that could drop down onto ramps at either terminus to allow dry access for passengers whatever the state of the tides.

Subsequently, Rendell set up similar chain ferries at nearby Saltash, across the Tamar between Devon and Cornwall, and at the major ports of Southampton and

Floating Bridge, Dartmouth.

61 This 'floating bridge' across the Dart estuary is a vehicular chain ferry, though not a busy one in this early twentieth-century view. The chain can just be seen rising out of the water on the right hand of the vessel

Plymouth. Other quite large chain ferries were also set up elsewhere in Britain using his basic principal, including two over the Clyde – at Erskine and Renfrew. The Torpoint ferry still operates and is being upgraded with new ferries. There are other vehicular chain ferries between West and East Cowes on the Isle of Wight; the King Harry Steam Ferry across the Fal in Cornwall; one across Poole Harbour; and a tiny one at Reedham – until the mid-twentieth century operated by hand – across the River Yare to the west of Great Yarmouth.

The remains of former ferry crossings vary. Some are only names in the landscape – Ferrybridge, Ferryhill, Queensferry, Stromeferry, Boat of Carputh, Boat of Garten (*Coit Ghairtean* – the Garten ferrying place – in Gaelic) etc. Others are marked by anomalies of footpaths on a modern map, whilst others have left virtually no record of any kind. Many, perhaps most, ferries would have had virtually no bank-side facilities at all, other than perhaps a partly paved path to the side of the water. Passengers often had to wade through the water and mud to reach the ferry boat, unless there was some form of pier.

62 The Corran Ferry to the west of Fort William was first recorded in 1411 but the first car crossed in 1934 on the *Tough*, a single-car carrier bought second-hand from the Ballachullish Ferry Company. The present ferry, fast to load and unload and taking many more – and larger – vehicles, forms an important part of the local transport infrastructure

Daniel Defoe, crossing the Mersey in the 1720s, recorded how his party landed 'on the flat shore ... contented to ride through the water for some length, not on horseback, but on the shoulders of some honest Lancashire clown, who comes knee deep to the boat side, to truss you up ...'. A much smaller foot ferry at Elford in Staffordshire, across the River Tame by the ford was alright in normal water levels but a petition of 1766 claimed that passengers 'in high floods are obliged to walk from the boats over the meadows, through the water'.

Vehicular ferries, developed especially from the nineteenth century, needed better access for wheeled vehicles and so generally needed ramps on each bank to accommodate the changing river levels or the changes of the tides. Usually constructed of stone – though sometimes of timber – and usually well-built and so difficult to demolish, these are one of the most common tangible reminders of the major ferries to survive.

Sometimes, the substantial post that held the rope or chain of a ferry may survive in isolation on a river bank; a timber post for a ferry across the Severn survives opposite a boat house in the Quarry park in Shrewsbury, for example, and outside the town, another post on the bank just outside the town and further downstream held the rope of the Preston Boats ferry.

Ancillary buildings related to ferries could include passenger shelters, toll-houses, ferry-keepers' houses and, very often, an inn built specifically to serve those travellers waiting for the ferry and benefiting when the weather was too bad for the service to run. The Buck brothers engraving of Gravesend in 1739 shows a fairly substantial 'Ferry House' set on its own to the east of Tilbury Fort on the northern bank of the crossing, and the inn at the Beachley end of the 'Old Passage' ferry across the Severn estuary was a very profitable establishment.

CHAPTER 8

Bridges

The bridge is the most iconic of all road-related features. It is not just a utilitarian structure – a fixed crossing of an obstacle, such as a river – but a symbol and metaphor for much else in many civilisations. In Irish mythology, the smith-god Goibniu was noted as a builder of bridges. For Roman Catholics, the Pope is the 'Pontiff', a name derived from pre-Christian times. In pagan Italy a legendary king, Ancus Marcius, built the Pons Sublicius over the Tiber and appointed a priest to look after it; he acquired the name Pontifex Maximus, or chief bridgemaker. Later, this was the bridge, according to legend, where Horatius and his two colleagues made their legendary stand against the might of the Etruscan army in the sixth century BC, ensuring the survival of the infant Roman Republic.

Even today the symbolism of the bridge can be potent. Sometimes, a major crossing, such as the Humber bridge, can be a symbol of engineering triumph and a country's pride. Sadly, a bridge can also symbolise a much less attractive side of human nature. A classic recent example was the totally unnecessary destruction in 1993, during the Bosnian civil war, of the magnificent mid-sixteenth century Stari Most bridge over the River Neretya at Mostar, built by Mimar Sinan, architect to the Sultans of Istanbul. It is to be hoped that the recent reconstruction of the bridge and its reopening in 2004 will herald better times for that blighted region.

The earliest bridges were presumably very small, simple logs spanning a brook or perhaps, if available, a flattish rock instead. There is evidence in antiquity of tethered reeds and inflated goat skins being used along with tree trunks. Such simple structures would have evolved gradually to allow more ambitious types of floating bridges, or *pontoon* bridges, across wider streams and rivers. The Persian army under Xerxes used a pontoon bridge that included triremes to cross the

63 Bridges have, from time immemorial, been symbolic as well as functional. The unique Trinity Bridge in Crowland, Lincolnshire, was built around 1350 to cross three streams which have since dried up. It was of course a religious symbol as well, and the meeting of the three arches was originally topped by a cross. This photograph probably dates from the 1880s

Hellespont and attack the Greeks in the fifth century BC; the Romans sometimes used pontoon bridges – *monoxyli* – in their campaigns; and many of the great bridges of the Arab world were pontoon bridges maintained for centuries. Whilst the Romans probably used such bridges in their British campaigns, the archaeological evidence for them is virtually non-existent, which is not surprising. At a much later date, on two separate occasions at the end of the thirteenth century, the English built pontoon bridges across the Menai Straits to assist in the pacification of Welsh strongholds on Anglesey.

Long before the Roman invasion of these islands, far more ambitious fixed bridges had been developed in the more advanced civilisations of the world. Amongst the most fabled was the bridge across the Euphrates in Babylon built in *c.*600 BC by the Chaldean king, Nabopolassar. This was the oldest bridge known to have incorporated the use of stone and brick as well as timber in its construction; it also incorporated a drawbridge and was one of the wonders of its age.

In Europe it was the Romans, typically copying, adapting and improving on the technology of earlier civilisations, who were the most prolific of bridge builders from the third century BC to the fifth century AD. They built bridges of timber, of stone, and composite ones that included both materials, throughout their expanding Empire; a surprisingly large number of their bridges and aqueducts survive.

In Britain, it used to be considered that it was the Romans that built the first sophisticated bridges in Britain following their invasion in the mid-first century. Recent archaeological work has suggested that there had already been a long history of fairly sophisticated native engineering that had managed to cross quite wide rivers by timber bridges before the Roman conquest – though the numbers of such bridges, their design and the reasons behind their construction are still being investigated.

The bridges the Romans built in Britain were related to their extensive road network and the evidence suggests that these were maintained, repaired and modified during the three or four centuries of Roman influence. With the withdrawal of the legions in the early fifth century AD and the gradual disintegration of Roman civilisation in the decades that followed, bridge maintenance ceased to be an important concern of authorities national or local. Few records have survived to indicate what exactly did happen to Roman bridges, but the archaeological and landscape evidence suggests that the larger bridges, in particular, proved to be too difficult to maintain once they had begun to fall into disrepair.

There are many examples throughout Britain of those Roman roads that did remain in use being diverted away from their bridge crossings to an easier ford site nearby, almost certainly after the bridge had collapsed and there was an inability for a variety of reasons – technological, economical and political – to rebuild it.

As well as the evidence on the ground, there is also the evidence of place names. It is thought, for example, that the name of the Yorkshire town Pontefract – spelt *Pontefracto* in a deed of 1090 – is derived from the debased Anglo-Norman for 'the broken bridge', possibly a ruined Roman one. Further north, the remains of two bridges on the line of Hadrian's Wall are now close to villages called Chollerford and Willowford, indicating that by the time they received their Old English names there were fords but no bridges across the rivers.

Sometimes the evidence for the survival of Roman bridges can be conflicting and confusing. A good example is that of Stamford Bridge across the Derwent to the east of York, the site of the battle between King Harold and Harold Hardrada, king of Norway, in 1066; King Harold won but then had to hurry south to face the greater dangers poised by William – and was, of course, defeated. At Stamford Bridge there was definitely a bridge extant in 1066 and it has sometimes been suggested that it was a surviving Roman bridge.

There was certainly a Roman road that needed to cross the river at this point, but the place name suggests that, by the Saxon period, there was only a ford and then a bridge was built later near to it; 'Stamford' is probably derived from the Old English *stan ford* – the 'stony ford' – sometimes considered, in the right context, to relate to a paved ford. As suggested earlier, such fords are, in turn, though to be of Roman origin, so was the original Roman crossing a ford and the 'bridge' element of the name only added in the later Saxon period?

The Saxons had the technological skills capable of building quite substantial bridges, as indeed did the Danes who held much of northern Britain – the Danegeld lands – during the later part of the first millennium. Both appear to have built their bridges in timber, and the most spectacular was presumably the one across the Thames in London burnt down by King Ethelred in 1014 as a defensive measure. However, the remains of very few bridges of this period have been positively identified. The fragments of a small timber bridge in Cromwell, Nottinghamshire, found in the 1880s, have been dated by modern tree-ring analysis to the late seventh century AD and, more recently, the University of Leicester Archaeology Service identified the remains of a narrow pedestrian bridge or causeway to the north of Leicester which was dated by the same technique to a period between the late fifth and mid-seventh century AD. Timber causeways of the Saxon period have also been found, but no doubt many more such structures will eventually be rediscovered where the environmental conditions help to preserve them.

In the medieval period, the provision of bridges was seen as a pious duty, and so many were built by the Church and various religious houses; this was also due in no small measure to the fact that the Church had access to the skilled workforce capable of building bridges. In France there was a special religious order, the *Frères du Pont*, that built bridges and organised ferries and hospices by river crossings in the twelfth and thirteenth centuries; they were responsible for the bridge at Avignon, made famous by the nursery rhyme.

In Britain it was mainly individual monasteries or benefactors that built and maintained bridges; for example, the Benedictine abbey at Ramsey is thought to have built the bridge across the Great Ouse at St Ives in Huntingdonshire and a sister house at Whitby built a bridge across the Esk. Often a convent would be granted land to provide income to build or maintain a bridge, either by the Crown or by a private benefactor. The other form of finance was through *pontage* – permission by the Crown for those responsible for a bridge to collect tolls from those crossing it.

Not all bridges were religious or private; others were built, for example, by borough or county authorities. Legislation as to who was responsible to provide and maintain bridges was rather vague until the mid-sixteenth century, although in general they were the responsibility of the landowners – the manors – at the end of the Saxon period. Bridges were even mentioned specifically in the Magna Carta that King John reluctantly signed in 1215, when it was agreed that only those who traditionally had to maintain bridges could be empowered to do so. With the decay of the feudal system, bridge maintenance tended to devolve to the local authorities, but it was not until the Statute of Bridges in 1531 (22 Hen. VIII, v) that some clarification was set out in law.

The statute decreed that Justices of the Peace were to look into the 'anoyances of bridges broken in the highe wayes to the damage of the Kynges liege People'. Where it was unclear which authority was responsible for the upkeep of a bridge – whether it was an individual, corporation, parish or hundred – the county was considered liable and their Quarter Sessions were allowed to impose a rate on the parishioners in order to do so. Given the sudden demise of the monastic order to fund Henry VIII's extravagances, this was an important statute and set the pattern for the next few centuries.

There are hundreds of surviving medieval bridges throughout Britain, though most have been altered over the years. The distribution of bridges in the medieval period was very uneven. Whilst most of England was well supplied with bridges, parts of the south-west and the north were not. There were far fewer bridges in medieval Wales or Scotland and in both countries, the bridges that did exist, whilst of a quality generally equal to those in England, were usually in or near the major towns and cities. Even by the early sixteenth century, according to John Leland, the only bridges over the Wye, one of the largest and widest rivers in Britain, below Builth were at Hereford and Monmouth, and there were very few road bridges at all in Scotland until the early eighteenth century.

Many medieval bridges were defended; they were vulnerable parts of any defensive circuit – be that of castle or town – and in the medieval period it was common for them to have gatehouses either at one end, or both or on the bridge itself. Many such defended bridges survive abroad, but in Britain there are only two examples still substantially intact – the late fourteenth-century bridge over the Coquet at Warkworth, Northumberland, protected by a gatehouse at its southern end and, more spectacularly, at Monmouth, where the Monnow Bridge of *c.*1272 has a fortified gatehouse on the bridge itself that was added in about 1296.

Most stone medieval bridges appear to have been sufficiently substantial and wide enough to carry the traffic for which they were designed for many centuries, so that there was not a need for wholesale replacement of bridges in the post-medieval period. It should be remembered that not all bridges were built to take vehicular traffic, and many were simply designed to carry either pedestrians or pack horses, particularly at ford sites. In Charles Cotton's sequel to Izaak Walton's *Compleat Angler*, written in 1676, the character Viator complains

64 The Monnow Bridge in Monmouth is the only one in Britain to retain a gateway on the bridge itself. It was probably built around 1272 and the gatehouse was added slightly later; the bridge has since been widened

that 'a mouse can hardly go over' a typical Derbyshire bridge, adding ''tis not two fingers broad'.

From the later medieval period onwards there was a gradual increase in the number of bridges and some replacement of stone bridges – but in the later seventeenth and eighteenth centuries one of the main reasons for rebuilding was in order to replace a decaying timber bridge with a more substantial stone structure. During the same period, many fords were replaced by bridges, as well as some of the smaller ferry crossings.

Scotland, in particular, has a large number of eighteenth and early nineteenth-century bridges, due in part to the provision of military roads following the 1715 and 1745 uprisings, and, subsequently, to the growing prosperity of the country from the later eighteenth century onwards. Indeed, for its size, the country has the best collection of such bridges in Britain and many are fine pieces of architecture as well as vital parts of the transport infrastructure.

The turnpike system provided a demand for more bridges, but often the roads used existing bridges rather than go to the expense of building new ones. By the late eighteenth century, technological advances in construction had led to the use of iron, especially after the success of the famous iron bridge of 1769–71 in Shropshire; this, across the Severn in what is now called Ironbridge, is another much used iconic bridge symbol representing the Industrial Revolution.

The new technologies led in the nineteenth century to far more ambitious bridges spanning waters that had previously been considered unbridgeable – such as Telford's Menai Bridge and Brunel's Clifton Bridge. However, from the middle of the century onwards, the major technological advances were not related to roads, but to railways. Only at the end of the century, in the early experiments in concrete bridge construction in France, can the origins of many of the great bridges of the twentieth century be seen.

Up until this time, most road bridges were built across water – from the simple stream to the broad estuary. If the waterway was navigable, then the bridge could not by law impede navigation. In general, at least one of its arches had to be built high enough to allow the normal barges used on the waterway through; this was the 'navigation arch', often, but not always, in the middle of the bridge. Sometimes that arch, especially in smaller bridges, could be very exaggerated, as in the bridge over the Thames at Sonning, Berkshire, or at Stopham, over the Arun in Sussex; normally, the differences are subtler. Many multi-span bridges have arches at one or other of their ends that were not over water at all but were nevertheless integral parts of their structure; these are called 'dry' or 'land' arches and were usually of smaller spans.

A few bridges inevitably spanned more than one channel, or a boggy area or a deep valley, and were long enough to be considered viaducts, rather than bridges. The often-debatable difference between the two is partly one of length and partly one of geography; in general, a bridge will span a specific obstacle, such as a river, whilst a viaduct will span a broader and less well defined area, such as a river valley. Viaducts really begin to be important in the railway era, when retaining a level route was far more important than it was for road traffic.

Nevertheless, several pre-railway structures can be considered to be viaducts, such as John Smeaton's low and utilitarian viaduct finished in 1770 to take the Great North Road across the flood plain of the River Trent at Newark; Thomas Telford's rather taller and more elegant, if shorter, Dean Bridge on the outskirts of Edinburgh built in 1832; and George Manners's viaduct across the River Avon at Limpley Stoke to the south of Bath, finished in 1834. In London, demolition on a massive scale was required to construct the new Holborn Viaduct in the 1860s, which crosses Farringdon Street; the scheme cost over £2 million. The advent of the motorway and faster motor traffic from the mid-twentieth century has made the viaduct ubiquitous and virtually unnoticed by those using it; much of the motorway system around Birmingham, for example, is built entirely on viaducts.

Prior to the development of the motorways, the late eighteenth to mid-nineteenth-century period saw the largest growth in the numbers of road bridges ever seen – due not to the increase in road traffic, but to the building of thousands of miles of, firstly, canals, and subsequently, of railways. These new transport arteries needed, by law, to respect the needs of the existing roads and even footpaths and this required tens of thousands of bridges, generally quite small, often quite steeply arched, but of a huge variety of designs.

Roads built over other roads – often now called flyovers – were rare until the twentieth century, simply because there was little need for them. A few were built, almost for fun, on the drives of some stately homes; this was sometimes to make sure that those using such drives were well segregated from the common people of their common lanes, or sometimes as follies. For example, there is a good example of such a flyover in the grounds of Alton Towers, Staffordshire, where the main drive between the house and the distant stable block (called 'Ingestre' after the family's other Staffordshire home) crossed over the main access drive to the now world-famous gardens on an elegant bridge.

One of the earliest flyovers in the 'real' world was the result of the collapse of the tunnel at Highgate Hill, London, where a bridge was built to take a road over the new turnpike in 1813. A far more elegant flyover, the Regent Bridge over Waterloo Place was built shortly afterwards in Edinburgh, designed by Archibald Elliot and part of the eastern approach to Princes Street and the New Town; it has a graceful single arch over the street below, whilst the main roadway is flanked by Doric porticos and screens.

It has only been with the development of special fast trunk roads in the 1920s and, later, in the development of motorways and faster dual carriageways, that road bridges have taken on the similar terminology used by the railways. To keep the motorway traffic running fast and safe there is a need for hundreds of footbridges, flyovers, and junction bridges. Now road bridges can be termed *underbridges* or *overbridges*, the former taking the road over something and the latter, something being taken over the road. Other fairly new terms include *accommodation* bridges, built purely for private use to link portions of an individual's property separated by the construction of the road, and *occupation* bridges built to carry an existing right of way over or under a new road.

On a modern motorway, the cost of the bridge work can be between a quarter and a third of the total construction budget, but it will also include the various and often complex sections of bridgework in the junctions. The first modern flyover junction in Britain is usually claimed to be on the Winchester Bypass, opened in 1939. By far the most complex junction has to be the Gravelly Hill Motorway Interchange on the M6 at Aston, on the eastern edge of Birmingham known to all and sundry as 'Spaghetti Junction', opened in the early 1970s.

BASIC BRIDGE TYPES

Historic bridges can represent a real challenge to the archaeologist even if much of the fabric survives. Sometimes it is relatively easy to see, by studying differences in masonry, construction breaks, changes in arch design, and so forth, how a bridge has been widened, or where an arch has been rebuilt, but many bridges are very difficult to interpret.

Although the materials and design of bridges built during the past 5,000 years varies enormously, there are really just three basic structural types of bridge – beam, arch and suspension – though one or more of these basic elements can be used in the same bridge structure.

Beam bridges are, theoretically, the simplest form of all, but range in sophistication from a simple log thrown across a stream to the two-mile long multi-million pound Tay Road Bridge linking Dundee and the Kingdom of Fife. In a beam bridge the main structure consists of a horizontal member or members laid between the bridge abutments or, in a multi-spanned structure, between abutments and the intermediate piers. The main force on the beam is compression from its own weight and the weight of the traffic on it, but that will force the beam to bend in the centre, which then creates tensile pressure in its lower section.

If the beam is a single slab of stone, a substantial enough timber or a sufficiently large iron girder, then it will be strong enough to do its job singly or in conjunction with others; if not, it will either eventually break or require additional support, either in the form of additional vertical supports under it or in some form of trussing. This can be either in the form of braces up to the beam from the piers and abutments, or the use of additional sections creating an integrally trussed structure using the strength of triangles to spread the loads more evenly. This can be done in timber, iron or concrete bridges in a large variety of ways; in iron bridges of the nineteenth and twentieth centuries, for example, it led to the development of different types of trussed girder forms such as the Fink, Pratt, Warren and lattice trusses.

The cantilever bridge is another version of a beam bridge, but one in which the beam has one end firmly fixed into a bank or abutment – or in engineering terms, *encastré* – and, depending on the strength of the beam and its length, the other end need not be attached to anything. Usually, however, a cantilever bridge is made up of two such beams, either joined in the middle or with an additional section of beam in between. Hundreds of motorway bridges have been built of this design in Britain.

Until the nineteenth century, the best bridges were those of the arch variety. These were usually of masonry, but timber arches were also built and the earliest iron bridges were also built as arched structures. Early arch forms, in brick, have been identified in Mesopotamia dating to around 3500 BC, but saw little development in Europe for another 3,000 years. The introduction of the arch form to Britain was presumably a direct consequence of the Roman occupation, though it is uncertain to what extent their engineers used proper arched construction in their road bridges.

The arch is a more sophisticated structure than the beam and capable of taking a great deal more weight. In a masonry arch, the downward forces of the loading are transferred into horizontal ones that are transferred by the stones making up the arch to the abutments on either side; the whole arch is thus in compression. The integrity of the arch is vital to its stability. A typical stone arch is made up of specially shaped stones called *voussoirs*. The first of these on either side are called the *springers;* at the crown of the arch is the *keystone*, often given due architectural prominence on the external flanks of the bridge and made larger than the rest.

Until the end of the twelfth century, most arches were semicircular; this was the Roman way and the semicircular or round arch in buildings is one of the main *motifs* of Romanesque architecture. Subsequently, pointed or 'two-centred' arches were developed that allowed greater spans. Both of these forms, however, tended to mean that the centre of the bridge had to be taller than the ends, unless it was built up of a whole series of fairly small arches.

Providing that the arch is well constructed, a full semi-circular arch is no more efficient than one that is only a segment of an arch. The oldest surviving stone bridge to incorporate a segmental, as opposed to semicircular, arch is thought to be one built across the Chiao Shui river in China by the engineer Li Chu'un, in about AD 610. Taddeo Gaddi's far more famous Ponte Vecchio in Florence, built around 1345, is the oldest major example of such an arch in Europe.

By the end of the sixteenth century other arch forms were being developed, including the three- and four-centred varieties and the elliptical arch. Bartolommeo Ammanati's Ponte Santa Trinita of 1567, with its amazingly flat four-centred arches, was spitefully destroyed in 1944 during the German retreat from Florence – the present one is a virtual replica. All of these various types of arches can be seen in British bridges. In general, the two-centred arch tended not to be used after the end of the medieval period, though there were inevitably exceptions.

In Britain the suspension type of bridge has never been particularly common, despite producing some of the most dramatic engineering structures on its roads. In this form of bridge, the bridge deck is usually suspended on vertical supports from a chain or chains supported at either end on tall pylons. The chain achieves a natural curve between the supports – effectively an arch upside down – and is usually continued past the end pylons and then downwards to be embedded in a substantial abutment at either end of the crossing.

Simpler suspension bridges have been developed in many parts of the world in which the decking is supported directly on the chains, but the materials of the 'chains' do not have to be sophisticated – rope is very commonly used and the whole structure can be made from materials growing to hand. A suspension bridge of sorts was built across the Tees in 1741, consisting of a pair of suspended chains supporting a planked footway barely 2ft (0.6m) wide with a 70ft (21.7m) span; it was not a bridge to inspire confidence and the earliest significant suspension bridges were not built in Britain until the start of the nineteenth century. Even then, with a few notable exceptions and many footbridges, it did not become important as a major road type until the 1960s.

As well as these main types, there are also several variants of bridge design that defy easy categorisation. A *bow-string* bridge, for example, is in some ways similar to a suspension bridge, but consists of the deck being supported partly by the strength of its own girders or beams – the string – but also by hanging supports from an upside down arch – the bow – which can either stop level with the roadway or continue on downwards below it to the abutments, depending on the design. This design can in some ways, therefore, be seen as a combination of all three of the major structural bridge types, although the relative importance of the three elements varies according to the design and the materials used. Examples are usually made of iron, steel or reinforced concrete.

Variations of moveable bridges have a long history for defence; in medieval times it was far better to have a drawbridge section that could be lifted or slid out of the way than to have to partly or completely demolish a bridge when an attack was imminent. In post-medieval times there were instances where a bridge could get in the way of something else – such as when it was over a navigable waterway. If a fixed bridge which allowed sufficient headroom for navigation was either undesirable or impractical, a moveable bridge was required. Typically these were of two sorts – swing bridges or lifting bridges.

In a swing bridge, the girder deck of the bridge pivots on a vertical axle either on one bank or on a central pier to allow boats through. These range in size from small hand-operated farm bridges (often made of timber) on smaller canals to quite large steel-framed structures over navigable rivers or ship canals – such as the massive bow-string swing bridge over the Tyne at Newcastle built in 1876 to the designs of John Ure.

In a simple lifting bridge, such as the typical castle drawbridge, the deck is lifted by ropes or chains from the horizontal to a vertical position. By introducing the basic principle of the lever and using counterweights and an off-centre pivot, the lifting of the deck is made simpler; the technical term for this type of bridge is the *bascule*, and examples also vary from the small, simple, timber examples – seen, for example, to take lanes over the former Ellesmere Canal and its branches in north Shropshire – to the most famous bascule bridge of all: Tower Bridge in London. Built by the engineer Sir John Wolfe Barry and the architect Sir Horace Jones in 1885 it was erected at the height of Empire with all the worst architectural pomp and pseudo-medieval trimmings it could muster hiding its sophisticated engineering, it has, nevertheless, become a much-loved icon.

Mention must also be made of perhaps the strangest form of bridge, though one that enjoyed a very brief vogue in the early years of the twentieth century. The *transporter* bridge was a type of moveable bridge in which the traffic was taken on a cradle or 'gondola' slung underneath the tall bridge structure and hauled from one side to the other. This allowed the bridge's fixed span to be as tall as required to allow shipping – including the sailing 'tall ships' – through, and it could also cope with the changes in the tides. Only a handful of such bridges were built, and only four were built in Britain – the largest at Runcorn opened in 1905 with a span of nearly 1,050ft (320m) (demolished in 1962) and others included one at Newport, Monmouthshire, opened in 1906; Middlesbrough, opened in 1911; and the smallest and latest, a private one in a chemical works in Warrington opened in 1916 and has long been out of use.

65 One of the attractive features of Amsterdam is the city's famous lift bridges. These are not unique to Holland, and there were even a few in English cities in the early eighteenth century. This particular example is depicted in the Buck brothers' 1741 engraving of Great Yarmouth, Norfolk

66 Another moveable form of bridge across water is the swing bridge, where the bridge turns horizontally; this one is across the Sharpness Canal near Frampton-on-Severn, Gloucestershire

MATERIALS

The different types of materials used in bridge construction varies tremendously, and often several different materials were used in the same structure. Up until the later eighteenth century materials used were mostly natural, such as stone and timber, or of relatively easy to make man-made materials such as brick. Since that period, rapid technological advances have seen the introduction of man-made materials such as iron, steel, and reinforced concrete.

Timber

A log or plank bridge is the simplest version of a beam bridge, and timber lends itself naturally to beam bridge design rather than to the more sophisticated arch. Simple trestle type bridges, or plank bridges with masonry or concrete supports, are still being built in large numbers in Britain, generally as footbridges. However, in many other parts of the world quite substantial timber bridges still take vehicular traffic on main roads.

Until fairly recently, it was generally accepted that in prehistoric Britain, smaller streams and rivers would have been crossed by primitive timber or 'clapper' type bridges with little engineering involved. It was not really considered possible that any ambitious bridge projects pre-dated the Roman Conquest of the mid-first century AD.

However, the archaeological evidence related to raised timber causeways and other prehistoric timber-built features has grown steadily over the past few decades. One of the most exciting prehistoric transport-related discoveries was the probable remains of a bridge across the Thames near Vauxhall. This was investigated by the Thames Archaeological Survey, a joint venture run by the Museum of London and the Institute of Archaeology. The fact that there two parallel lines of very substantial posts roughly 16ft (5m) apart were identified suggested to the archaeologists that they were dealing with a bridge, rather than a jetty or causeway.

The timbers were set into the bed of the river on the diagonal, presumably to form a series of saltire or 'St Andrew's' cross-type trusses or trestle piers of the type known to have been used in prehistoric causeways. The timbers were dated by radiocarbon dating to around 1500 BC, a period when the Thames would have been wider but shallower than it later became. What is slightly confusing is the lack of any mention of a bridge near London in Caesar's chronicle of his brief foray into England in 54 BC or in later accounts of the Claudian invasion of nearly a century later.

Remains of a slightly later, smaller and narrower bridge than that at Vauxhall, dated to about 1300 BC, were recently identified by the Oxford Archaeology Unit spanning a small tributary of the Thames further upstream at Eton. These two structures suggest both a settled and a sophisticated society capable of impressive civil engineering; they also indicate that road transport was of some importance to those responsible for the construction of the bridges. No doubt, further prehistoric bridges will be discovered in the future.

Throughout most of Britain, good quality timber for construction was readily available and it was a logical building material for bridges. Indeed, up until the medieval period, most bridges in Britain appear to have been made either entirely of timber, or to have been of composite construction with stone abutments and piers and timber spans. From the available archaeological evidence it seems that this latter technique was the one favoured by the Romans, certainly for their larger bridges – although it is likely that initially all-timber temporary bridges, and pontoon bridges, were used. These types of structure are documented as being used elsewhere in their expanding Empire.

Foundations for good quality piers and abutments have been identified on Roman bridge sites, including several associated with Hadrian's Wall across the north of England. At Chollerford, immediately to the east of Chesters, the route of the wall was interrupted by the River North Tyne, and a bridge was built to link the sections on either side; the river has since changed its course a little, confusing the interpretation. On the east bank, the bridge abutment is some distance from the present bank but is a substantial structure of stone blocks reinforced with lead-set iron bands. It is of two separate phases, as is at least one of the three pier bases that still survive; these were rectangular with cutwater or angled ends only on their upstream side.

The evidence indicates that in its later stage it was a composite bridge of four timber spans, but the discovery of what appear to be voussoir blocks in the vicinity could indicate that the first narrow bridge had arched spans. The earlier work seems to be better than the later and is presumably contemporary with the construction of the wall in the early second century AD; the date of the second phase is unknown, but was presumably in the later Roman period and could have been associated with repairing problems of the original design caused by the scouring action of the river. There was also some system of water management in the structure, possibly associated with a water mill.

More impressive are the remains of the Roman bridge at Piercebridge, which carried the main road to the north-east across the River Tees. Excavations in the early 1970s exposed the southern abutment, some of the piers and a section of paving on the river bed. Again the bridge appears to have been a composite structure of wooden spans and stone piers, although recently further questions have been raised about the function of the structure.

Traces of a longer Roman bridge of similar construction across the Tyne at Newcastle were claimed to have been found when a later bridge was being demolished in the mid-nineteenth century, and the foundation of a pier with cutwaters at each end was encountered supported on the remnants of iron-stiffened oak piles. It was also claimed that this bridge had survived until the fire which destroyed much of the city in the middle of the thirteenth century.

Elsewhere, Roman bridges have remained remarkable elusive, as have definitive indications of the fords that must have existed if bridges did not. One site that has been the subject of much debate is at Wroxeter, once the major regional capital, *Uriconium*, on the banks of the River Severn a few miles downstream of Shrewsbury. A road is known to have crossed the river at this point, and timbers have been found in the river bed roughly on the right alignment; once these were thought to be either the foundations of a completely timber-built bridge, or the pilings of a composite bridge with stone piers. However, it is more likely that the timbers are related to a much later medieval or post-medieval fish-weir – one of many along the upper stretches of the river.

One logical inference from the lack of evidence for purely stone-built Roman bridges is that in Britain good quality timber was in bountiful supply and that Roman engineers used their carpentry skills for the necessary bridges of their new road system. The use of the phrase 'timber bridges', in the Roman and later periods, is perhaps a little misleading; there were bridges constructed entirely of timber, especially in the early road-building campaigns, but often timber was used in the spans of the bridges whilst the abutments were of the high quality masonry for which the Romans were renowned.

Completely timber-built bridges would have had piers made up of timbers piled deep into the river bed, usually forming the corners of trestle-type structures that supported the timber bridge decking. Sometimes, rubble would be introduced to stabilise such piers.

It is likely that many of the larger bridges described as being wooden in medieval and later deeds were, in fact, of composite construction rather than being made entirely out of wood. The basic construction of their abutments and piers was similar to those of masonry bridges described below, though in some the piers rose up to deck level whilst in others they ended lower down to provide a base for timber-framed piers rising to the deck. In some bridges the stone work stopped below the water level and the whole visible section of the piers were of timber. That seems to have been the case when a new bridge across the Trent at Newark was needed in 1485 after the old one had been destroyed in floods. Built by the carpenter, Edward Downes, the surviving contract included references to a sill-plate under water, presumably on top of a stone base, to take the main posts of the piers

By the nature of the material, timber would need quite frequent repair and replacement, especially when exposed to the constant flow of water and seasonal flooding and associated floating debris. A particularly bad flood could sweep away the entire bridge – as happened in 1673 when the Wharfe flooded in Yorkshire and destroyed six major wooden bridges. Even without such natural disasters, constant repairs and replacement would have been needed to the timbers due to a variety of causes, including wear and tear and rot.

In general, a stone bridge would have been more expensive to build but probably stronger than a timber one; they would also have been perceived to be of higher status. Nevertheless, there was not simply a chronology of timber bridges being replaced by stone ones in the medieval period. For example, in 1422 three masons, Thomas Ampilford, John Garette and Robert Maunselle, were contracted to build the new stone bridge over the River Swale at Catterick, Yorkshire. This new bridge, which still stands though much altered and widened, was built 'be twix ye old stane brigge and ye new brigg of tree [i.e. wood]'. Clearly, in this case, the wooden bridge that was about to be replaced had, in its turn, replaced an older stone one.

Timber or composite bridges remained very common on major roads as well as minor ones well into the eighteenth century, partly because of their cost and partly because of their ease of construction. In the early sixteenth century, John Leland mentions many he encountered in his travels, including one over the Wye at Builth which was a 'bridge newly repayryd with tymbre'; others had been destroyed and not replaced including 'one of tymbar at Chepstow', Monmouthshire. Ogilby's maps of the late seventeenth century similarly mention many timber bridges on the main highways.

One of the longer all-timber road bridges of the post-medieval period in Britain was probably that across the Thames at Fulham. Over 650ft (200m) long, but with 26 quite narrow spans, the piers were constructed of timber uprights, the decking between was flat and the roadway was guarded by a simple timber handrail. Built by the master carpenter Thomas Phillips and designed by Sir Joseph Acworth, it replaced an ancient ferry in 1729; it was replaced in turn by the present bridge, usually known as Putney Bridge, in the 1880s. Hampton Court Bridge, a little upstream, was built in 1753 as a rather bizarre Chinese bridge in timber with stone abutments, but was then rebuilt in the late 1770s and replaced by the predecessor of the present structure in 1865.

Increasing sophistication in timber construction led to a serious design being put forward by a carpenter, James King, in 1737 to build a bridge across the Thames at Westminster in timber. It would have had spans of 'arches' made up of tangentially and radially trussed timber braces rising from low stone piers to support the timber decking. The bridge seems to have been started but, after damage when the river froze, a stone bridge was decided on instead. King was rewarded with the lucrative contract to construct the necessary centrings for its arches – which were built to virtually the same design. A much smaller bridge of similar design was built across the Cam in the Backs of Cambridge University by Queen's College.

Constructed in 1749 by James Essex the Younger, it was to a design of William Etheridge, James King's assistant, and is known as the 'mathematical bridge'; it was rebuilt in 1866 and 1905 to more or less its original design.

As late as the 1830s the *Penny Cyclopædia* claimed that timber bridges were 'much more common than bridges of stone, on account of their greater facility of construction and their cheapness'. Even great engineers were not adverse to building timber bridges; Telford built a wooden toll bridge over the Severn at Cressage, Shropshire, in the late eighteenth century and Brunel built dozens of sophisticated laminated timber bridges above and below his railway lines in the 1830s and '40s.

Quite large timber road bridges were still being built in the nineteenth century, with several examples to be found in Norfolk. The Shaldon Bridge across the Teign in Devon was built in 1827; it had 34 spans and was over 1,600ft (488m) long – the longest wooden bridge in Britain when it was replaced in 1931. One of the larger surviving examples is the Penmaenpool Toll Bridge across the head of the estuary of the Afon Mawddach, not far from Barmouth. Built as late as 1879 to replace a ferry, it is one of the few surviving toll bridges in Britain and is built to a basic design of timber trestle piers and timber decking that could have been built centuries before. An even later bridge is that at Shoreham-on-Sea, Sussex, across the Adur – a trestle bridge constructed in 1916 to replace a virtually identical toll bridge built in 1781.

67 Timber was used for bridges of quite considerable size, as shown in this Frith postcard of about 1920 of the Shaldon Bridge across the Teign estuary in Devon. Built in 1827 it was replaced just over a century later

Timber bridges have continued to be constructed into the twenty-first century, either as simple pedestrian bridges on stone piers or more sophisticated structures using arches of laminated timber – a style developed in the mid-nineteenth century especially for railway bridges rather than for roads.

Once they have been demolished or, in the case of composite bridges, partly dismantled, the designs of timber bridges are difficult to properly assess from the archaeological evidence. This is simply because that evidence is slight even when associated masonry has survived, and the documentary evidence that does exist generally has little information about the construction methods used. In general, it would seem that most of these bridges were of the girder form, albeit with a degree of bracing and propping from the piers, rather than true arches.

Stone

Although the Romans, having developed the arch, were known masters of masonry construction, in stone, brick and concrete, littering Europe with extraordinary engineering feats of bridge design, no such examples survive from the four hundred years or so in which they dominated Britain. Nowhere in Britain are bridges such as the five-arched Bridge of Augustus at Rimini of *c.*AD 20, the extraordinary bridge over the Tagus at Alcantara in Spain of *c.*AD 110 or towering aqueducts such as the Pont du Gard, near Nîmes in France of *c.*AD 14.

Clearly, their British province was not a backwater, and there are some notable examples of stone construction, not least of which was Hadrian's Wall. However, whilst there are a few tantalising bits of evidence – such as stones cut to voussoirs found at or near some known Roman bridging points – no definite evidence for stone bridges from the period have yet been discovered. Research is always ongoing, new evidence awaits discovery and existing evidence can always be reinterpreted, so it is not possible or wise to rule out the existence of such bridges.

The simplest form of a stone bridge is the *clam* or *clapper* bridge, which is a stone version of logs or planks spanning a crossing; the origin of the name is not really understood, and this type has also been called by several other names, such as *slab*, *lintel*, or even *cromlech* bridge. It has been claimed that 'clapper' is a dialect word for plank in Sussex and Berkshire, and was sometimes applied to plank bridges; similarly 'clam' could be derived from the Old English for branch or bough and was once used to denote rough timber pedestrian bridges in Devon and Cornwall. In general, the term 'clam' bridge is used for the simplest single span form and 'clapper' bridges are of similar construction but with two or more spans.

A simple clam bridge consists of a single slab of stone across a stream, usually supported on stone abutments, however primitive, on each side to prevent it sinking into the banks. In a clapper bridge there are two or more such slabs supported by stone abutments at either end and crude stone piers between the spans. More sophisticated versions could incorporate two or more rows of slabs laid parallel to each other.

In all cases, the stone slab or slabs used needed to be reasonably flat and of a reasonable length and breadth to span the spaces between the banks or the upright stone piers. As most of the earlier ones were not built for wheeled traffic there was no need for smooth approach ramps, and this type generally have stepped approaches on either side instead.

This simple form of bridge is one known to have been used in early Aegean cultures, and by the ancient Greeks – a sophisticated people who never seem to have understood or found a need for the arch. In Britain, the primitive nature of these bridges has generally led to their origins being placed in the prehistoric period, even in the Bronze Age. As there are certain obvious affinities with the construction of Stonehenge, for example, or on a less ambitious scale, with the masonry cores of burial barrows and cromlechs, the technology and organisational ability was certainly available in these islands several thousands of years ago.

One of the most primitive surviving examples of a clam bridge in Britain is that across the Wallabrook (a tributary of the Teign) on Dartmoor, in Devon, and there is a simple clapper bridge across that river at Teignhead. Also on Dartmoor is one of the most famous examples of a clapper bridge, at Postbridge, on the edge of the moor crossing the infant East Dart river; the name, incidentally, is probably derived from a guide post sited to indicate the position of the bridge to travellers in this bleak landscape.

That bridge is made up of three spans, each roughly 15ft (4.8m) long, consisting of single slabs of local granite a little over 6ft (2m) wide and supported on rough stone piers. At each end it is approached by steps, so could not take wheeled traffic. Its date is unknown, and there are similarly undated clapper bridges elsewhere on Dartmoor at Grimspound and Bellever Tor. Over the River Barle on Exmoor in neighbouring Somerset is a much longer example of a clapper bridge, seventeen spans in all, known as the Tarr Steps near Hawkridge.

These simple bridges in the south-west of England have been considered to be prehistoric and another example, the six-spanned and much repaired Pont-sarn-ddu taking a farm track over the Afon Lledr in north Wales, has been considered, wrongly, to be Roman; indeed, the local station on the former London & North Western Railway line is called Roman Bridge. Also in Wales, but in the south of the country, is the small clapper bridge across the Afon Alun just to the south of

68 The simplest of all stone bridges is the clam bridge – a single slab of stone; this one is just outside Wycoller in Lancashire and is impossible to date

69 A multi-span version of the clam bridge is generally called a clapper bridge, and this example is just downstream of the clam bridge in the previous illustration, in the village of Wycoller

Bridgend in Glamorgan; two of the limestone slab spans appear to be primary, the other two are the result of later repair, and it has been dated to the tenth century. A *pons lapidus* – stone bridge – in Cornwall mentioned in a deed of 1170 was probably a clapper bridge.

However, the truth is that the dates of most of the surviving bridges of this type are not really known at all, and whilst some may be of considerable antiquity, others are much later. Several in the Pennines, for example, appear to be post-medieval and built for packhorse traffic. There are good examples of such post-medieval clapper bridges over a stream at Wycoller, Lancashire and over the Wharfe at Linton, Yorkshire. An extremely simple slab bridge across the Bar Brook on the desolate Big Moor to the south of Sheffield bears two dates – 1742 and 1777 – though both probably relate to parish boundary markings rather than to the date of the bridge. Other much smaller examples appear to be a simple improvement on stepping stones, the steps being spanned by stone slabs; there are a number of such examples at fords where stepping stones appear to have been upgraded in this way.

In the northern Highlands of Scotland, at Aultbea in Ross & Cromarty, there is a restored stone clapper bridge of seven spans by the sea which is of eighteenth- or nineteenth-century date; clearly designed for wheeled traffic, it bore modern motor vehicles until recently. This is a much wider and more sophisticated structure than the pedestrian bridges in England and Wales and also has parapets on both sides; however, the basic construction techniques are the same. There is a handful of other late clapper bridges of this basic design in the north of Scotland, including one at Achriesgill in Sutherland built in the mid-1830s.

The arch represented a huge breakthrough in engineering. As with many things, it was not a Roman invention, but something taken by them from earlier cultures and improved upon. In this case they adapted a form being pioneered, in Europe at least, by the Etruscans. By the first century BC the Romans were able to build extremely large and ambitious arched bridges and aqueducts throughout much of their Empire, and developed arched vaulting in both stone and brick in their buildings to a degree that remains impressive two thousand years on. However, as already noted, the available archaeological evidence suggests that they appear not to have used the masonry arch in many of their bridges in Britain, despite claims that this or that simple stone arch bridge could be a genuine survival of the period or that some pier remnants and fallen masonry indicate an arched structure.

Saxon masons knew how to handle the masonry arch, and used it in their more important stone churches. But, possible Roman bridges apart, the earliest use of a masonry arch for a bridge in Britain was probably not until after the Norman Conquest of 1066. There is a tradition that the first stone arched bridge in England was built at the behest of Matilda, the erstwhile queen, in the twelfth century after she got soaked crossing the ford at Stratford-atte-Bowe – Bow Bridge being the result. However, Ranulf Flambard, Bishop of Durham between 1099 and 1128 was credited by a contemporary chronicler with linking 'the parted banks of the river Wear by building an arched bridge of massive stonework'.

Arched stone bridges are generally not, despite appearances, built of solid stone. Instead, their abutments and piers are usually made up of *face work* – generally of worked or ashlared stone – infilled with *core work,* usually of rubble and mortar, the quality of both depending on the quality of the design. In some medieval deeds, the better-faced stone is sometimes referred to as *freestone* (a technical term more restricted in its use today) and the core work, quite appropriately, *filling stone.* The Romans used concrete in their core work abroad, but there are too few remains to indicate to what extent that did so in their British bridges. Piers and abutments are, structurally, usually hollow masonry shells infilled with

70 An ancient packhorse bridge stands by the ford close to the Dorset village of Fifehead Neville across the River Divelish. Probably medieval, it is needed by modern pedestrians; the ford, on a bend in the lane, is both deep and swift

71 Ayleswade Bridge was built in the 1240s and was vital in the prosperity of the new city of Salisbury established by the Bishop to replace the earlier hill-top settlement in Old Sarum. The construction of the bridge led to the diversion of the main road from London to the south-west of England away from both Old Sarum and Wilton, through Salisbury. The original medieval work is partly hidden by the widening of the bridge in 1774

rubble. The abutments on the bank sides could be built in a standard manner off foundations, and were designed to be sufficiently substantial to take not just their own weight and that of the roadway over them, but also some of the forces transmitted to them by the arch of the adjacent bridge span.

Building foundations for the piers in the river or stream was obviously more difficult. A normal method to obtain a stable footing for the pier was to sink vertical timber piles, often of oak or elm and sometimes tipped with iron 'shoes', deep into the river bed; there are early references to special machines, or pile-drivers, being used in the process. Usually the piles were rammed home close together, but sometimes an outer 'frame' of piles could be created and the middle section infilled with large blocks of stone sunk into the mud between them. In either case a level and reasonably solid surface was then created on which a solid stone 'raft' footing was built from which construction work could begin.

Obviously the water had to be diverted around the pier footings, and this led to some of the most dangerous aspects of bridge construction. The use of *caissons*, specially built enclosures around the footings from which water was then excluded, appears to have been developed early on, otherwise most of the fine multi-spanned medieval bridges simply could not have been built.

Piers were usually designed in plan with pointed projections, or *cutwaters*, on their upstream ends. These deflected the force of the river around the piers. On the downstream side, cutwaters were also useful in resisting the natural inclination of the water to eddy back once through the narrowing of the arch, but were not always used. The cutwaters could be used for decorative effect but, more usefully and especially on narrower bridges, if their shape was continued up to parapet level, the resulting triangular recesses by the side of the roadway formed useful *refuges* for pedestrians. Some bridges had additional protection on their upstream sides, usually of open timber frames, to deflect debris floating down river, such as fallen trees, away from the piers; these are known as *starlings*.

Once the pier was being raised and the abutments were ready, the arches needed to be formed. These were of solid interlocking masonry, as the strength of the whole bridge relied on their structural integrity. To build them, however, a temporary formwork of timber in the right profile for the arch was needed. This work, by master carpenters, took a great deal of skill and yet is usually forgotten for few traces, other than the odd redundant slot in a masonry pier, survived once the formwork was 'struck'.

After the arch had been built using specially chosen and shaped stones carefully laid on top of the formwork, the timbers were no longer needed as the complete arch then had inherent structural integrity. Providing the stones are well laid and the abutments sufficient, it is difficult to collapse an arch. The rest of the bridge structure above the arches is, like the piers and abutments, generally only a shell. The side walls, or *spandrels*, between the arches are built up to the level of the roadway, but the space in between below the final deck level is usually made up in rubble and other fill.

Early medieval arches were fairly narrow in their spans and so early medieval bridges tended, on longer crossings, to have many of them. This resulted in many piers as well, which not only impeded navigation but also restricted the flow of the river. Old London Bridge had so many arches on such a broad river that it acted almost as a weir; the water upstream was kept fairly static, allowing it to freeze in really bad winters. The water shot between the piers, especially at

72 Forming the timber 'centring' on which masonry arches could be built was a highly skilled and vital craft; this is the centring for the 'Strand Bridge' across the Thames in London, designed by John Rennie and opened in 1819 as the Waterloo Bridge. It was demolished in 1938

low tides, and made navigation somewhat hazardous. It is also thought that the scouring below the bridge helped to create the deeper area of the river that became the Pool of London, a vital part of the city's development as a port.

A large number of small arches did, however, allow for a fairly level roadway and, in the case of London Bridge, this allowed the development of housing on either side of the roadway. Other examples of very long medieval multi-span bridges included two that no longer survive – the Long Bridge over the Torridge at Bideford in Devon, widened and virtually rebuilt in the nineteenth century, and the 35 span bridge across the Trent at Burton-on-Trent, nearly 1,640ft (500m) long.

By the fourteenth and fifteenth century, masons were capable of building wider arches, especially of two-centred, or 'pointed' form. These resulted in a less bulky and more graceful structure, such as the fifteenth-century Brig O'Doon, near Ayr. Wider arches were also made more achievable by the development of the use of arch ribs. These were long and narrow arches, separate and self-supporting structures in their own right. They formed the support for other blocks of stone spanning the spaces between the ribs. The result was that the bridges could use less masonry, and be lighter as a result, and that broader spans were possible. Some of the most elegant bridges in Britain are built to this system, such as the magnificent Twizel Bridge over the River Till near Berwick-on-Tweed, with a single span of 90ft (27.5m) built around 1500, and Warkworth Bridge over the Coquet, built around 1379. It is noticeable that the wider arch was more commonly used during the medieval period in the north of England and in Scotland than it was in southern Britain and Wales, but regional differences in bridges, as in any other building, are to be expected.

Ribs continued to be used in stone bridges after the medieval period – for example in the late seventeenth-century Bridge of Dye to the south of Banchory in Grampian or the deliberately anachronistic Edensor Bridge over the Derwent in the grounds of Chatsworth House, designed by James Paine in 1760 – but in general this form of construction seems to have died out gradually and full-width arches became the norm. The basic construction techniques used in stone bridges continued virtually unaltered until well into the twentieth century and the main changes were in their architecture rather in their engineering.

73 The grace and elegance of a Georgian bridge – in this case, John Gwynne's bridge (opened in 1776) carries Holyhead Road across the River Severn at Atcham. Note the pronounced 'hump' that proved to be a problem for traffic until a new bridge was built alongside in the early twentieth century

Brick

Bricks have a long history, and bridges using brick in their construction are known in the ancient civilisations of the Middle East and in the Roman Empire. It was the Romans that introduced bricks to Britain, though the archaeological evidence suggests that they do not seem to have been particularly common. No brick bridges of the period have been identified and up until the end of the eighteenth century, brick was a far less common material for bridge construction.

This was mainly because of the availability of both timber and stone throughout most of Britain. In some areas, particularly the south-eastern part of England, there was relatively little good quality building stone, and timber supplies had been depleted by the demands of the charcoal industry, ship-building, and construction from the sixteenth century onwards. In such areas, bricks were sometimes used to form the arches, or even just the sides of the arches, of otherwise completely rubblestone built bridges. One not uncommon form from the late medieval period in this region was the brick-built moat bridge to replace a timber drawbridge, such as the fine mid-fifteenth century example as Hurstmonceux Castle in Sussex.

The late eighteenth century saw the ready acceptance of brick as a bridge building material, but the vast majority of brick bridges were fairly small and built to carry roads over the increasing numbers of canals. The rather old-fashioned multi-spanned brick bridge over the Thames at Sonning, built in 1773, was more of an exception. Other bridges from this period incorporated structural brickwork but were, for architectural effect, faced with stone. An early example of this was the Godstow bridge in Oxford of 1770.

The improvements to transport of heavy goods that the canals brought about, followed by yet further improvements of the railways from the mid-nineteenth century onwards, led to bricks being readily available throughout Britain. The development of railways, in particular, led to the construction of tens of thousands of brick-built over and under bridges to keep established roads and other rights of way intact. Bricks were either used for the entire bridge structure, often with stone decoration, or in conjunction with other materials – particularly cast iron. A common design, in railway-related road bridges in particular, was the series of parallel brick jack arches springing from cast-iron girders to support the deck.

Iron & steel

Iron, as a building material, was firmly established by the success of the famous 'Iron Bridge' over the navigable River Severn in Shropshire; the bridge gave the developing riverside settlement its present name. Contrary to popular history, this was not the first iron bridge to be designed; plans for a bridge in Lyon, France, had been made in 1755 and one iron arch, at least, cast; the project was cancelled. In Scotland, Robert Mylne designed an iron bridge to be built at Inverary in 1775, but it too was never built. Thus it was the iron bridge across the Severn that became the first of any note to be finished.

The bridge, with its 100ft (30m) main semi-circular span, was almost certainly designed by local Shrewsbury architect Thomas Farnolls Pritchard in conjunction with local ironmaster Abraham Darby the Third. Revolutionary in its material but, structurally, not very sophisticated, the jointing was based on well-established carpentry techniques but using iron pieces instead of timber ones. The main castings were ready by 1779, after Pritchard's death. It is perhaps worth remembering that, when the main cast-iron arch of the bridge was opened for traffic in 1781, the two side spans on the south bank were of timber. Nevertheless, the bridge has become an iconic symbol of the Industrial Revolution.

74 The famous 'Iron Bridge' across the Severn gave its name to the riverside settlement of this part of what was then Madeley. Designed by Thomas Pritchard, no doubt with assistance from Abraham Darby, it was cast in 1779 and opened in 1781. It can claim to be the first significant iron bridge in the world

This new form of bridge had also proven to be very expensive to make, and the cost, together with the inevitable risks perceived in such a new technology, meant that the design did not catch on immediately. However, the fact that it was one of the few bridges to emerge unscathed after a huge flood in 1795 that destroyed other bridges along the Severn inevitably led to other engineers realising the possibilities of this 'new' material.

There are two basic types of iron – *cast* and *wrought*. Cast iron consists of iron 'cast' when molten into moulds and allowed to harden. The moulding process allowed for a huge variety of shapes and forms, including arches and girders, and the opportunity was afforded for integral decoration. It has good resistance to rust and is strong in compression – that is, it can take heavy loads acting vertically down onto it – and in this respect it has similar properties to masonry. Arched ribs formed from cast iron are as strong and far lighter than masonry arches, allowing for slightly less substantial abutments and piers. However, it is not strong in tension, and it is also quite brittle.

Wrought iron, on the other hand, is a more expensive but more utilitarian form of iron and needs more work to produce it – including constant rolling and hammering in the foundry – and it is more prone to rusting. However, it is stronger in tension and better able to resist bending and lateral forces. By the end of the nineteenth century, steel became more widely available and, in combining the best qualities of both cast and wrought iron, rapidly replaced both in major civil engineering works, including bridges.

The second great iron bridge was built across the River Wear in Sunderland and had a span more than double that of the Shropshire iron bridge. Designed by Thomas Wilson, it used some second-hand parts – arch castings produced for a bridge designed by the philosopher Thomas Paine and intended to be shipped to the United States for use there on yet another aborted project. In its design, it took up the use of iron hoops in the spandrels of the Shropshire iron bridge but used them in both the arches and spandrels as structural bracing; although the Wear bridge was demolished in 1858, the smaller Tickford Bridge at Newport Pagnell of 1810, clearly influenced by it, survives. Subsequently, other designers used different types of inter-arch bracing.

Iron bridges were still seen as slightly risky, especially after Wilson's bridge over the Thames at Staines, opened in 1803, had to be dismantled in the following year due to structural failures. However, other engineers developed the concept to produce several quite spectacular iron bridges in the early years of the nineteenth century. Telford had strong Shropshire connections and, although by training a mason and a builder of many fine masonry bridges, his first iron bridge was built at Buildwas after the medieval bridge had been swept away in the floods of 1795. This was a distinct engineering improvement on the one downstream at what had become Ironbridge, using far less iron in its construction.

75 A detail of the cast-iron work of Joseph Potter's High Bridge across the Trent at Armitage, Staffordshire. By the time it was opened in 1830 iron construction techniques had improved considerably

It was demolished in 1905, but Telford also designed several other fixed arched iron bridges that have survived. These include, in Scotland, the Craigellachie Bridge over the Spey in Grampian with a single 150ft segmental span; in Wales, the Waterloo Bridge at Bettws-y-Coed across the Afon Conwy, dated 1815 but finished a little later with decorative cast-iron foliage representing the national floral emblems of Britain; and in England, the Mythe Bridge over the Severn just upstream of Tewkesbury, opened in 1823 with a span of 174ft (53m). Telford also developed a type of cast-iron 'kit bridge' of simple castings that could be used for minor road bridges in the county, and one of these survives, happily bypassed and preserved, at Cantlop, on the narrow road between Shrewsbury and Acton Burnell.

Another great engineer of the time, John Rennie, also designed several iron bridges, including the five-arched bridge across the tidal Wye at Chepstow – a composite bridge in which the piers were of masonry; this opened in 1815 and replaced a wooden bridge. His Southwark Bridge across the Thames in London is of a similar design, but the central arch was a massive 240ft (73m) – the largest to be built in cast iron; opened in 1819, the bridge was replaced in 1921. Rennie had also built a bridge of wrought iron at Boston, Lincolnshire in 1800.

Wrought iron was more expensive to make and initially more difficult to use in bridge construction, especially before advanced rolling techniques were available in the ironworks. It could be used bolted together to create box-girders, and Robert Stephenson took this idea to the extreme when he built the Conwy and Menai railways bridges at the start of the 1850s, creating box girders big enough to take the trains inside them. This form of construction really came into its own after the development of steel. The earliest example of a large motorway bridge using this method of construction is the Samlesbury Bridge to the east of Preston, opened in 1958 and carrying the M6 motorway in three unequal spans across the Ribble valley; it is over 425ft (130m) long. The development of steel also led to the construction of very large bridges of varying form, from simple girder and trussed girder bridges to massive structures such as the Tyne Bridge in Newcastle, the Wearmouth Bridge in Sunderland (1929), and the Runcorn Bridge over the Mersey built as recently as 1956.

The trust placed in iron by the early nineteenth century, and the vision of some of the great engineers of the time, also allowed for the construction of the great suspension bridges, many of which are still impressive nearly two centuries later. The first large suspension bridge capable of taking normal traffic was the Union Bridge across the River Tweed near Horncliffe, a few miles to the west of Berwick-on-Tweed. Designed by Captain Samuel Brown it was opened in 1820 and has a massive single span of 360ft (110m). Still in use, the main change has been the substitution of steel cables for the original suspension chains.

This bridge was soon dwarfed by one designed by Telford as part of the Holyhead Road improvements in north Wales. This was to replace the often dangerous and erratic ferry across the Menai Straits linking mainland Wales with Anglesey. The bridge has carefully worked arched approaches on either side and then a central suspended span of 580ft (177m) between the two tall pylons. Telford used wrought, rather than cast, iron in its construction, mostly from William Hazeldine's Upton Forge on the River Tern in Shropshire. Incorporated into the eastern abutment of the bridge was the bridge-keeper's house and the toll-house. Still in use since it opened in 1826, it has been subtly altered and strengthened on several occasions, and virtually none of the original ironwork survives. The original deck was replaced in 1893 and the chains, rods and walkways between 1938–1940. The overall character of the bridge, however, has been retained, and some original iron fencing survives on the mainland bank. In the same year that

76 Iron or steel bridges in the twentieth century have tended to be rather more utilitarian. This is a typical example, built between the world wars to carry the main road across the river near Ingleton, Yorkshire

77 A large suspension bridge for wheeled traffic, the Union Bridge across the Tweed in Northumberland, designed by Captain Samuel Brown. Opened in 1820 it has a massive single span of 360ft

the Menai Bridge opened, a second Telford suspension bridge opened not far away at Conwy; this is now traffic free and in the care of the National Trust.

An even longer suspension bridge was designed and begun by Isambard Kingdom Brunel to span the Avon Gorge to the west of Bristol. Work started in 1836 but stopped for financial reasons; it was then completed after Brunel's death as a memorial to him – ironically using the chains of his short-lived (1845–1861) Hungerford suspension bridge across the Thames in London. Opened in 1864, its span is over 700ft (213m), made even more impressive by the fact that it is nearly 250ft (76m) down to the river below.

That was the last of the great suspension bridges in Britain for nearly a century; most of the subsequent bridges of this type were fairly humble affairs, including many footbridges. The main reason for that was the fact that the roads had been eclipsed by the railways and that the suspension bridge was not a particularly suitable form of structure for them. One major change in technology was the introduction of first wire and then steel rope in place of iron chains.

78 Thomas Telford's Menai Bridge was one of the marvels of its time and an important part of his Holyhead Road improvements. It opened in 1826; this is the view from the Holyhead side of the Strait

The great resurgence in suspension bridge technology began in the United States, and that led to the construction of several great bridges in Britain, including the Tamar Bridge between Devon and Cornwall of 1959 with a main span of 1,100ft (335m), towering over Brunel's railway bridge alongside; the Severn Bridge opened in 1963 with a main span of 3,240ft (988m); the Forth Bridge of 1959, with a slightly longer main span of 3,300 ft (1006m); and the Humber Bridge of 1972, with a main span of 4,625ft (1,410m) − until recently the longest in the world.

Concrete

Concrete is considered to be a modern material, particularly when related to bridge construction. However, concrete has been used in bridge construction for over two thousand years. Much of Roman masonry techniques in continental Europe relied on concrete, mainly used in the core work of structures, but little conclusive evidence of its use has been identified in their British bridges. As a building material, concrete did not really become significant until the later nineteenth century, due largely to the pioneering work of French engineers – although it has been claimed that Sir Charles Fowler built a temporary concrete bridge in Cromwell Road, London, in 1869 and Philip Brannon certainly built the three-arched bridge across the estuary of the Axe at Seaton, Devonshire, from mass concrete and blocks in 1877.

Both concrete blocks and shuttered concrete – that is, concrete simply poured into moulds and allowed to set – could be used in small bridges where the sheer weight and mass of the material was capable of dealing with the stresses involved. Indeed, in railway construction, both of these simple techniques could produce quite large structures, including several major viaducts on Scottish lines built at the end of the nineteenth century. However, it was really with the development of reinforced concrete that the material came to be important. This gave the material the tensile strength that it had hitherto lacked, and allowed the various elements within the design to share the loads more equally.

Several patents had been granted for the introduction of ironwork into concrete prior to the successful work of François Hennébique in the 1890s; he used steel, rather than iron, reinforcing rods and invented new types of connectors between them, including the 'stirrup beam' patented in 1892. In 1898 Hennébique built the first ambitious reinforced concrete bridge, the Pont de Chatellerault, which had a span of over 50m. In Britain, some of the early pioneering work in reinforced concrete was undertaken by L.G. Mouchel, one of Hennébique's former assistants. The two earliest identified reinforced concrete road bridges in Britain are considered to be one at Chewton Glen in the New Forest, built in 1901, and another at Satterthwaite, Cumbria, built in the following year. Both are relatively modest structures.

Shropshire was a county that built some of the earliest reinforced concrete road bridges in the early twentieth century, including a small one over the Rea Brook in Minsterley, and two more ambitious ones over the River Severn both built by the Mouchel partnership. The first of those was the recently demolished Free Bridge at Jackfield in 1909; the second was built in 1913–14 at Cressage and still stands.

This graceful structure of three segmental arches replaced another rarity – the timber bridge designed by Telford; it was deliberately designed to look like a traditional stone bridge, complete with ornate balustrade. Only decades later, when the iron reinforcing has begun to rust and 'blow' or crack the concrete, is the deception revealed and repairs are needed. At the end of the 1920s the same company built a considerably larger bridge to the designs of the county surveyor, William Butler, a little upstream to take the main Holyhead Road across the

79 At first, Cressage Bridge looks to be a rather graceful stone bridge, rather old-fashioned for its opening date of 1913. It is actually made of reinforced concrete, one of several across the River Severn built by Shropshire County Council in the early twentieth century

river at Atcham; in this, the construction is more honestly, if not attractively, expressed.

The 1920s and '30s saw many reinforced concrete bridges being built on British roads, generally with their ribs and framework expressed honestly as in the Atcham bridge. One of the largest examples is the Royal Tweed Bridge of 1928 over that river at Berwick-on-Tweed, another Mouchel construction but with one span of 361ft (110m) being the largest built by that date in Britain. Several bridges were built on the new roads built during this period to relieve unemployment, such as a pair of bow-string type bridges on the road across Rannoch Moor in the Scottish Highlands.

By the middle of the century the shape of reinforced concrete bridges began to change. A much shallower segmental arch began to become more common; an interesting early example was built to link collieries on either side of the River Severn in south-eastern Shropshire at Alveley. Built by the British Reinforced

80 The Bridgnorth Bypass bridge, here seen approaching completion in the early-1980s, is of pre-stressed reinforced concrete; the two sides of the main arch could be built cantilevered out from their abutments with no need for centring

Concrete Engineering Company in 1936–37, it originally took a pair of narrow gauge railway tracks and pedestrians; lorries later used it but since the collieries closed in 1969 it has served as a footbridge. Now in need of urgent repair, it is facing demolition.

After the Second World War a new form of reinforcing was developed which involved pre-stressing the reinforcing rods or wires before the concrete was poured; this meant that the reinforcing was already in tension. A small bridge at Fishtoft, Lincolnshire, of 1947 is thought to be the first road bridge in Britain of this type, but they have since become ubiquitous. In the past fifty years there have literally been thousands of reinforced concrete bridges of all shapes and sizes constructed, especially with the huge demand for such bridges in motorway construction.

PART IV

BUILDINGS

There are and were many different types of buildings associated directly or indirectly with road transport, though these are far more difficult to categorise than the built heritage of other forms of transport, such as the railways or the canals. Some, such as toll-houses, are obviously entirely road related. Others, such as the coaching inns, could have a more local function not directly related to the travellers staying at them – but owed most of their prosperity to such passing trade.

CHAPTER 9

Inns

The direct antecedents of the modern motorway service station were the special posting stations established along the Royal Road of Persia by the Emperor Cyrus in the mid-sixth century BC; these were vital in allowing those carrying the post a fresh change of horses every set number of miles and thus speeding the official lines of communication. Herodotus later praised the royal rest stops and excellent lodgings on this main highway between Sardis and Susa. It was a system admired but not really copied by the Greeks, but taken up and improved by the Romans.

There is little evidence, archaeological or historical, relating to the accommodation of travellers in Roman Britain. Evidence from other parts of the former Roman Empire is more forthcoming. This shows that there were inns in towns at least – Horace mentions one at *Beneventum* that caught fire when he was staying in it – and there were also strategically placed posting stations along the major roads supplying fresh horses and accommodation for the Imperial mail – the *cursus publicus*.

Posting stations, or *mansiones*, in the larger towns appear to have also been used by the more important official travellers as well, usually situated close to one of the main gates. Presumably similar facilities were available to those using the roads of Britain. In some Roman towns, the ruins of certain buildings have been considered to be those of hostelries, sometimes with their own private courtyards and bath houses. A particularly large complex has been identified as a *mansio* in the former Roman town of Silchester, Hampshire, and others tentatively identified at Caerwent, Gwent; Chelmsford, Essex; and Aldborough, Yorkshire.

Even less is known of the way that travellers were dealt with in Britain and western Europe during the so-called Dark Ages and the Saxon period that followed, though in the Byzantine Empire the Roman road system with its posts and inns seems to have continued to function and in Arabia, the expansion of the Muslim empire from the seventh century AD onwards led to a similar system of staging posts for the state mails – the *barid* – along the roads stretching out from the Cailiph's palace in Medina.

In medieval Christian states, one of the duties of the monasteries was that of hospitality, particularly for pilgrims and the poor. That tradition continued until the end of the monastic era in the early sixteenth century. The way in which a traveller might be treated at a religious house depended on his status. The wealthy lord would be a guest of the abbot and be dealt with accordingly, especially if he had a connection with a benefactor of the house. It was not uncommon for some of the aristocracy to abuse monastic hospitality, arriving uninvited and staying for days or weeks – despite occasional efforts by the Crown to prevent this happening.

Members of a wealthy man's retinue would, like the poorer traveller, be accommodated elsewhere, usually in the specially constructed *Guesten Hall* or *Hospitium*. These were often very grand buildings, though undoubtedly the quality of the hospitality itself must have varied from place to place. Some seem to have had more private chambers off the main hall, but in most the travellers probably slept in the hall itself, probably on crude straw mattresses laid out on the floor. Guests were not expected to pay, but were expected to give an appropriate donation according to their means.

As well as the monasteries, there were other religious foundations that would help travellers. Some provided food for travellers, such as the twelfth century Hospital of St Cross to the south of Winchester. Celia Fiennes noted at the end of the seventeenth century that the inhabitants of this almshouse 'by their foundation … are to give relief to any Travellers that call there so farre as a Loafe of bread … and a Draughte of beare and a piece of money, I thinke its value of a Groate …'; that tradition continues to this day.

There were also medieval hostels set up specifically to cater for pilgrims heading for or arriving at the main religious shrines dotted throughout Britain. These varied in size and grandeur; one of the oldest recorded is the Angel, Grantham, set up by the Knights Templar in the early twelfth century for pilgrims but frequented by royalty; King John is said to have held court at the Angel in 1213 and Richard III also visited in the late fifteenth century by which time some of its present components would have been built.

Slightly lower down the scale were the *maisons dieu*; these were hospitals – the word was not then specifically associated with the care of the sick and elderly – whose main purpose was to cater for less wealthy pilgrims. The numbers of *maisons dieu* – sometimes also known simply known as *domus Dei* or *God's houses* – increased in the late twelfth century following an increase in domestic pilgrimages in the aftermath of the murder of Thomas à Becket at Canterbury. These hospitals varied in size and layout, depending on their charters; most probably had resident brethren to cater for the pilgrims, as well as facilities to look after the infirm.

God's House in Brentford had beds and other facilities 'for the entertainment of poor travellers' and the *maison dieu* in Dover had fixed beds for travellers in the hall; fragments of this establishment have survived. There are other surviving buildings associated with medieval hostels and hospitals but it is often difficult to assess whether or not these were specifically related to travellers; typical examples are the surviving church of the God's House in Portsmouth, founded in the early thirteenth century, and Barnaby House, in Ludlow, thought to be a pilgrims' hostel.

Throughout the fourteenth century the urge for pilgrimages seems to have declined as, indeed, did the population due to the successive outbreaks of the Plague. This led to the gradual decline of the hostels and *maisons dieu*. In addition, the monasteries seem to have become slightly less willing to cater for pilgrims within their walls. Nevertheless, they still had to be housed and one common solution was for the greater religious houses to establish their own inns outside their precinct walls, where normal commercial practices usually applied. Quite a few of these have survived and, in most respects, were little different than the contemporary secular inns; indeed, most seem to have continued as inns after the dissolution of the monastic house that established them.

Most inns would have been too expensive for the poor and were mainly used by the merchant and middle classes. It was usual for the guests to bring their own provisions, but they could also buy food on site. There were many recorded complaints against the high prices charged in inns and accusations about innkeepers and their staff over-charging and stealing from their guests. In 1354 Edward III passed a statute aimed at ending 'great and outrageous cost of victuals kept up in all the realm by innkeepers and other retailers of victuals, to the great detriment of the people travelling through the realm'.

Accommodation seems to have been fairly communal in the medieval period, with guests sharing not only the main hall of the inn, but also beds, which were usually set out in large chambers or dormitories. Gradually, in common with domestic living, privacy became more important so that individual rooms were being provided in some inns by the end of the sixteenth century.

Like many businesses in the largely illiterate medieval period, inns selling ale had their own distinctive sign – a long pole with a bush tied to it, the 'ale-stake'. This symbol was shared by the less salubrious ale-house, which also stood by the road side, often at junctions, to serve travellers. The ale-house offered no

81 The George Hotel in Glastonbury, Somerset, is one of the most famous pilgrims'
inns in Britain and was built by the local abbey in the very early sixteenth century. It is
unusually richly decorated and, equally unusual in being of three storeys with its main
floor at first-floor level

82 A medieval engraving of the inside of an inn, showing the rather cramped and communal conditions faced by travellers and pilgrims alike

overnight accommodation and was often no more than a roadside hut, catering for people like Chaucer's Pardoner who, at the end of the fourteenth century, kept his fellow pilgrims waiting before beginning his tale:

> But first, quod he, her at this ale-stake
> I wil bothe drynke and byten on a cake

83 A medieval sketch of a roadside ale house, with its traditional bush on the end of the pole signifying its function

A tiny fourteenth-century miniature of an ale house has survived. In the country, the 'ale-stakes' could be as long as needed to catch the travellers' attention, but in the crowded and narrow streets of London their length was limited by decree in 1375 to 7ft (2.2m).

The greed and extravagance of Henry VIII led to the dramatic demise of the monasteries and most other religious houses in England and Wales in the 1530s and '40s. Whilst this eliminated the need to go on pilgrimage, it also eliminated an important source of accommodation for travellers. Inns appear to have been on the increase prior to that. Following the dissolution of the monasteries and their great estates, and the increase in commerce and trade in Elizabethan England – with the resultant increase in the numbers of those travelling on the roads – this trend accelerated.

By the late sixteenth century, according to William Harrison, all of the towns along the busier roads of England had 'great and sumptuous inns builded in them for the receiving of such travellers and strangers as pass to and fro'. He added that these were not just for the rich, but that 'every man may use his inne as his owne house in England, and have for his money how great or little variety of vittels, and what other service himself shall think expedient to call for'.

Whilst inns varied in size and status according to their site and clientele, the larger ones had begun to develop a fairly standard form by the later medieval period. Usually they were built of local materials and in the style of the better local town houses – typically with their most elaborate elevation to the street.

Thus it was common for timber-framed buildings to have jetties and close-studding on their main elevations and much plainer framing to the rear, or a stone building would have an ashlared facade to a plainer rubblestone carcass.

Where space was available, there would be a carriageway through the main range leading to a courtyard beyond, often quite narrow because of the typical thin medieval burgage plots that formed the property boundaries in most towns. This yard would be flanked on one or both of its long sides by rear wings. Again, depending on the length of the curtilage, these could have additional chambers close to the main frontage block with the various services beyond, or stabling on one side and chambers on the other, or even stabling below chambers. Usually facing into the courtyard were the necessary kitchen, brew-house and stores. The increase in individual chambers for guests led to the development of external galleries, usually timber-framed, to the courtyard. These provided independent and separate access to the rooms on the upper floors.

There was, however, no real set pattern for inns and each developed in an often *ad hoc* manner. This can be misleading to later archaeologists. For example, the Saracen's Head in King's Norton, once a large village outside, but now part of Birmingham, looks, at first glance, to be a typical medieval inn. It has a late fifteenth century timber-framed main range, a slightly later frontage set back between two projecting wings, and a passageway through it to a rear courtyard. Yet this was one, or perhaps two, private houses originally and only seems to have become an inn during the eighteenth century.

In Elizabeth's reign, in order to improve the speed of royal messengers, the first posting houses were established – perhaps recreating those of the Roman era. For a small stipend from the Crown, inns stabled fresh horses for the messengers, an idea that soon spread to private individuals especially after this was made legal in 1583. Fixed charges were made by statute of 2d per horse per 'stage', but the riders also had to hire a guide with a horn riding another horse that also carried the luggage for 4d. By the early seventeenth century the fixed charges were abandoned and more market-led agreements made between the inn and the traveller. The use of 'post horses' meant that greater stabling accommodation was needed at the inns involved.

Another development in the latter part of the sixteenth century was the use of the carriage or coach for travellers, and this led in some inns to adaptations of their outbuildings to house such expensive pieces of equipment. A rare early example of a known purpose-built coaching inn was built in Norfolk during the Commonwealth period on the main Norwich to London road at Scole. Known originally as the White Hart, it is a large building in the 'artisan mannerist' style dated to 1655 and built by a wealthy merchant, John Peck; built mainly of brick, but with some rendered timber-framing to the rear courtyard, it still has many

84 The Scole Inn, in the Norfolk village of that name but originally the White Hart, was one of the first purpose-built coaching inns and opened in 1655 on the then busy road between London and Norwich

of its original fixtures and fittings, fine rooms and a grand staircase. Apart from the replacement of many of its original cross-mullioned windows with tripartite sashes, its appearance has changed remarkably little, though it is no longer on the line of the main road. It is now called the Scole Inn.

With the improvements brought about by the turnpikes, coupled with improvements to vehicle design and comfort, more and more people began to travel by stagecoach, post coach, and post chaise. This led to the need for more and more inns along the main roads capable of serving their needs, accelerated still further by the introduction of the mail coach in 1784. In the larger towns there would be several inns, often all in fierce competition.

In some cases, new establishments grew up where needed at intervals along the newly turnpiked roads. Sometimes these could, in turn, lead to the establishment of small villages clustered around them. A case in point is that of Craven Arms,

85 The Craven Arms opened as a coaching inn outside an insignificant village called Newton in the late eighteenth century at a junction of the main Shrewsbury–Ludlow road in Shropshire, part of the main highway along the England–Wales border. Behind the main frontage block was spacious stabling for the many horses required for road travel at that time. In many ways it was a motorway service station of its day

Shropshire. The small market town got its name from a coaching inn of that name set up in the late eighteenth century at a junction of newly improved roads a short distance from an existing hamlet. The new settlement closer to the inn was sufficiently important by the time the railway arrived in the early 1850s to be chosen as the site for a station, and a small town grew up around this new focal point as a result.

Usually inns were privately built and run, but the inn on the Anglesey section of the Holyhead Road in the 1820s was built by the government Commission responsible. Thomas Telford's new main route bypassed an earlier coaching inn nearby and a new one was needed towards the centre of the island. A site was chosen at Mona, and a new inn with two courts of stabling was built. In many respects, it was the 1820s equivalent of a service station on a new stretch of motorway. Its immediate prosperity was, like that of the road it served, short-lived and quickly taken away by the new-fangled railways.

In general, inns continued to be built or rebuilt to the same courtyard design well into the early nineteenth century, though this was by no means universal. Where space was not at a premium, such as at the Craven Arms Inn mentioned above, a completely separate stable block could be built. This was sometimes also the case where the layout of a site, particularly in towns, made any expansion of a courtyard impossible, as in the case of the Rutland Arms in the centre of Bakewell, Derbyshire, built in 1804; its stables were on the opposite side of the street.

The frontages of inns continued to be their most important elevations and were often upgraded whilst the rest was not. Thus many ancient timber-framed inns were simply given fashionable new brick or stone facades. Some had completely rebuilt frontages, such as the former Swan Hotel in Lichfield, rebuilt in the later eighteenth century but retaining late-medieval and seventeenth-century rear ranges. The frontage block of another former coaching inn, the White Hart in Chipping Norton, looks to be a fine early eighteenth-century building but is the re-fronting of an earlier building with a stone facade and timber-framed rear wall.

Inevitably, opinions of the quality of inns varied, depending on the true attributes of the inn and on the even-mindedness of the observer. Perhaps it has always been the case that those who commit their thoughts about such things in writing are the ones who usually want to complain. There were certainly many bad inns of the type satirised in the poet Thomas Hood's 1826 poem, 'Our Village'; of the many taverns in Bullock Smithy professing to be inns, the Green Man was the only one 'that for love or money could raise/A postillion, a blue jacket, two deplorable lame white horses, and a ramshackled "neat postchaise"'.

A little earlier the much travelled John Byng, later Viscount Torrington, often had little good to say about inns in his late eighteenth-century journals. An inn in Haslingden, Lancashire, was simply described as 'the worst in the world' and the largest inn in March, Cambridgeshire, 'looked so shabbily, and the casements so broken' that he refused to stay there. Unlike most writers of his time, he also commented on the stabling as well. He stayed at the George, in Huntingdon, despite it being 'an old and unfashionable inn' because it had good stabling. In contrast, in Baldock, Hertfordshire, he changed inns 'having quarrell'd with the ostler at the White Horse', the George in Rye was 'a dirty seaport inn with a wretched stable', the stables at the Three Cranes, Chepstow, 'were a wretched dungeon, everything bad and charged high'.

It was the development of the railways that led to the general downturn in road traffic in general and, inevitably, to a fall in demand for the services provided by the roadside inns. The loss of stagecoach traffic, in particular, hit the grander inns very hard, whilst the transfer of goods and farm animals from road or drove trail to the railways hit those slightly lower down the social scale. Many closed, or became public houses serving their communities rather than relying on people passing through.

The first signs of a revival in the roadside inn came in the 1890s, but not because of the motor car — which was a very rare and expensive thing at that time — but because of the bicycle. Cycling became relatively safe, popular and cheap and led to the development of tourism, fostered by new organisations such as the Cyclists' Touring Club. This, in turn, led to the need for good quality accommodation, vetted by the CTC and other cycling organisations who produced lists of recommended premises. The old and mainly rundown roadside inns were the ideal places. Within a few years, the bicycle was followed by the motor vehicle — initially a novelty but quickly an integral part of the nation's transport system.

Early in the twentieth century, the development of the car, coach and lorry led to a more radical revival of the roadside inns. P.H. Ditchfield's book *Vanishing England* was published in 1910. After lamenting the end of the old coaching inns in the nineteenth century, he noted, with little enthusiasm, that 'Now the wayside inns wake up again with the bellow of the motor car, which like a hideous monster rushes through the old-world villages, startling and killing old slow-footed rustics and scampering children, dogs and hens, and clouds of dust strive in very mercy to hide the view of the terrible rushing demon'.

An interesting development a little before this time had been the proposal by the 4th Earl Grey to set up a countywide network of Public Trust House Companies to take on old inns and refurbish them for the travelling public, offering accommodation, food and soft drinks as well as alcoholic ones. The first was set up in Hertfordshire, and the first inn upgraded in this way was the Waggon & Horses at Ridge Hill on the main Holyhead Road in 1904 which became very popular with cyclists. Other similar enterprises followed and these combined to form a national chain of Trust Houses — the first proper chain of hotels. By 1913 they operated 43 houses and by 1938, well over 200; the company merged with that of the Forte group in 1970 to become Trust House Forte, one of the biggest hotel chains in the world.

Usually, and if it was possible to do so, well-established inns converted most, if not all, of their underused or redundant stabling to garages to cater for the new age. The horse was not completely ignored, even after the First World War, and as late as 1949 the influential architect Francis Yorke was recommending in his book, *Public Houses*, that in country areas provision still be made by inns for 'hack or guest horses, and for a riding school'.

In the early years of motoring, when motor cars had to be serviced after virtually every trip, some hotels could provide that service too; for example, in

1904 the Clydesdale Hotel in Lanark had a repair pit, petrol and oil on the premises and the Great Western Hotel in Oban boasted a resident engineer. In more congested towns, there might not be room in the hotel grounds, so cars could be parked elsewhere, often in converted livery stables or carriage workshops.

Not all hostelries could rely on providing overnight accommodation for their guests, as the car could travel far further and faster than the carriage or horse ever could and the amount of overnight stops travellers needed was reduced. However, they could provide suitable areas in which the motorists could rest for a while, and perhaps eat.

Whilst older establishments adapted to serve the new traveller, a new type of inn rapidly evolved, especially between the world wars. These new roadside inns, or road houses, were usually sited on the newly improved main roads leading out of towns, sometimes with the expectation of also serving the inevitable spread of suburban development that such roads fostered. A new road or bypass almost inevitably led to the construction of a new road house, and others were established at suitable sites along the main roads to serve both travellers and tourists.

In 1949, Yorke defined the top quality road house as having a 'generous car park, gardens and outdoor and indoor amusements, sometimes including a swimming bath, a lawn for outside dancing, a floor for inside dancing etc., and catering generally for food'. At the bottom end of his scale were the much plainer small road houses 'catering principally for transport drivers with constant passing trade and perhaps some local trade'. Some of the larger road houses had separate public rooms for private motorists, lorry drivers, and charabanc or coach-passengers.

The most distinctive feature of these establishments was the provision of large areas of car parking, often well-lit and with elaborately formed entrances off the road. The facilities offered varied enormously, as did their design. These inns, perhaps more than any other form of twentieth century building, clearly demonstrate the schizophrenic nature of British architecture. Many were built in what could be described as 'Brewer's Tudor' – a generally insipid and nostalgic recreation of the ancient hostelries of the past. These dripped with mock timber-framing or aspired, usually with limited success, to Georgian elegance. A few architects did manage to develop these historic design elements into quite elegant designs, but they were few and far between.

In complete, and refreshing, contrast, the latest mode of rapid road transport in a new and exciting era was celebrated by quite radical, crisp, modern and excitingly designed road houses. These included the distinctive road houses by E.B. Musman, such as the Ace of Spades in Surbiton (1932), the Nag's Head in Bishop's Stortford (1934), and the Comet in Hatfield (1936); the Comet

86 The motor age brought about a revival of the moribund coaching inns and also led to the creation of a new type of road-side hostelry – the road houses. Their design varied from 'Brewer's Tudor' and derivatives to more up-to-date styles such as this modernist inter-war Toll House on the main Birmingham Road just outside Coventry

was described at the time by the Architecture Club as 'Beautiful brickwork in a streamlined design apt beside a modern highway yet, carrying on the Pickwickian tradition of the coaching inn, cheerful and solid'. The distinguished modern architect, Oliver Hill, designed the equally elegant Prospect Inn at Minster-in-Thanet, Kent, opened in 1938. As with any style of architecture, these modern designs could be, and were, copied by lesser architects and produced some quite ugly buildings.

One of the more common forms of accommodation for the motorist in North America is the motel, where each room or individual chalet is next to the travellers car parking space. This idea has not really caught on in Britain, though there were several attempts at hotels specifically catering for the motorist since the 1930s. It has been claimed that the first proper motel in Britain was the Royal Oak in Hythe, Kent, though the terminology is open to interpretation. In general, the British seem to have preferred 'motor hotels' instead, such as the Breakspear Motor Hotel in Hemel Hempstead designed for Trust House by Nelson Foley in 1964, or the Dover Stage, just off the seafront in Dover. The distinction between

87 Some of the new motorway service stations built in the 1960s aspired to architectural pretension, reflecting the excitement of a new era; this is the viewing tower at Forton Services on the M6 to the south of Lancaster – originally a restaurant but sadly now closed

these and, especially given the more recent 'lodges' at motorway service stations, and motels in the American sense of the word is slight.

To a certain extent, the service stations on the motorways and the smaller ones on main roads are the modern equivalent of the coaching inn – a rest area providing fuel and food for travellers and their steeds and, sometimes, accommodation as well. These had been built on and across motorways in other countries, the first being on the original *autostrade* between Milan and Verese in 1924.

In Britain, the government sensibly decided to only lease the potential sites of motorway service stations to potential operators. The new rules for the motorways insisted that the service stations could not be too close together, and that they had to be serviced off normal roads. The first was that at Newport Pagnell, Buckinghamshire on the M1, opened in 1960 by Forte & Co. Ltd, followed by the Watford Gap services further north in Northamptonshire, operated by the Blue Boar (Motorway) Ltd.

Although architecturally indifferent, these were followed by a series of more dramatic designs on the expanding system in the rest of the 1960s. Vetted by the Royal Fine Art Commission, these were often as bold and confident as the 'new age' of travel the motorways were thought to bring about. By the end of the twentieth century, their originality and individuality had largely been superseded by safer and less exciting corporate designs. There has also been a tendency to move away from the earlier arrangements of 'mirror-image' services on either side of the motorway only accessible by slip roads from one direction – but linked by a pedestrian bridge – to one common set of services generally reached from a roundabout and often at junctions with other main roads. Incidentally, one of the Thatcher government's very first privatisation schemes in 1979 was the sale of the freeholds of the motorway service stations.

CHAPTER 10

Bridge chapels

In medieval times, bridges were expensive and represented a considerable investment in materials and costs. They also had a degree of religious symbolism as well as commercial utility, and this did not only apply in Christendom. Construction of bridges was generally seen as a pious act – though to what extent the expected profits from tolls diminished the purity of the act is less quantifiable.

In this period, when travel was not part of the everyday lives of most people but when religion was, the construction of chapels associated with major bridges was fairly common. Bridge chapels offered spiritual comfort to those about to undertake a journey and a place to give thanks at journey's end. The alms given helped to maintain the bridge and pay for the upkeep of the chapel – as did the more formal tolls, or pontage, that became common in the medieval period. These were often 'farmed' out to the priest or hermit looking after the chapel.

One of the earliest documented bridge chapels in England was the chapel of St James at Burton Bridge over the River Trent, Staffordshire; it seems to have been built in the twelfth century. Research has identified nearly 50 bridge chapels in medieval England, though there could have been more.

Whilst the Church was actively involved in the building and maintenance of bridges, they had no monopoly on the work. Secular individuals and organisations also built and maintained bridges and sometimes established bridge chapels; the fact that a medieval bridge had a chapel did not necessarily mean that it had been endowed by the Church or a religious house. In 1445 for example, the burgesses of Appleby, Westmorland, granted to John Marshall, a chaplain, the 'certain ruinous chapel upon the west end of the stone bridge' across the River Eden – a chapel that had been built by the town. Some bridge chapels were founded as chantry chapels in which travellers could pray for the soul of their founders.

These bridge chapels varied considerably in size – from the large two-storey chapel on London Bridge, 60ft (19m) long and 20ft (6.3m) wide with its pinnacles rising to 110ft (35m) above the river, to the tiny chapel on the Chantry Bridge at Bradford-on-Avon just a few feet square. Some chapels were built as part of a new bridge, but many more were later additions to one – sometimes replacing an earlier chapel.

Sometimes a bridge chapel would either be at the landward end of the bridge, as was the case with those at Appleby-in-Westmorland, Barnstaple, Rochester, Torrington and Bungay. More commonly they were built onto the bridge itself. This was usually on one of the piers especially enlarged for that purpose, a typical case being that of St Ives, Huntingdonshire. The restored bridge chapel of St Mary's, Derby, is now isolated on the bank of the Derwent between the ends of an eighteenth-century bridge on one side and a rather ugly late twentieth-century bridge on the other, but was originally on a pier of the demolished medieval bridge; that pier had been enlarged when the chapel was enlarged in the later medieval period. An unusual, and probably unique, chapel was that at Droitwich, Worcestershire, which seems to have been timber-framed and built above the bridge deck below.

As well as the chapel itself, most bridge chapels also had accommodation for the chaplain or hermit. Whilst these are usually well-documented in medieval deeds, the changes made to most chapels that have survived make it difficult to fully understand the domestic provision which, in any case, presumably varied from chapel to chapel. The fact that a chapel had to be accessible from road level often meant that there was space below that level for accommodation.

At Wakefield, built in the fourteenth century, the chaplain seems to have lived in an undercroft under the east end of the chapel reached by a spiral stair (or 'vice') that also rose up to a turret providing access to the roof; the situation at St Mary's, Derby, may have been the same and the lower section of the stone spiral survives. Similarly, there was room for a lodging under the chapel at St Ives, Huntingdonshire. Conversely, the late fifteenth-century chapel at Rotherham had a small priest's chamber in a gallery at its southern end (the liturgical west), and at Appleby-in-Westmorland there was 'a certain chamber or oratory over the said chapel'.

The dissolution of religious houses in the 1530s and 40s brought an end to the religious role of bridge chapels, and to most of their endowments. Many were demolished or left to become derelict, but others were adapted for secular uses and altered accordingly – the chapel of 'Our Lady of the Brigge' in Leicester became a house and that at Appleby-in-Westmorland became a prison. Only six bridge chapels have survived reasonably intact in Britain – at Bradford-on-Avon, Wiltshire; Derby; Rochester, Kent; St Ives, Huntingdonshire; and two in

Yorkshire, at Rotherham and Wakefield – the latter heavily restored in the mid-nineteenth century. There are fragmentary remains of others, for example on the Derbyshire Derwent at Cromford.

These surviving chapels vary in their positions in relation to the bridges, their styles and their archaeological complexity and most have been fairly heavily restored. The uses to which they were put after the dissolution have been various. The bridge chapels at Bradford-on-Avon and Rotherham, for example, were prisons at one time or another and that at Wakefield was let to a second-hand clothes dealer. The chapel at St Ives, Huntingdonshire, was raised in brick by two additional stories complete with sash windows and chimney when it was a house; these were removed in the early twentieth century when the building was restored to something like its original form. St Mary's Bridge chapel in Derby was converted into three small houses and then into workshops. This chapel, incidentally, is perhaps the least known of the surviving ones yet well worth seeking out; it is restored and reconsecrated and well cared for. One of its unusual features is a small squint in the former bridge-side wall, assumed to allow travellers to see the altar before passing over the Derwent and out of the town.

CHAPTER 11

Toll-houses & toll gates

Ever since the first toll was levied on road users there has been a need to accommodate the toll-keeper, and this pre-dates the era of the turnpiked roads. The earliest tolls of road users, excluding market tolls levied as they passed through town and city gates, were those of pontage designed to help maintain medieval bridges. It is not certain how the toll-keepers, where needed, were housed, although where a bridge had an associated chapel, the priest in charge would presumably also take the tolls.

Clearly it was only with the development of the turnpiked roads that toll-houses and toll gates needed to be built in large numbers. The earliest barriers appear to have been horizontal poles, or 'pikes', and from this the terms 'turnpike' and 'turnpiked road' evolved. The *Oxford English Dictionary* considers the origins of the word 'turnpike' to have been related to military defence; a spiked bar placed across a road to prevent a sudden attack, particularly from cavalry. It adds a quote from the playwright Ben Jonson – 'I move upon my axel, like a turne-pike'. A legal action of 1642 in Cirencester mentions 'a strong straight boom which our men call Turn pike. A barrier with short metal spikes along the upper surface, placed across a road to stop passage till the toll has been paid'. A little over fifty years later, Celia Fiennes noted that the East Anglian turnpike she was travelling on was 'secured by a barr'.

Such bars or pikes, and sometimes, iron chains, were quickly replaced by gates, usually of the typical barred farm type and made from wood, on the main roads but simple barriers were still used on by-ways. The gates would need to be replaced periodically but continued to be mainly made of timber until the end of the turnpike era. A typical gate, hung on iron straps, would have oak posts and main frame, with soft-wood bars, though the types of wood used varied considerably. Iron gates seem to have been far too expensive for most trusts but, inevitably perhaps, Telford specified them for his Holyhead road improvements

88 Most toll gates were timber and required occasional replacement. Few survived the closure of the trusts. However, Telford, typically, over-engineered his gates on the Holyhead Road and used in many places specially designed 'sun-burst' iron gates. After these long-lasting gates were made redundant they could make useful farm gates – and this one in Denbighshire is many miles from the former turnpike

of the 1820s. The fact that several of these distinctive 'sun-burst' pattern gates, especially in the area around Bangor, have survived, often reused as farm gates, is testimony to their longevity.

At some toll gates, there were steps or a stile provided to let pedestrians climb over the toll gate or adjacent barrier instead. Other trusts provided smaller pedestrian gates to save having to open the main gates across the road when it was not necessary. Again, Telford's Holyhead road improvements were more sophisticated, and included turnstiles in some places instead of side gates. Incidentally, the use of the smaller pedestrian gates was, and still is, continued in the later development of level-crossings of the railways where pedestrian access is separate to that of vehicular traffic.

It is likely that the earliest accommodation for those collecting the tolls at the 'pikes' consisted of little more than primitive roadside huts or sheds, and a very rare eighteenth century example of such a shelter, built of stone and not dissimilar to a soldier's sentry box, survives at Yealmbridge in Devon; it was built by the Modbury Turnpike Trust which was set up in 1759.

As roads were public highways, even though all but the pedestrian public were now charged to use them, they had to be open all the time. This meant that, unless the trusts were willing to allow free access to travellers at night, toll-keepers had to be on call all the time. It was thus sensible to provide them with a building that served both as a toll-house and a home. The toll-house and its grounds were usually the only part of a turnpike that actually belonged to the trust, as the road itself usually did not.

Occasionally, a suitably sited existing roadside cottage would be adapted as a toll-house, sometimes with a bay-window or extension added, but this was relatively uncommon. Most toll-houses were newly built of local materials – in this period, usually of stone or brick and sometimes rendered – and at as low a cost as possible, given that the initial term of most trusts was for just 21 years.

The variety of the styles used was vast, but certain standard elements began to evolve. Most were single storey, partly for cheapness but also, one assumes, to ensure that, even when asleep, the gatekeeper would not be far from the gate as he had to sleep at ground-floor level. Often they just consisted solely of a single living room–cum–kitchen and a bedroom, with a small outhouse, though most had slightly more generous accommodation. This does, however, have to be seen in the context of the general domestic conditions then prevailing.

To allow a good view of approaching traffic, toll-houses tended to have fairly large windows and often had either a bay window from which this could be seen, or were commonly designed with a polygonal bay front – usually a half-hexagon or half-octagon – with windows in the two main flanking sides and a recess with the toll board in between. Rarer examples had semi-circular, or bowed, fronts for the same reason and other, more adventurous designs, were entirely round or polygonal in plan.

Most toll-houses, as well as displaying the obligatory board of charges (often in a purpose-built recess), would also have had a bracket for a lamp for night work and some of the more enlightened trusts provided deeply overhanging eaves or an attached shelter to protect the toll-keeper from the worst of the weather. Sometimes this would be simply a projecting porch, but in a handful of others, a fuller loggia – such as Telford's well-known example at Llanfairpwllgwngyll on the Holyhead Road in Anglesey.

Although small and cheaply built, the toll-houses did often allow the trusts to introduce a degree of architectural pretension – and they would sometimes be obliged to do so if a toll-house was close to the property of an important landowner. Fashionable *motifs* of the day could be used, such as, at the turn of

89 A typical and well-restored late eighteenth-century toll-house; this one at South Cheriton, Dorset, built by the Vale of Blackmoor Trust, was a fairly late example of 1824, but the same basic polygonal design allowing the toll-keeper good vision up and down the road had been used throughout Britain

90 Not all toll-houses were built to the standard style and some turnpike trusts occasionally built rather grander structures, such as this octagonal toll-house on the Sheffield to Hathersage turnpike at Ringinglow, Yorkshire. Although the eastern section of the road is fairly straight, the descent into Hathersage was steep and dangerous and the main road is now the A625 further south

the nineteenth century, Gothick battlements or *cottage ornee* detailing. In this respect they shared many features with the gate lodges of the country residences of the gentry. In some places, a trust built on a slightly grander scale, producing buildings like the Tower Toll-house on Clopton Bridge in Stratford-on-Avon in 1814 or the elegant Ashton Gate of the 1820s in Bristol.

Originally, most toll-keepers – or 'pikemen' – were employed directly by the turnpike trusts, but it soon became more convenient to 'farm' out tolls to others for fixed periods of time. An announcement in the *Shrewsbury Chronicle* on 1804 would have been typical – 'Notice is hereby given that the tolls arising at the Toll Gates and Weighing Machine upon the Turnpike Road in the parish of Caynham in the county of Salop, will be let by auction'. These 'toll farmers' appointed and paid their own toll-keepers, agreed a minimum income to the trust, and either kept or divided out any surplus income. It was in their interests to keep the wages of their toll-keepers as low as possible.

Toll-keepers, mainly because they were taking money off people, tended to be unpopular in the same undeserved way that traffic wardens are today – though clearly a minority deserved their unpopularity. They could also, in troubled times, be liable to attack because of what they represented. In the more remote rural areas, the toll-houses were often quite isolated and the life must have been lonely and generally boring for those without families.

Mr Weller, in Charles Dicken's *Pickwick Papers*, published in 1837, tells his fellow travellers that 'pike-keepers … [are] all on 'em men as has met vith some disappointment in life … Consequence of vich, they retires from the world, and shuts themselves in pikes; partly with a view of being solitary, and partly to rewenge themselves on mankind, by takin' tolls …' In his account of a journey on foot round Wales in 1854, George Borrow related that the poet Twm o'r Nant once kept a toll-bar in south Wales but gave up after seeing ghosts, goblins and phantom hearses pass through his gate, without paying, in the middle of the night.

By the mid-nineteenth century, reduced tolls and reduced wages for toll-keepers meant that many had to diversify. Dickens, in the *Uncommercial Traveller* of 1859, passed a 'Turnpike-house … all covered with ivy; and the Turnpike-keeper, unable to get a living out of the tolls, plied the trade of a cobbler'; his wife sold ginger beer and sweets from the open window. Even before the rapid demise of the turnpikes in the second half of the nineteenth century, a toll-house might become redundant after a diversion to a turnpike route was made, or the road ceased to be a turnpike.

In the later Acts there were usually clauses to cater for this. For example, in an 1835 Acts approving diversions to turnpikes in the Merioneth area of Wales, a clause was included that accepted that some toll-houses would then 'become useless and unnecessary, and of little or no Value, unless … sold standing and as

Dwelling Houses … together with the Outhouses, Gardens, and Appurtenances thereto belonging …'. The trustees were allowed to dispose of them as they wished. As the number of turnpikes declined, the numbers of redundant toll-houses increased rapidly. Many were just too small and too inconveniently situated to be adapted as normal family dwellings without substantial change. As a result, many were demolished as soon as they became redundant or simply left to become to fall down on their own.

Many others have since been lost to various road improvements, especially to road widening schemes, and some used as dwellings, usually extended, often quite radically and unsympathetically. A handful have been carefully taken down and re-erected elsewhere, usually in an open-air museum. Despite this, it is quite surprising just how many have survived reasonably unscathed and in their original positions. Nevertheless, survive they do throughout most of Britain, and many are now protected by their listed status. In general, extensions that may be needed to ensure their long-term fitness for domestic use, and thus their long-term futures, are handled far more sympathetically than used to be the case.

91 Most of the toll-houses throughout Britain that have survived have only done so because a different use was found for them. Because of the differences in marriage law between England and Scotland, many couples fled to Scotland to wed. Several toll-houses just across the border offered wedding services, including this one at Gretna Green, seen here in a photograph of the 1930s

Weighbridges

The carriages and carts using British roads obviously varied in weight, but until an Act of 1741, this was not taken into consideration by the relevant highway authorities or the turnpike trusts. Thereafter, heavier vehicles had to be weighed, and means developed to do so. Several enterprising manufacturers began to make and advertised suitable apparatus and weighing machines of varying types were erected throughout the country.

Although details of the early examples are scarce, it would appear that they were more than capable of being improved. For example, in 1771 James Edgell of Somerset was claiming in his advertisements that his 'Engines ... are of a new Construction, and may be placed where those of the old Construction cannot,

92 The weight of wagons using their roads was of concern to the turnpike trusts and weigh houses were built in order to check suspect loads. Telford built several on the Holyhead Road; this one at Lon Isa on the opposite side of the road to the surviving toll-house, was opened in 1824. In the foreground, the layby feature is one of the many 'depots' along the road built for the storage of road mending material; others had hedge or slate boundaries and many of these survive on the Welsh section of the road

a Space of Ground 15 Feet Square, and Four Feet in Depth, being sufficient for erecting one of these'; his machines could weigh anything from just one pound to over nine tons.

Very few of these eighteenth- and nineteenth-century examples have survived. The most obvious and well-known is probably the one that stands rather dramatically outside the aptly named Olde Bell & Steelyard in Woodbridge, Suffolk. It probably dates to the mid-eighteenth century, in design at least, and is based on the steelyard system – a pivoting, asymmetrically balanced arm. The apparatus is supported on a huge timber gibbet or cantilevered bracket that carries the balance, or steelyard, which is about 20ft (6.2m) long; a system of pulleys, housed in a small open-sided shelter to protect the operator, is attached from the end of the outer, shorter section of the steelyard to the wagon and the lead weight can be moved along until the whole thing is balanced and level, and the weight recorded.

Two out of the original three weighbridge houses on the Welsh section of Telford's Holyhead Road have survived, at Lon Isa near Bangor and Ty Isaf, a few miles to the west of Llangollen. Their superstructures, or engine houses, survive but the machinery does not and there are no records of how it worked. Both engine houses are well-crafted in locally derived rubblestone with simple ashlar detailing, and are built where there road runs on a revetted terraceway; that meant that they had a basement level as well as a ground floor. Both are sited opposite original toll-houses and were thus next to turnpike gates. Weighbridges, of different types, have continued to be built in the twentieth century as heavy goods vehicles continue to grow in size.

CHAPTER 12

The manufacturing industry

THE PRE-MOTOR AGE

Early road vehicles were probably made on a very local basis, usually by a local craftsman carpenter with help from the blacksmith; the history of wheeled vehicles in Britain dates from at least the fourth century BC from the archaeological evidence, but it would not have been until the seventeenth century that the manufacture of carriages or carts could be described as an industry as such. Even then, the workshops were probably not particularly specialist in their layout, though by the nineteenth century some workshops for carriage manufacture were purpose-built. Seldom, however, were such enterprises of any large scale.

One of the first manufacturers of vehicles other than carriages, carts and coaches, was a London coachmaker called Denis Johnson who built hundreds of 'hobby horses' – the early form of bicycle – for the Regency dandies from 1818 onwards. The demand for bicycles in the later part of the century led to the establishment of a fairly large industry, particularly in parts of the Midlands, such as Coventry where the Coventry Machinist Factory is considered to have been the first large-scale bicycle factory when in opened in 1869.

A few workshops used for, or associated with, bicycle manufacture have survived, by far the most impressive being the premises on Far Gosforth Street of the Calcott Brothers, founded in 1886 as cycle manufacturers. They went on to build motorcycles from 1904 and then cars from 1914. The vaguely Tudorbethan brick frontage block with its shaped gables and terracotta decoration still stands like a slightly off-key miniature country house, its formal grounds a roundabout on a busy junction. Other major companies included Sunbeam of Wolverhampton, but by 1900 the largest was Raleigh, established in Raleigh Street, Nottingham, whose 850 staff were producing around 12,000 bicycles a year.

94 The interior of the Coventry Machinists' Company bicycle works in around 1900. Note the mainly female labour force, the north-lit roof, miles of belt-drives, and complete lack of safety equipment or clothing

Opposite 93 Coach making, as opposed to wagon making, was undertaken in the eighteenth century by the separate trades of body-building and carriage-making. This is a contemporary print showing a high-status carriage nearing completion

CAR FACTORIES

Although there was already a very well-established tradition of transport-related heavy industry in Britain – manufacturing railway locomotives, carriages and wagons as well as ships – the embryonic car industry was initially completely different. Early motor cars were hand-built with basic assembly techniques in small workshops little altered from those of carriage makers. As a result, there was a great variety of design and size of workshops, which did not really become 'factories' in the modern sense until the start of the twentieth century.

Whilst some of the pioneering makers were already established as carriage makers, a greater proportion had already been manufacturing bicycles. This was subject to the whims of the public and to seasonal change and it made sense for the more far-sighted manufacturers to diversify, using their existing skills and equipment to produce the new-fangled motor vehicles. It is estimated that around 130 car manufacturers were at work at one time or another in Coventry alone in the early twentieth century, mostly small in scale and many with bicycle-making origins. Of the once major car companies whose origins were also in the city's cycle industry were Rover, Triumph, Riley, Humber and Sunbeam.

Not all car companies had made bicycles; Royce & Co, later partners in the most famous brand of all, Rolls-Royce, built electric dock cranes in a factory in Liverpool before they were involved in cars and Wolseley, perhaps appropriately, made sheep-shearing equipment in Birmingham. Some companies were set up with little or no engineering background, merely assembling parts made by other works and often set up by entrepreneurs wishing to capitalise quickly on what was still seen, at the very start of the twentieth century, as a sporting craze.

In the early days, the workshops in which the cars were made differed very little from the cycle factories, and many were, as outlined above, just cycle shops converted to produce motor cars. A variety of other premises were also used. The earliest cars built by one of the more famous marques in British motoring – Hillman – were built in a shed in the grounds of William Hillman's home in Coventry, Abingdon House, before moving to his Auto Machinery Works in Hood Street where bicycles, roller-skates and sewing machines were already being produced. Both Daimler, which had begun selling engines in 1893 from under a railway viaduct by Putney Bridge station, and the short-lived Great Horseless Carriage Company shared a disused mid-nineteenth century cotton mill near Coventry for a short time from 1896, claiming that their 'Motor Mills' was then the largest car factory in Britain and employed 200 workers. Henry Austin first built the cars that bore his name in a former tin-plate and tin-box factory at Longbridge from 1905.

Curiously, what was probably the first purpose-built motor car factory in Britain had been set up well away from what became the main car producing areas. Instead it was built, at great expense, in Granton, one of the port areas of Edinburgh, in 1899. Even more unusually, it was at least a century ahead of its time because it was built to produce the electric cars of the Madelvic Motor Car Company – set up by the city's official astronomer, William Peck.

Peck's car was essentially an adapted horse-drawn brougham, fitted with an electric motor turning a central, fifth wheel; the vehicles were even supplied with fixings for shafts so that a horse could be used should the motor fail. Unfortunately that was not uncommon as the cars proved unreliable.

Nevertheless, the factory in which they were assembled was a pioneering state-of-the-art and ambitious complex. It had a frontage office block built mainly of brick with stone decoration. Behind were the main workshops, a large two-storey block with large work spaces on both levels and an adjacent single-storey block with abundant natural light.

Despite the design of the buildings, the processes involved in manufacturing the cars were as inefficient as they were and, with a huge capital investment to repay, the business was bankrupt by 1900. Other companies continued to build internal combustion-engine cars on a small scale at the site up until about 1912 and during the war it became a torpedo store; for over 75 years it was used as a wire works and was recently bought by Waterfront Edinburgh Ltd, a major undertaking by several local authorities to regenerate this part of the city; the country's first purpose-built car factory appears to have a reasonably secure future.

Scotland could also claim to have once had the largest car factory in Europe, and the second largest in the world, by 1906. The early 1900s boom in car production led to several spectacularly grandiose factories. Argyle cars began to be built in Glasgow in 1900, the same year that the Madelvic concern failed; its founder was Alexander Govan who had worked for the Scottish Cycle Manufacturing Company and in 1904 it turned out over 150 cars. The ambitious company then invested nearly a quarter of a million pounds in a new 25 acre site at Alexandria-by-Glasgow – between the Clyde estuary and the south end of Loch Lomond. Opened by Lord Montagu in 1906 the new factory had, as well as the necessary workshops, the added benefits of an elaborate 760ft (236m) long frontage block of several architectural styles with a fine central tower, a main hallway with a marble staircase up to the directors' offices and a huge dining room and lecture theatre that could be used for classical concerts. The new site was far too large for the company, which by the end of 1908 was bankrupt; production of its 'simple, silent and comfortable car' lingered on until 1914 before the factory finally closed; coincidentally, it too was taken over by the Royal Navy for torpedo work, remaining in military hands until the 1970s. It is now a retail outlet and has a motor museum as well.

Scotland also has another two important pioneering pre-World War One car factories still standing, heavily influenced by North American practice. A company called Arrol-Johnston Cars Co. Ltd In Paisley, managed by Thomas Pullinger, had a new 'greenfield' factory in the rural south-west of Scotland, just outside Dumfries, built by the Trussed Concrete Steel Company in 1913; multi-storey and well-lit the war halted car production virtually straight away and afterwards it only staggered on until the end of the 1920s. It is now a rubber factory.

A similar, but smaller, factory built by the company in Tongland, in an even more rural part of Dumfries and Galloway, had been used for war work but in

1919 a separate subsidiary, Galloway Cars, was created to manufacture cars at the plant. Most management and workers were women – a fact no doubt influenced that one of those in charge was Dorothy Pullinger, Thomas Pullinger's daughter; of similar construction to the Dumfries plant, the factory looked after its workers and even boasted a tennis court on the roof! It too had closed by 1928, was then used for the production of silk and is now used for light industry.

It was the early failure of these companies, coupled with the fortunate reuse of their premises, that has led to the buildings being retained. Clearly, the failure of these early Scottish car factories was not due to the quality of their products or to any want of ambition or innovation in their design and construction. Instead, it seems that the industry north of the border simply lacked the necessary infrastructure of local suppliers within a convenient and concentrated area. In England, most of the successful car factories prospered in the English midlands, or in the environs of London or the industrial north-west where all of the components required for the manufacture of a vehicle could be obtained relatively quickly and cheaply.

Many of the key factory sites – at Longbridge, near Coventry, Cowley in Oxford, or Dagenham, Essex – have been constantly altered and upgraded so that older buildings become altered significantly or demolished as manufacturing techniques change. The major change to affect the industry quite early on was the introduction of assembly lines to replace the older and far less efficient 'batch' method of construction.

Although the demand for motor cars increased from the early 1900s, initially the same old-fashioned craft techniques were used; the workshops simply grew larger to meet demand. The development of the Sunbeam Factory in Wolverhampton would have been fairly typical of one of the larger companies. John Marston bought a bicycle factory in 1887 and renamed it the Sunbeamland Cycle Factory. In 1899 his assistant, Thomas Cureton, built a prototype motor car and soon afterwards persuaded Marston to start production using mainly imported components in a disused building on Upper Villiers Street. Success led to the expansion of this site and to the construction of a new factory in 1905. Then, in 1906, the company built a far more ambitious factory on the opposite side of the street that became known as the Moorfields Works.

Opened in October 1907 this was, for its day, a state of the art complex; the buildings were designed by local architect Joseph Lavender and were mainly constructed in brick, with large trussed iron and steel roof girders allowing a series of wide and uninterrupted interiors. The layout was probably designed by the company's new chief engineer, Angus Shaw who, incidentally, had in the previous year undertaken a remarkable round-trip in one of the company's motor cars from John o'Groats to Land's End, a successful endurance test that was something of a marketing coup for Sunbeams.

95 This part of the large Moorfields Works complex in Wolverhampton was opened for the manufacture of Sunbeam cars in 1907, but within a few years, the mass-production techniques introduced by Henry Ford had made it virtually obsolete

The narrow main gatehouse with the central main entrance, offices, boardroom, mess-room, bicycle racks, timekeeper's office and three small workshops for casting, polishing and plating, was built parallel to Upper Villiers Street. The only part of the site with any architectural pretensions, it was flanked by two additional entrances allowing cars in and out of an inner yard. To either side of the gatehouse were the large paint shop, on the north, and the repair shop, on the south. These were physically linked to five separate workshops running back at right-angles to the frontage block, with room for a narrow yard in between; from south to north these were the smiths shop, the body shop, the trimming shop, the finishing shop and the erecting shop. Although these had brick walls, their rear gables were deliberately built of sheeted studwork to allow them all to be lengthened as demand increased – which was virtually straightaway. None of these separate shops were originally linked, and there were no doorways in the walls between them. Components and partly completed cars had to be manhandled through openings in the gable ends to be taken to the next stage in the manufacture.

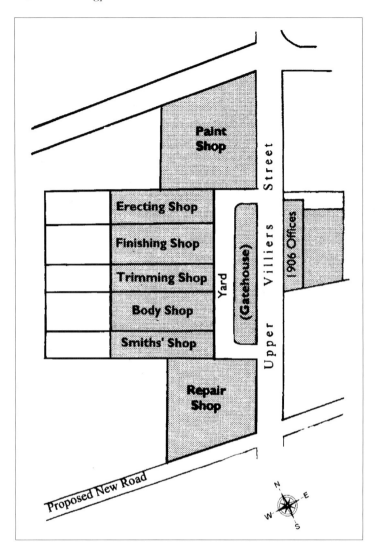

96 This very basic plan of 1906–07 shows the layout of the Moorfields Works, and how little integration there was in even large car factories of this date before the development of the production line

Henry Ford developed the concept of the assembly line for motor car manufacture in the United States and opened a 'line' in Detroit in 1913. Shortly afterwards his English branch at Trafford Park, Manchester, was similarly updated; the new buildings were designed by Charles Heathcote but their layout was the work of the company's engineers. The new process, using less skilled labour and streamlined assembly processes, was far more efficient – in terms of volume, at least – than the old batch system. The moving track and overhead conveyors would gradually become more and more sophisticated and require radical change or complete rebuilding of existing old-fashioned car factories. What the system did require was very large buildings capable of housing the whole line and its feeders, well-lit through side windows and roof lights. Ford had made even the largest of the old-fashioned car factories obsolete.

Other companies simply had to change if they were to compete with the price of the Ford products. The Austin factory at Longbridge was radically altered in 1919 and designed to allow further expansion. In others, change was less swift and sometimes rather *ad hoc*. This can be seen at the Sunbeam's Moorfields Works, where attempts were made to update the existing buildings in the same year. However, the company remained aloof from the mass-produced market occupied by Ford, Austins and Morris and their more expensive cars continued to be produced in a more leisurely way; they also built racing cars and world land-speed record holders which were good for publicity but little else. In 1920 a financial crisis had led to the company being amalgamated with two others – Talbot of London and the French firm, Darracq – and becoming part of the new STD company. In the financial crises of the early 1930s the company finally succumbed and in 1935 production at the Moorfield Works ceased. Subsequently, trolleybuses were built in the works until the 1950s and until recently, part was being used by the engineering firm Timkins, makers of special bearings for railway wheels.

Despite the inefficiency of the British car industry in the 1930s, it was still second only to the United States in output. This was due in no small measure to its dominance in the supply of vehicles to the Empire. For a short while after the Second World War the British industry enjoyed another period of prosperity. This was due to two main economic factors. The first was that much of the car production capacity in Europe had been devastated by the war, with many factories destroyed. The second was that in order to try and alleviate the chronic problem of national debt that the war had caused, the government actively encouraged any potential export trade – and that included cars. By 1950 nearly 80 per cent of old-fashioned British-produced cars were being exported. However, by the mid-1960s the British car industry, with largely obsolete plants, poor management, and even poorer industrial relations, began a decline that has continued into the twenty-first century.

In direct contrast to the larger firms' factories were the workshops of hundreds of smaller manufacturers turning out small cars assembled from bought-in components. Many companies produced the hybrid 'cyclo-cars' that were very popular in the 1920s until the costs of mass-produced 'proper' cars fell to a level that effectively put an end to those often rather dangerous and uncomfortable vehicles. Despite the rationalisation of the industry from the 1930s onwards, some smaller car companies did survive, working quite inefficiently in workshops of all shapes and sizes. A few such companies still produce cars today, none more evocative that the world-famous Morgan Company of Malvern, whose cars are still hand-built by craftsmen in a manner that pre-dates the mass-production of Henry Ford, with cars in varying states of completion being trundled between the various workshops in an apparently haphazard manner.

As well as car factories, there were also other factories that produced motor lorries, motor buses, and motor bikes – all in workshops built or adapted for their specific needs. In addition, factories also produced traction engines, trams and trolleybuses and, of course, continued to build cycles. The variety of road vehicles has been as varied as the factories used for their production, but the later twentieth century has seen the development of fairly similar computer-designed cars being produced in fairly similar computer-designed and semi-automated factories.

97 Morgan Cars of Malvern, Worcestershire have continued to stick to their traditional way of working, and their premises respect this. For anyone from the outside it is difficult to understand how the whole production process works in what is, superficially, a haphazard collection of buildings

There can still be exceptions, though generally short-lived. Two fairly recent – and certainly short-lived – examples can be mentioned. The first was the production of the odd three-wheel Isetta 'bubble' cars in a former railway locomotive works in Brighton in the late 1950s. The second, the infamous Sinclair C5 mass-produced three-wheel electric 'trikes', assembled during 1985 in a washing-machine factory in Merthyr Tydfill – a vehicle either far ahead of its time, or dangerous and quite barmy, depending on your point of view.

COMPONENT FACTORIES

The rapid increase of numbers of bicycles from the later nineteenth century and, especially, of motor cars from the early twentieth century led to the need for a huge component industry supplying the basic parts used both in their manufacture and maintenance – everything from engines to number plates. Most of these were made in factories and workshops of varying sizes but seldom of any architectural pretensions.

There were a few exceptions. The multi-storey 1930s Lucas Factory (where alternators and other electrical equipment was assembled) to the north of Birmingham city centre – recently converted into apartments – does have a distinct period honesty about it. More obvious exceptions were the workshops of one particularly common and public component – the tyre.

The development of the pneumatic tyre at the end of the nineteenth century, replacing the solid rubber ones used beforehand, was a major innovation for both cycles and motor cars. Tyres inevitably wear out and consumers had a choice about which brand to choose. As a result, the major tyre companies became adept at advertising their wares. This was not confined to straightforward advertisements, but extended to various forms of related sponsorship – the famous Michelin guides being an early example – and was expressed in architecture.

Michelin's impressive former headquarters in Fulham Road, London, designed by F. Espinasse in 1905, survives virtually intact. The up-to-date utilitarian concrete-framed structure is masked by its rich brick and terracotta façade with tile panels and jokey *motifs*, including the famous Michelin Man or 'Bibendum' – literally, 'the tyre that eats up obstacles' – which was quite *avant garde* for the time and thus suited to the new age; the interior has more tiled panels and fascinating original mosaics on the floors and part is now a restaurant. Far larger and more austere, Fort Dunlop in Birmingham was originally founded in 1917 and the main building still dominates the view from the M6 motorway; it is no longer associated with the company and has recently been redeveloped.

A third important tyre factory was build by the Firestone Company on the Great West Road in Hounslow, west London. The wide new road had been laid out as a new arterial route in 1925, and was zoned to be lined by factories or by housing. The Firestone building was begun almost at once and opened in 1927; in front of the fairly utilitarian workshops was a long, low office block of rendered reinforced concrete painted bright white. The art deco centrepiece with its clock and pillars was vaguely Egyptian in style and was faced in faience. The building was wantonly destroyed the weekend prior to being listed in 1980.

CHAPTER 13

Garages

The term 'garage' can now mean several different things: a place in which vehicles are housed overnight, ranging in size from a large bus garage to a domestic one in the garden; a place where vehicles are serviced and mended; or, most commonly, a petrol filling station. Some of these functions have parallels in a pre-motor vehicle age in stables or blacksmiths. Indeed, perhaps the earliest reference to the road side running repairs of vehicles occurs as early as the fourth century BC in Xenophon's *Cyropaedia*, a biography of Cyrus of Persia; he wrote that the Emperor ordered his armies to take spare wood and fixtures for wagons and chariots, as well as craftsmen to mend them, as they would inevitably need repairs on their journeys. However, the word 'garage' is now confined almost exclusively to sites serving the motor vehicle.

The complex and sensitive early motor vehicle required far different facilities than the horse or pedestrian and few stables were sufficiently adaptable to cope. The term 'garage', which came to mean a place where cars could refuel, be maintained and, if necessary, repaired, came from France. It is derived from the verb *garer* meaning 'to shelter', but had generally been used to signify places along the French canals, *garages*, where barges could moor or pass; it had been taken up by the French railways for their locomotive depots and subsequently became part of the pioneering French motorist's vocabulary.

The first use of the word in England appears to have occurred in 1899 but other terms were still being used in the early years of the twentieth century, including, logically, motor-stable and depôt. The earliest garages were quite small and generally built either for those wealthy enough to be able afford a motor car in the same manner as they would have previously built a coach house or stable, or by those who supplied and maintained the vehicles and often part of their main showroom complex.

In the first decade of the twentieth century it was clear that the 'fad' of the motor car was not going to fade away, and there was a clearer need for businesses dedicated to looking after them when away from their dealers or from their home bases. In many of the larger towns there were already well-established businesses dealing with cycles, and it became logical for these, with the mechanical skills they possessed, to branch out as motor repairers. In other cases, established carriage repairers also took to looking after the new motor vehicles, as did a variety of light engineering firms, such as those involved with agricultural implements, and occasionally a village blacksmith would take on the role. In addition, some of the larger hotels also provided garage services.

These various trades also mean that a wide variety of premises were initially adapted as garages. Partly because of this, and because of regional pride, there is still a degree of controversy about the site of the first purpose-built British garage dedicated to the motor vehicle. One claimed site is that of H.W. Egerton and G.N.C. Mann in Prince of Wales Road, Norwich, opened in 1901; this became the Mann Egerton company, one of the most important in the early years of the motor car and still going today. Another contender was the Imperial Motor Works in Lyndhurst, Hampshire, certainly in business by the spring of 1902.

However, both were preceded by the City & Suburban Electric Carriage Company premises near London's Piccadilly Circus in 1901, one of a small number of different forms of garages confined to the larger cities. In such cities, initially in London and then others, there were a handful of fairly large buildings built from 1901 into the early 1930s that combined the needs of servicing vehicles with the parking of them. These gradually became more important for their car parking role than for their garaging role and have been dealt with in the appropriate section of the book.

Elsewhere, more and more garages sprang up throughout the whole country to cope with the growth of the numbers of motor vehicles; by the 1930s there were around 36,000 garages. Between the 1930s and the early 1960s, even the smallest village usually had at least one garage – the tiny village of Denstone, north Staffordshire, with two garages despite not being on a main road was by no means unique. The major towns had several garages of various types from large purpose-built premises with showrooms, pumps and workshops to less glamorous sites in the back streets or workshops under the arches of railway viaducts. Up until the 1950s, most of the garages, however small, would also be able to service vehicles and undertake minor repairs to both cars and bicycles.

In market towns and villages a typical garage would have one or more large and generally cheaply built workshops with inspection pits and perhaps a small office. Town garages tended to be on more restricted sites, often facing directly onto the street; occasionally their premises would be adapted from an existing

98 A rare photograph of the interior of an early London garage, taken in about 1901. At this time the cars would need a fairly full service after each trip and premises like this offered to service and store the vehicles for their wealthy owners

99 A typical small rural garage in the 1920s; this one is at Stickney in south-eastern Lincolnshire

building. Several fine Georgian town houses had their ground floors gutted to be converted into workshops and a well-established garage near the abbey in Shrewsbury was, until very recently, housed in a medieval cruck-framed building. Rural garages, because land was cheaper, had rather more spacious plots and would often provide other services, such as a taxi service, car or bicycle hire and general repairs for household appliances.

As early as the 1920s a separate form of more specialist 'garage' had developed along the major routes. These were, appropriately, known then as filling stations – for obvious reasons – and their role was mainly that of supplying petrol; maintenance and servicing was secondary. The first of these is claimed to be the one opened by the AA at Aldermaston, Berkshire, in 1919, the first of seven that it opened in England. This was not a simple a gesture as it first seems; the AA were, in fact, keen to promote cheaper home-refined benzole as an alternative to imported petroleum, and this is what the filling stations sold. Benzole, a by-product of the gas works, could be used in conjunction with petrol and had not been subjected to tax in 1909.

Oil companies and others quickly followed suit and the AA quickly ceased being a retailer. Filling stations were largely made possible because of the development of the petrol pump. Up until the First World War, petrol had to be bought in two-gallon cans from garages, shops or even hotels – a wasteful and potential dangerous process with cans often piled up in potentially lethal columns on the street. The first hand-cranked petrol pump in Britain was installed outside F.A. Legge's garage on the Abbey Foregate in Shrewsbury in 1914 and by 1930 there were nearly 30,000, rising to around 100,000 by the outbreak of the Second World War. In 1930, Legge may have become the first person in England to install an electrically powered pump, and these soon replaced the older style ones.

In an indirect way, filling stations were responsible for the development of conservation laws in rural areas. With so many opening up on the main roads in the countryside there was great competition amongst them and each tried to make the motorist aware of their existence. Huge signs sprouted up on the approaches to the filling stations, and the buildings, often cheaply and rapidly built structures covered in corrugated tin or weatherboarding, would be plastered with more signs, wooden or enamel, often advertising several different brands of petrol, oil and tyre.

An Act of 1927 brought in some rules governing safety issues and licensing for petrol pumps and the Petroleum (Consolidation) Act in the following year gave local authorities the powers to govern the design of garages. Advice was also produced by the Council for the Protection of Rural England, of which the architect Guy Dawber was an influential member. The net result could, if local authorities insisted, be an assured quality of design and less advertising – though this could lead to a degree of twee-ness, hinted by W.H. Auden's lines on the state of the countryside in which there were '… Filling stations/Supplying petrol from rustic pumps'.

After the Second World War there was a general tendency for independent filling stations to be taken over by the major petrol companies, selling only their own products. Gradually, their house styles swamped the older piecemeal architecture and such filling stations tend to be radically upgraded and rebuilt every ten years or so. The domination of the market by the major companies, allowing them through their sheer bulk of sales to make money out of tiny profit margins, coupled with the effects of the oil crisis of 1973, has led to a reduction in the number of garages – especially in rural areas and especially amongst the independents.

This has also affected rural garages that relied on petrol sales to supplement their other activities, and as cars became more and more sophisticated, the equipment required to service them became more sophisticated and expensive too. As a result, there are hundreds of abandoned garage sites throughout Britain. Many are being demolished and redeveloped for housing or light industry; others have been adapted for new uses; and others are simply falling into decay. Few are of sufficient architectural merit or historical interest to excite the interest of any pressure group and most, it has to be admitted, are becoming eyesores.

SHOW ROOMS

The earliest car show rooms in Britain were, not surprisingly, in those places that had clients wealthy enough to buy the cars on show – which initially meant London. Usually these also included facilities for servicing and storing cars for clients and for others as well; they were thus multi-functional buildings. Before the First World War there were showrooms in other major towns in Britain, as well as in some less expected places.

One of the best preserved is the remarkable showroom, built as the Automobile Palace in 1913, in the town of Llandridnod Wells, Powys, then a fashionable Spa in a very rural and very hilly part of mid-Wales. Tom Norton, an inventor, engineer and salesman, had started a bicycle business there in 1899 and then expanded into cars and the even newer craze – aeroplanes. The faience-faced showrooms retain original lettering indicating the wares on view, and part is now the National Cycling Museum.

Another, larger, show room is that designed by William Curtis Green, an architect that had earlier built several buildings for electric tramways. The fine

100 Tom Norton was a remarkable Edwardian pioneer, interested in most forms of transport from the bicycle to the aeroplane. His showrooms in Llandridnod Wells in mid-Wales have survived more or less intact and the oldest sections opened in 1913

and vaguely neo-classical car show-room for the Wolseley Motor Company in Piccadilly was opened in 1921; it won Green the Royal Institute of British Architects' first Street Architecture Medal in the following year and was later converted into a bank. Edmund Wimperis and W. Begg Simpson designed Macy's Garage in Balderton Street, London, to a design that combined a degree of neo-classicism with art deco; it opened in 1926 and although no longer a garage, is used by the Ford Motor Company.

CHAPTER 14

Car parks

The problem of parking has been around for thousands of years, though one of the earliest solutions did not, fortunately, catch on. Around 700 BC, Sannacherib, King of Assyria, had a simple if ruthless way of preventing parked chariots on the broad paved processional road between the main temples in Nineveh; the owners were executed. He was eventually assassinated, but it is not known if his death could be classed as a traffic-related fatality.

Although there were a few problems of parking carts and wagons in towns on market days in Britain in the horse-drawn era, it was only really with the advent of the motor vehicle that parking became a serious issue. The first recognised temporary car park is claimed to be one set up at the Henley Regatta in 1898, for by that time there were sufficient numbers of cars owned by the wealthy enthusiast to warrant such a convenience at such events.

In the early years of motoring, motor cars required constant repair and would be usually garaged overnight rather than left to the vagaries of the weather. As a result, the covered car park – usually called a garage – was a fairly early innovation and pressure of space in the major towns where they would be needed led to the development of the multi-storey car park.

The first multi-storey car park in the world was opened in 1901 on Denman Street near Piccadilly Circus in London by the City & Suburban Electric Carriage Company, suppliers of early motor cars, and was solely for their customers' use at first. It was built on seven floors and had a lift capable of taking the small lorries of the time; it also claimed to be the largest garage in the world. The London Motor Garage Company opened their 200 car capacity garage in nearby Wardour Street in 1903 with a facade influenced by the 'Queen Anne Revival' style popular at the end of the nineteenth century. Within a few years, other combined car parks and garage complexes opened in the capital and larger towns and the Scottish Motor Garage Company boasted that their Renfrew Street garage could house and repair 200 cars and was open day and night.

With the rapid increase in car numbers after the First World War, the problems of where to park them became a real town-planning issue. As early as 1919 the police in London were concerned about the lack of car parking space in the capital, and this soon became a problem in most towns throughout the country which were simply not designed to accommodate the motor car.

A handful of other garages-cum-multi-storey car parks were built in central London in between the wars. These include one on the King's Road, Chelsea in 1924 and another in Herbrand Street, Bloomsbury, opened in 1931. When the Bluebird Motor Company opened their Bluebird Garage on the King's Road it was claimed to be the largest in Europe with room for 300 cars as well as large workshops; built with a long and low well-windowed art deco style, faced with faience, in front of the main garage area and workshops, it had separate lounges and writing rooms for different classes of clientele – owner drivers and chauffeurs – as well as numerous petrol pumps and dozens of tyre inflation points, indicating the relatively unreliable nature of tyres of the time. In the later twentieth century it was used as an ambulance station but has more recently been rather cleverly converted into the high-class Bluebird Cafe.

The former Daimler Car Hire garage on Herbrand Street, Bloomsbury, was designed by the then fashionable firm of Wallis Gilbert & Partners. With its distinctive smooth facade of angles and curves, this was designed to house cars owned by Daimler on the upper floors and privately owned cars below in a basement. Around 500 vehicles could be catered for and as well as usual garage, fuel and repair services, facilities included waiting rooms, toilets, telephones and advanced electrically powered car-washes. After being used as a base for taxis, it has recently been converted into offices.

Both of those buildings were recently listed and, in 2002, so was another – the little-altered four-storey car park in Brewer Street, Soho. Designed by Robert Sharp and James J. Joass and opened in 1929, it has a distinctive octagonal corner tower and retains its original ramps; it once had a separate room for chauffeurs and a changing room for lady theatre-goers – a reminder that motoring was still then the preserve of the wealthier members of society. At the time of writing this car park is still under threat of demolition, though its listing should have helped to preserve it.

The largest inter-war car park in London was in many ways more of the prototype for what was to follow from the late 1950s onwards. The Olympia Garage in Maclise Road, Kensington, has eleven floors arranged as mezzanine half-storeys linked by cleverly-designed ramps and with wide open floors virtually uninterrupted by the structural columns. It was the work of Joseph

Emberton who in 1929 had built the nearby Kensington Olympia complex; with exposed concrete to the inside and yellow brick exterior with long and narrow window bands, it could take up to 1,200 cars and was claimed to be largest car park in Europe when it opened in 1937.

Not all towns wanted or required or had the space for large multi-storey car parks. The first underground car park in Britain of any size was opened under Carlisle Parade in Hastings, Sussex, at the end of 1931 to cater for the increasing numbers of cars being used for day trips to the seaside; it is still in use. To cope with the exhaust fumes from the cars, this was fitted with a pair of ventilation towers cleverly designed to appear, at ground level, as matching public shelters on the promenade. Building underground, however, was a very expensive option.

Instead, most car parks tended to occupy any available areas of open ground in towns and even before the Second World War, campaigns of slum clearance could free up formerly built-up streets for this purpose. This happened, for example, in Shrewsbury in the 1930s when dozens of old and mainly timber-framed buildings were, in retrospect unfortunately, pulled down in the Barker Street area to form a new bus station and car parks.

After the Second World War, more 'windfall' areas in some towns were available because of bomb damage or more radical campaigns of slum clearance and urban redevelopment; these supposedly temporary car parks could survive for many years and many are still in use. In historic Worcester, for example, the area around Newport Street, once a main thoroughfare, is still blighted with acres of open 'temporary' car parking.

Whereas open car parks, purpose-built or making use of available land awaiting eventual redevelopment, are both generally aesthetically unappealing and wasteful of valuable space, the alternative, built in large numbers from the 1950s onwards – the modern breed of multi-storey car park – is seldom an architectural asset to any town, ancient or modern. Some early ones were steel-framed, but most are of reinforced concrete with the various levels accessed by ramps.

In theory, these new structures offered a chance for innovative architecture that would combine form and function to create something necessary yet aesthetically pleasing; that had been achieved in the London car parks between the wars. One of the earliest post-war multi-storey car parks did just that and should have been the hallmark that other designers aimed for; sadly, it was in Germany. P. Schnieder Esleben's elegant concrete, glass and steel structure built in the ruins of Dusseldorf opened in 1950 and took 500 cars. In Britain, the occasional car park could, with the right architect and sufficient funds, aspire to a degree of architectural style and quality; one of the best was the bold circular car park with continuous spiral ramp built in the centre of Hemel Hempstead, Hertfordshire, in 1963 to the designs of Maurice Bebb.

Sadly, a more usual combination of uninspired design, cost-cutting and, above all, inappropriate location, has resulted in dozens of ugly car parks, often prone to vandalism and neglect, in towns and cities throughout the land. Again, poor Worcester, a fine but car-blighted medieval city, has the dubious distinction of having one of the ugliest and least sympathetically positioned multi-storey car parks of the 1960s, dominating one end of medieval Friar Street.

At least it and the other car parks of the 1960s and 70s were architecturally honest and of their time. The more recent trend in the post-modernist world has been to disguise multi-storey car parks as anything but car parks, resulting in some bizarre pseudo Georgian 'terraces' or other architectural nightmares. There are a few exceptions, such as the controversial but at least architecturally bold and interesting Avenue de Chartres car park in Chichester, Sussex.

Another unfortunate but related trend has been the location of large shops and retail parks away from the crowded town centres, to sites generally accessible only by car. These require vast numbers of car parking spaces and, almost invariably, the cheaper option of open-air parking rather than the potential opportunities for innovation has led to vast acreages of countryside being buried below tarmac.

PART V

SIGNS

CHAPTER 15

Milestones

Not surprisingly, it is the Romans that are credited with the introduction of milestones to Britain in the first century AD. These had been a feature of Roman roads in Italy long before the Conquest, some of the earliest being attributed to the road-building schemes of the Emperor Gaias Gracchus. The word 'mile' is derived from the Latin *mille*, a thousand, and each Roman mile was a thousand standard paces, generally accepted as being 1,618 yards (1,536m) long. Thus on a milestone from a Roman road near Llanfairfechan, Gwynedd, preserved in the British Museum, the distance from *Kanovium* – Caerhun – is inscribed as being 8 *milia passuum*, or 8,000 paces.

This is slightly shorter than our modern British mile of 1,760 yards (1,671m), established by decree in 1593, but 'miles' in post-Roman Europe varied widely until the development of the metric system from the late eighteenth century onwards. Indeed, miles in Britain varied considerably too, until well into the eighteenth century, and this needs to be taken into account when studying early milestones. It is not always appreciated that the statute mile was not set as a proper standard mile until as late as 1864.

Although it is generally accepted that milestones were an important element in the long-distance Roman roads, very few have survived in Britain. If every Roman road in the country had milestones, there should have been in the region of 10,000 of them. To date, only a little over 100 have been identified. Clearly many would have been reused after the departure of the Romans, but the disparity between the supposed amount of stones and those that have been found is enormous.

Even the surviving milestones are not that informative. The mileage and distances, where still legible, are usually quite secondary to the typically grovelling tributes to one ruling emperor or another, and even the dates of the inscriptions are difficult to verify as being primary. All of these milestones are, obviously, of stone, and several are cylindrical, such as the most famous example still *in situ* at Vindolanda close to Hadrian's wall.

The departure of the Roman legions led to the gradual abandonment of their roads and of long-distance travel in general, and milestones of any sort became quite redundant until the post-medieval period. A handful of roads appear to have been given milestones or markers in the early seventeenth century, generally by private benefactors, and Ogilby created the first accurate maps based on the modern mile in the 1670s. Ogilby even marked each mile along the routes in his *Britannia* but there is no evidence that these indicated actual milestones. Some major towns had special milestones or markers exactly one mile out from their centres on the main highways, and the earliest dated stone to indicate distance is one such stone, erected in 1667 in what is now Morrell Avenue, Oxford. Daniel Defoe, writing in the 1720s, reported that every mile between Grantham and Stangate was marked 'by stones set up by Mr. Boulton which he designed to have carried on to London for the general benefit'.

However, the main impetus for their widespread use was the development of the turnpikes from that period onwards. In order to charge, and to be seen to charge, people the correct amount for the use of their roads, the turnpike trusts had to accurately locate milestones along them at standard mile intervals. This was made compulsory for most turnpiked roads by an Act of 1744 and for all following another General Turnpike Act of 1766. The use of milestones also allowed the increasingly important coach traffic to regularise their schedules along the route, using the milestones as timing markers.

Carl Moritz, the German traveller, wrote, in 1782, 'The English mile-stones give me much pleasure; and they certainly are a great convenience to travellers. They have often seemed to ease me of half the distance of a journey, merely by telling me how far I had already gone; and by assuring me that I was on the right road. For, besides the distance from London, every milestone informs you that to the next place is so many miles ….'

Excluding some of the fancier individual examples, most milestones were relatively simple and generally of a standard 'house style' of the trust that set them up. These designs, however, could and did vary enormously.

The earlier milestones were, as their name suggests, made out of stone; it could be argued that all other 'milestones' made out of different materials – cast-iron, wood or concrete, for example – should technically be referred to as mileposts or mile markers. Wooden mileposts, presumably painted, were certainly used by some of the early turnpike trusts but must have required constant replacement; in some cases they were used as a temporary measure in anticipation of being replaced by ones that were more durable.

Stone continued to be used for milestones well into the nineteenth century and was only gradually supplanted by cast-iron. Stone had the advantage of being relatively cheap, readily available in most parts of the country and easy to work. The quality of the design of the milestones depended on the aspirations of the individual or trust that erected them, and varied enormously.

Earlier stones can be both square – sometimes diagonally set to the road – or cylindrical, but by the mid-eighteenth century the most common, inevitably, were the simple 'gravestone' type – a low upright slab, generally with a square or rounded top and a minimal degree of carved information on the face. This basic type continued to be used throughout the turnpike era and can still be seen, for example, on the Minsterley-Churchstoke turnpike route laid out as late as the 1830s.

Depending on the quality of the stone, the inscriptions would weather to a greater or lesser degree, requiring renewal of either the inscriptions or the stone. By the later eighteenth century, the manufacture of cast iron had

101 A typical stone milestone of the later eighteenth century. Often the names would mean little to the outsider; in this case 'Sarum' means Salisbury and 'Shaston' is Shaftesbury. Note that the distance to London is to Hyde Park

102 A composite milestone, with a cast-iron plate on a stone pedestal; this one, near Beverley in east Yorkshire, has a dual purpose – it is also a convenient mounting block for horse riders

become sufficiently reliable and relatively cheap to allow the use of composite milestones, made up of a plain stone on which cast-iron plates with the necessary information could be fixed. These plates could be plain or decorative, depending on the whim of the turnpike trustees. Usually the plates were fixed by iron dowels fitted into leaded sockets drilled into the stones; sometimes, the surface of the stone would be cut back, or rebated, to give a better and more secure bedding for the plate.

A logical progression was the development of all-iron mile markers, which became very popular from the early nineteenth century onwards and continued to be used well into the twentieth century. The material allowed a great deal of flexibility and durability at a very reasonable cost in comparison to stone. There were many different shapes and sizes of such posts, some only used by a single trust, others more commonly adapted, especially after the county-based Highway Boards took over general road maintenance towards the end of the Victorian period.

103 The all-metal milestone (or technically, milepost or mile marker) became available at a reasonable cost from the early nineteenth century and this triangular sectioned type became one of the standard forms. This one is on the western edge of Yorkshire, high in the Pennines

By the middle of the nineteenth century one particular type had become very common – the triangular sectioned milepost, usually with a 'hipped' top. Some of the more elaborate stone milestones had been of a similar section, or cylindrical, and that had allowed information to be displayed to travellers approaching in either direction along the road. The cast-iron versions did the same, and also allowed room for further information on the 'hipped' section or fin at the top as well.

The demand for milestones of any type in the twentieth century, when increasing traffic speeds virtually made them redundant for all but administrative purposes, meant few further developments in design or materials. Thin enamelled metal sheet mile markers, in their own house colours, were used in the early twentieth century by motoring organisations such as the AA and RAC and usually fixed to the wall of a convenient roadside building.

In between the two world wars, on some road improvements and new road building programmes, a variety of concrete mileposts and markers were used,

104 The speed of the motor vehicle effectively made milestones redundant, but some continued to be installed between the World Wars, such as this concrete one designed for Worcestershire County Council in the late 1920s

including, for example, the traditional triangular sectioned ones on the road over Rannoch Moor in the Scottish Highlands, and the rather attractive ones with a hint of art deco style used by Worcestershire County Council.

The information on milestones and markers varied considerably, both in its presentation and in its quantity. Some were basic in the extreme, with simply an initial for the towns and the number of miles beneath; sometimes, local versions and abbreviations of the destinations were used, probably confusing those from other areas as much then as they can do now. Others were much more informative, giving a variety of information that could include the full names of several destinations, the distance to London (often to Hyde Park Corner), the name of the turnpike trust or road and, later, the local authority responsible for its maintenance, or a date. Cast-iron plates or mileposts often have their maker's marks boldly or subtly displayed.

On earlier milestones, Roman numerals were often used, sometimes in a debased form and with the lesser measures – fractions of miles or furlongs – in the more common Arabic numerals. Arabic, or modern, numerals became the norm after the eighteenth century and many milestones were recut accordingly. By the end of the eighteenth century it was normal for the series of milestones along a route to be started off at one end at mile intervals. Thus, all the milestones would be in proper mile distances from the town at that end, but, unless the other destination was exactly so many miles away, the distances back from it would include a repeating fraction of a mile, sometimes expressed in furlongs.

The surviving milestones and markers on our roads are subject to constant damage or destruction by road traffic, road maintenance and, above all, road widening. Most of them date from the nineteenth century, though many are earlier still. Some present individual archaeological problems of their own, where stones have been re-carved or moved, and castings added or altered. They represent an important and, until quite recently, overlooked part of our transport heritage. Fortunately, the value of the better ones has been recognised by the listing legislation, and more individuals and groups are beginning to appreciate and protect them both on a local, and since the recent establishment of the Milestone Society, national level.

CHAPTER 16

Direction signs

The origins of direction signs to aid travellers are lost in antiquity and myth. In prehistoric societies, once travellers left the relative safety of their settlement or area, they would need to remember how to get back. Normally, a series of natural landmarks could suffice – a group of trees, a hill, a particular bend in the river, for example. Even in the early twenty-first century, there are tribes and groups throughout the world that have no need of the maps and signs of our 'civilised' society. The aboriginal people of northern Australia and various tribes of the Congo rainforest are cases in point.

In the bleaker and often relatively featureless uplands of prehistoric Britain, however, it was, as it is now, easy to get lost, especially when the weather closed in or at night. The earliest form of man-made direction aid is probably the simple pile of rocks – the cairn – which can still be found all over upland Britain. These are virtually impossible to date, and as more and more walkers have ventured onto the uplands for recreation rather than for trade, many hundreds have been piled up in the modern era; indeed, it is likely that the vast majority of cairns, especially in areas such as the Lake District, are no earlier in date than the nineteenth century. Many, however, seem to be of more antiquity and undoubtedly, some are prehistoric.

A more sophisticated version of the cairn is the single upright stone waymarker, often a combination of waymarker and boundary marker, erected to delineate the boundaries of medieval monastic estates. Another medieval development was the erection of stone crosses, usually by the Church, in part designed for the benefit of travellers but also sometimes boundary markers of ecclesiastic estates or parishes. Some crosses were of proper cruciform shape, others simply tall stones with a cross carved into them.

All of these stone features, probably augmented in the past in some areas by long-lost timber versions, would have been vital to show travellers at least where

105 The earliest and most primitive form of signpost is the simple stone cairn, used from prehistoric times up until the present; this is a fairly modern one to guide walkers on the Stiperstones in south-western Shropshire, but there are far more ancient ones along the ridge as well

106 At certain points along the more remote tracks, especially in upland areas, rather more sophisticated markers were placed – especially crosses sited by some of the monastic houses. This is the medieval Aiggin Stone on the top of Blackstone Edge in the Pennines; in this case the cross is carved into the stone. It is likely that there were many more such crosses in the medieval period, and many would have been of timber and thus vulnerable to replacement and decay

they were, if not how to get to where they wanted to go. There are also some surviving examples of deliberately laid out lines of marker stones indicating the route across a particularly bleak section of moorland. Examples of all these features survive, and whilst some, especially later, are recorded in old deeds, in general their dates or provenance are not easy to determine. Some are probably ancient but others relatively modern – such as some of the marker stones marking the routes of the military roads in Scotland constructed through challenging terrain in the eighteenth century where snow, in particular, was a problem for travellers. Their modern equivalents are in concrete or steel and generally painted.

It is assumed that there would have been at least some Roman road signs, though their frequency and form is not known. Indeed, very few such signs have been found in Europe on what was a very extensive road system, even though there is a possible mention of road signs – *tabellarii* – in a record of 132 BC related to the road between Regium and Capua in Italy.

High on the North Yorkshire moors in England, a few marker stones – tall and narrow – have holes, usually square or rectangular, cut through them near to their tops; a particularly good example of a series of six such stones survives along a lane on the ominously named Murk Mire Moor near Goathland. Many

107 Several different theories, from astronomical siting posts to candleholders have been put forward to a series of pierced upright marker stones on the remote Wheeldale Moor to the south of Goathland in Yorkshire. One other explanation is that the slots were designed to take wooden finger posts

theories have been put forward, including, almost inevitably, convoluted ones connected with ley lines and astrology. A more prosaic explanation could be that the holes were simply slots to take wooden signposts showing the way, an explanation made more plausible by the fact that two stones are set quite close together at the only junction along the route.

One of the earliest documented *direction* signs, a type later officially designated as 'guide posts' by the Ordnance Survey, was that on a crossroads on the Cotswolds ridge where the main road from Oxford to Worcester (now the A44) was crossed by a lane from Snowshill to Chipping Campden, just to the south of that town. Dated 1669, and with iron arms, it is known as 'Joseph Izod's Post'; the original has been preserved and been replaced by a copy. This was sufficiently unusual to be specifically mentioned in John Ogilvy's finely detailed strip maps published in 1675; labelled '*A Hand for Direction to Winchcomb*'; it seems to be the only signpost included in that work.

Up until the later seventeenth century, most of those travelling long distances were the wealthier classes and their entourages, and they could afford to employ

108 One of the earliest recorded finger posts is Joseph Izod's post, dated 1669, with a stone stanchion and iron arms between Broadway and Oxford. This is a replica put up in place of the preserved original

local guides to show them the way. Less wealthy travellers tended to be those on traditional routes, such as the drovers and packhorse men, who knew their own well-trod ways. Local landmarks were thus important in finding the way, and form an integral part of Ogilvy's strip maps. He marks and labels a wide variety of features in the landscape, including windmills, beacons, inns, gallows, mines, mills and, above all, bridges – usually indicating what they are made of and often how many arches they have. Some of his landmarks are rather less substantial – an ash near Farringdon, an oak near Coventry, or an elm near Yate, for example, and 'a Great flat stone by ye way side with a Sundial on it' in Suffolk.

With the gradual increase in road traffic in the later-seventeenth century, the absence of direction signs, particularly in the remoter areas, became a problem for travellers venturing out of their own localities. As a result, an Act of 1697 authorised Justices of the Peace to erect direction or guide posts at junctions of roads outside towns and villages. Shortly afterwards, Celia Fiennes, whilst riding through Lancashire, was impressed to note 'that at all Cross wayes there are Posts wth hands pointing to each road wth ye names of ye great town or market towns that it Leads to, wch does make up for ye length of ye miles y^t [that] strangers may not Loose their Road and have it to goe back againe'.

Not all counties immediately set about erecting signs, and not all signs were of what became the traditional 'finger-post' type – with a post carrying the arms pointing in the relevant direction and bearing the names and distances of the destinations. Many, especially in the Midland and southern counties of England, were probably of timber and the information would have been painted on. Not surprisingly, virtually none have survived. In addition, fewer such direction signs would have been needed in this more populous part of the country, as settlements were relatively close together and travellers could simply ask the way or follow well-trodden tracks between villages.

Most of the direction signs of the late seventeenth and eighteenth centuries that have survived have been in the remoter areas, and are almost invariably of stone – with the relevant information carved into them. In the southern Pennines these were called 'stoops' and more survive in this area than anywhere else in Britain. This is partly because of the hard local millstone grit generally used to make them, and partly because it was then one of the busiest upland areas, crisscrossed with packhorse paths in particular.

Typically the guide stoops were around 4–5ft (1.4m) high and generally square in section, though shallow triangular ones and even a six-sided stoop have been identified. Some have pointing hands to guide the traveller, many do not; if there were no carved fingers to show the way, it was normal to assume that, when reading one side of such a sign, the direction to take for the town or towns mentioned was to the traveller's right. Information varied; sometimes only the

109 A typical guide stoop, in this case at the junction of two formerly busy lanes to the north-east of Bakewell in the Derbyshire Peak District. Both are now very minor lanes, one virtually impassable for motor vehicles. This stoop has carved hands, but many did not

town was indicated, often in abbreviated form. Sometimes the stone is dated, and sometimes the local surveyor's name is added. Seldom were the distances to the towns added until later in the period. Most of these 'Justices' direction signs date to the period between the passing of the 1697 Act and the 1750s.

Many of the upland stoops, in particular, are now literally off the beaten track, the routes they served having been abandoned or bypassed. Redundant examples could conveniently be reused as gate-posts, especially in these drystone walled areas, and can sometimes be found being used as such. Others remain where they were set, providing evidence for a once busier route over the hills. The best surviving examples are in south-western Yorkshire, eastern Lancashire and, especially, the Peak District of northern Derbyshire.

Not all such guide stones or signs were erected on the orders of the Justices of the Peace, and other local benefactors occasionally paid for quite elaborate examples, especially in the eighteenth century. However, the next great increase in the numbers of direction signs was the result of the development of the turnpike system.

The need for accurate information regarding mileage on such signs was set out in the General Turnpike Act of 1773, which stated that the surveyor of each

Trust had to 'cause to be fixed, in the most convenient Place where …Ways meet, a Stone or Post with an inscription thereon in Large Letter, containing the Name of, and Distances from, the next Market Town or Towns, or other considerable Places or Place to which the said Highways respectively lead'.

By 1782, Carl Moritz, a German visitor who toured parts of England on foot, wrote that 'at crossroads there are direction posts, and it is virtually impossible to get lost walking'. The first recorded mention of the term 'finger-post', incidentally, according to the *Oxford English Dictionary* was in 1785; the first official use of the term in legislation was not until a government circular of 1975.

A wide variety of direction signs were erected from the mid-eighteenth century onwards, mostly cheap and plain and wooden, and a few extraordinarily elaborate and expensive. It is generally the latter type that has survived, resulting in a rather unbalanced heritage. Examples include the late eighteenth-century stone obelisk at Craven Arms in south Shropshire, listing, amongst the destinations, Edinburgh and Plymouth; another bulbous stone column

110 One of the grandest signposts of the turnpike era is the Egyptian style stylus outside the Craven Arms Inn in south Shropshire; the destinations carved into it would be virtually unknown to most of the locals

111 A privately funded fingerpost in south Shropshire, erected in around 1800, at Little Brampton near Craven Arms

with fretted iron arms a little to the west at Little Brampton, erected in 1800; and another obelisk, with inset and well-carved directing hands at St Ives, Cambridgeshire.

Wooden signposts continued to be common through most of the nineteenth century, and still remain in use in parts of the country; they obviously need constant replacement. As cast iron became cheaper, it provided a suitable, if still more expensive, alternative, and some cast-iron finger-posts still in use date from the end of the nineteenth century.

Up until the start of the twentieth century there had been no set standard or design for direction signs, and no official government guidance. With the relative decline in the importance of roads because of the railways throughout the second half of the nineteenth century, this was hardly surprising. The signposts that did exist were generally more than adequate to cater for the needs of those using the roads, and for the speeds at which that traffic moved.

112 A typical wooden finger post, this particular example being in north Wiltshire; although not particularly old, it is already in need of replacement because of the nature of the material, so very few such signs are of any great antiquity

113 This all-metal finger post, probably of around 1900, in Kikby Stephen, Cumbria, has remarkably accurate distances marked on it in miles and furlongs

However, the development of the internal combustion engine and the revival of the significance of the road system changed matters. More and more of the new breed – motorists – were travelling longer and longer distances, and faster. An early attempt at advice on a national level had been made in 1904, but that had mainly been to do with warning signs. Further attempts were halted by the outbreak of the First World War, but in 1919 a committee was set up by the government to look into all aspects of road signs.

The committee's report was refined by the new Ministry of Transport into a circular, issued in 1921, and this coincided with the classification of roads. It seemed logical to publicise the new road classification system, so the circular advised that the new road numbers – mainly just those of the 'A' or 'B' categories – be incorporated into the new direction signs. The new standard suggested plain rectangular fingerpost arms with 3-inch-high plain lettering on a white background, with the road numbers, where relevant, at the end of each arm. The 'A' road numbers were also to be black on white, but the 'B' road numbers were to be painted white on black instead. The local authority's name or initials could be added at the top of the post, either in the form of an upright ring – an *annulus* – or finial. Signs could be made of timber, but cast-iron was a longer-lasting material and one that became very popular.

While most of the local authorities responsible for road signs – counties, county boroughs, and rural and urban districts – followed the basic principles of the 1921 circular, there was still scope for local variations of the same theme. This partly depended on the materials used. Iron was common, but timber continued to be used and concrete was tried; there were also composite designs, particularly of concrete posts with wooden arms. Similarly, this individuality continued following another circular in 1930 which, amongst other matters, recognised that as road vehicles were getting faster, signs at major junctions should be supplemented with advance warning direction signs.

In the following year another committee met to review road signs and produced their report in 1933. For the first time, the usefulness of the road number system for faster moving traffic and route finding was recognised, and the road numbers took precedence over the destinations. The new advance warning direction signs – the so-called 'map' signs with individual rectangles containing the road number and destination fixed onto a basic map of each junction – were more in line with those that we are used to in the early twenty-first century, though still with black lettering on a white background. Capital letters only, of a new standard set – the Llewellyn-Smith font – were to be used. Another innovation was the 'route confirmation sign', usually of one or more road numbers on top of each other to show the traveller the road he was on and, beneath a simple chequer band, those he was heading for.

One anomaly in the first half of the twentieth century was the fact that, as well as local authorities, the two main motoring organisations – the AA and the RAC – could also put up their own signs at junctions and elsewhere with suitable permission. These included permanent direction signs as well as temporary ones related to special events or diversions.

Early in the Second World War, the AA and the RAC were given the job of removing and storing nearly 200,000 signposts throughout Britain – to confuse an enemy presumed to be geographically illiterate and short of maps; this caused more problems to British drivers and soon there were demands for the reinstatement of at least some. Following the end of the war there was yet another radical shake-up in road traffic signs, in line with the conclusions of yet another committee in 1944. More local advanced warning signs were recommended in 1950, similar to those of 1933 but set onto a black background, changed to yellow for most through routes in 1957 and blue for urban areas.

The most dramatic, and aesthetically damaging, changes followed. In 1962, a report by Sir Colin Anderson that had been specifically related to the signage of the pioneering motorways, had resulted in their now standard blue-backed signs with a carefully worked out new *sans serif* font. The detailed design work was under the direction of a graphic artist, Jock Kinneir. Another committee, chaired by Sir Walter Worboys, reported on the signage of the rest of the road network in 1963. The Worboys report emphasised the need for colour-coded signs and a different typeface and size for lettering, reflecting those used for the motorways. Unfortunately, and controversially, it also called for the wholesale and rapid phasing out of fingerpost type direction signs and their replacement by standard 'map' type signs. Enshrined in an Act of the following year, hundreds of old signs were replaced until the remainder were reprieved by the then Department of Transport in 1975; fingerpost signs were allowed on quieter junctions and since then many authorities have not only retained older examples, but also introduced new ones.

Older twentieth century signs can often be a palimpsest of their relatively brief history. The standard, or post, may remain, but sometimes a county finial or *annulus* has been altered or replaced to reflect changes in administration districts (especially after the Local Government Act of 1973), and the arms may have been replaced by modern ones. Sometimes, the reverse is true – old cast arms and finial being reset on a modern standard.

In other cases, the cast lettering may have been deliberately painted out – a once fairly common example being the directions to the nearest country railway station after so many were closed in the 1960s. Sometimes it is the road numbers that have been changed, due to reclassification of routes, and many of the original 'B' road elements that were originally of white letters on a black background have been repainted black on white. To confuse matters, in recent years replica fingerposts have been introduced, particularly in conservation areas, often based on original designs.

CHAPTER 17

Traffic signs

Traffic signs are distinguished from direction signs in being designed to assist or control traffic, rather than being used to show it the way. The slow speed of most road traffic until the advent of the motor car meant that such signs on roads were virtually unknown until the end of the nineteenth century. Nevertheless, signs of all types had, by that time, become not only common but vital on the railway network where speeds were much higher and safety issues far more critical.

However, it was not the needs of the motorist that first led to the widespread use of such signs on the roads, but those of the cyclist. Apart from some home-made examples of warning signs, the first real attempt to introduce them on a more ambitious scale was made by the various groups of cycling organisations that belonged to the Bicycle Union. In 1879 they adopted a simple enamelled sign on a timber post warning cyclists of steep hills, a very useful warning considering the primitive state of bicycle brakes at that time; the sign simply read '*To Cyclists – This Hill is Dangerous*'. The BU later became the National Cyclist Union and they, and other cycling bodies such as the Cyclists' Touring Club and the Scottish Cyclists' Union, continued to erect warning signs at the top of steep hills. Two scales of warning were used – 'Danger' and 'Caution' – and the words were usually in white on a red or blue background. Between them, the various cycling organisations had put up well over 4,000 signs throughout Britain by 1903.

There is some dispute about the first 'official' traffic sign directly related to the motorist, but the most usual candidate was a sign erected by what was still then the Automobile Club in October 1901. This was at the top of Birdlip, a particularly steep hill on the edge of the Cotswolds a little to the east of Gloucester.

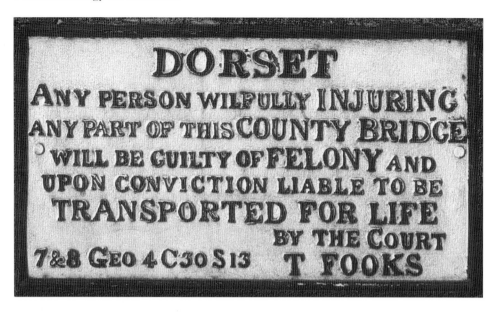

114 One of the more ominous warning signs in Dorset, dating to the early nineteenth century and affixed to many of the county's bridges

115 A typical weight restriction sign of the late nineteenth and early twentieth century; these are now virtually unknown on the roads and this particular one is in the Great Western Railway museum at Didcot, Oxfordshire

Following the passing of the Motor Car Act of 1903, the government issued a Local Government Board Circular in March 1904 that provided recommendations for a standard system of warning signs. Four different types of signs were suggested, identified by different tops above the information plates beneath. An 18 inch (7cm) diameter white ring, or *annulus*, was placed on top of speed limit signs; a solid red ring of the same diameter was placed on top of prohibition signs; a pierced red triangle with 18 inch (7cm) sides was placed on top of warning signs relating to 'dangerous corners, cross roads or precipitous places'; and all other signs, such as weight restrictions etc., were to be placed on diamond-shaped plates which had been used since an earlier Act of 1896.

Unfortunately, unlike the standards adopted by France in 1903, these recommendations were not compulsory. Whilst many local authorities adopted them, some did so only half-heartedly and some not at all. Others produced their

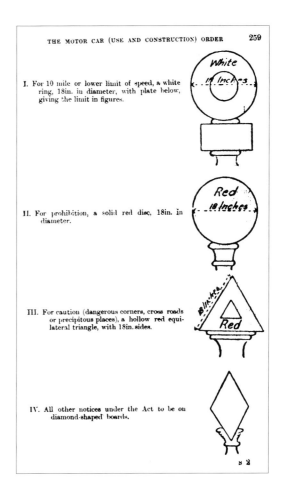

116 An extract from the warning sign recommendations of the 1903 Motor Car Act

own idiosyncratic warning signs. The proliferation of different signs continued, and the AA and the RAC continued to produce their own warning signs as well as their own direction signs, both being accused, with some justification, of using them as cheap advertising; their yellow or blue house colours and their logos were prominently displayed.

At the Convention on International Circulation of Motor Vehicles held in France in 1909, most European countries adopted a generally similar standard of traffic signs, using what is now the well-known red triangle for many of them and simple but effective symbols on the plates below. Britain did not sign the Convention and continued to go its own haphazard way.

Another non-binding memorandum was issued by the newly formed Ministry of Transport in 1921. This advised a standard layout of the warning information on signs; these were to be vertical rectangular plates with a warning symbol and lettering beneath to explain. In general these were not too dissimilar to the European examples – although the lit flaring torch to symbolise a school was rather confusing.

In 1930, another ministry memorandum was issued, another Road Traffic Act was passed, and another committee was set up. The Maybury Committee finally reported in 1933; its main finding – a rather obvious one in retrospect – was that signs 'should be designed and sited to attract the attention of those persons for whom they were intended'. The members did not approve of symbols unless they were readily understood, and recommended the use of explanatory wording. Under the auspices of the Act, the Traffic Signs (size, colour and type) Provisional Regulations were implemented to produce a new national standard for traffic signs. This introduced more types of warning signs – for narrowing roads, hospitals, roundabouts etc. – as well as 'no waiting' and 'no entry' signs, and black and white striped posts. Another committee, set up in 1943 by the emergency Ministry of War Transport and reporting in the following year, considered that the existing regulations were still working and recommended only a few minor alterations.

After the Second World War most European countries agreed to a new standard for traffic signs at a conference held in Geneva in 1949; Britain again opted out, although a few minor changes were made to traffic signs following legislation passed in 1950. It was only after the report of the Worboys Committee in 1964 that it finally decided to follow the rest of Europe.

This led to a radical change in road signs of all types, formed the basis of the signs of the present day and led to the final abolition of independent direction signs by the AA and RAC. By this time, the cast-iron road signs had begun to be replaced by cheaper aluminium alloy and this became the norm, with signs painted and flat rather than with any castings, and reflective paints replacing the rather attractive but primitive reflective studs that had appeared between the wars.

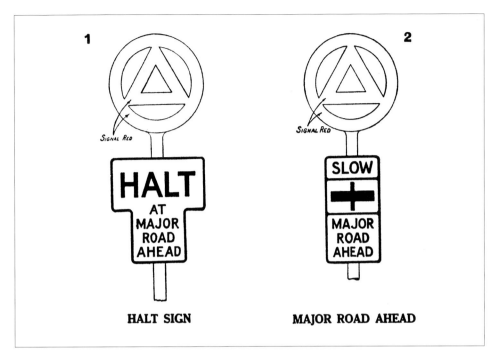

117 Typical warning signs in the earliest editions of the Highway Code, based on the 1933 recommendations of the Maybury Committee

TRAFFIC LIGHTS

The development of the railways in the nineteenth century, and the ever increasing numbers and speed of trains, had led to the development of sophisticated signalling. This was, in general, irrelevant for the road network. However, the first traffic light was installed long before the rise of the motor car, and by a company, Saxby & Farmer, that was one of the main suppliers of railway signalling equipment. In a short-lived experiment off Parliament Square in London, to allow MPs access without delay across to the Houses of Parliament, a red (stop) or green (caution) gas-lit lamp was directed at traffic by a duty policeman. The scheme was begun in 1869 and stopped in 1872.

Electric traffic lights were first used in America just before the First World War, and afterwards a set was introduced at a busy junction in Paris in 1923. The first traffic lights in Britain were set up in Piccadilly, London, in 1926, again controlled by a constable; the first automatic traffic lights were installed in Prince's Square, Wolverhampton, in the following year and they had become relatively common on the busier road junctions by the end of the 1930s.

PEDESTRIAN CROSSINGS

Another warning sign that resulted from the 1933 Regulations related to pedestrian crossings. Apart from the short-lived 'private' crossing for MPs and Lords by the Houses of Parliament, the first public pedestrian crossings had been set up in London in the winter of 1926–27. The prototype was in Parliament Square, Westminster. These were initially marked by a simple pair of parallel white lines, changed to hatched white lines soon afterwards.

The 1933 regulations introduced two lines of studs across the road and specially designed beacons on each pavement – black and white poles surmounted by glass globes painted orange; these were the 'Belisha beacons', taking their name from the then Minister of Transport, Sir Leslie Hore-Belisha. In the early 1950s the crossings were given their black and white stripes on the road surface and became instantly known thereafter as 'zebra crossings'. Subsequently, light-controlled crossings – pelicans, toucans etc. – have been developed.

PART VI

PUBLIC TRANSPORT

CHAPTER 18

Trams

The tram was a logical extension of the railway and the distinction between the two is fairly subtle. Both rely on vehicles, powered by animal or engines, running on a fixed track. Both forms can have separate locomotives or vehicles with integral engines and both can, theoretically, run in towns or between them. Even in law the distinction was blurred. For example, the railway running up the Glyn Valley in north-east Wales – a narrow-gauge steam-hauled railway in all but name – was classed as a tramway because it mostly ran on the broad verge of the adjacent lane, and the Camborne & Redruth Tramway in Cornwall ended up as a goods only railway. Conversely, the Burton & Ashby Light Railway, despite its earthworks and mostly dedicated track, was a rural tramway complete with double-decker electric trams that operated between 1906 and 1927.

The origins of the tram lie in the 'street railways' of the USA that developed in the 1830s, but it was not until 1860 that a public tram service was established in Britain – in Birkenhead by an American, George Train. Using 'L-shaped' plate-rails that projected above the road surface – to the annoyance of other road users – the horse-drawn trams were similar to the contemporary omnibuses of the day. The tracks had to be replaced by ones sunk beneath the road surface, but Train continued to use his 'L-shaped' rails on other systems – short-lived routes in London in 1861, another in Darlington, and a more successful one run by the Staffordshire Potteries Street Railway Company between Hanley and Burslem in 1864. Trams reappeared in London in 1870 and several more horse-drawn systems were then established in other parts of Britain, especially following the passing of the Tramways Act in that year which clarified their legal status and simplified their planning, financing and operation.

Introducing steam power to urban tramways was a logical step, given the success of the steam railway. On some cable-operated systems the steam engines

118 A typical early twentieth-century electric tram in Ipswich, Suffolk; it was not only London and the industrial cities of the north that relied on trams for urban transport

were stationary and hauled the cables. These were relatively uncommon in Britain and used mainly where steep hills had to be dealt with – for example in Edinburgh and Matlock. On other tramways, steam locomotion was used, but there were matters that needed to be dealt with – not least the perceived dangers from accidents in crowded thoroughfares. Most of the tramways that used steam locomotives were in the north and midland towns in England; the Bradford system had around 40 steam locomotives at the end of the nineteenth century.

It was the introduction of electric power that revolutionised the tramways, providing an efficient and generally reliable source of power. Werner von Siemens ran an experimental electric powered tramway in Berlin in 1879 and the first public line in Anhalt, Germany, opened in 1881. In Britain, the first electric tramway was in Blackpool, opened in 1885.

Electricity had another advantage. The tram companies, and subsequently the municipal authorities that had their own tram systems, needed electricity; at the time there was no national grid so they had to build their own power plants. These normally generated surplus electricity – and even more at the right times of the day; the trams were mainly busy in the day time and the main need for what was then power for street and domestic lighting was greatest at night. As a result the generating capacity was a useful sideline to the tramway. Conversely,

119 Matlock had one of the shortest but steepest tram systems in the world which opened in 1893. It was cable-hauled, and the main engine house and depot was at the top of the bank on Rutland Street. It survived closure in 1927 and is now partly used by a garage

some local authorities recognised that their new electricity stations could also be used for tramways systems.

The pioneering electric tramway in Blackpool had used a conduit system between the rail for power pick up to the motors on the tram cars, but only a few other systems, such as Wolverhampton, used this. Overhead wires were first tried in Leeds in 1891 and became the more standard method – considered less expensive, more reliable and safer.

In 1900 there were just over 1,000 miles of tram route miles in Britain, of which about three-quarters were electric, about 300 miles horse-drawn, and the rest steam hauled. The systems operated nearly 6,000 tram cars and in that year 35,987 horses and 539 locomotive engines are recorded as being in use on what was a very disparate system. Although trams were mainly used in the major towns, there were a few inter-urban routes and some tramways in the most surprising places – such as Rothesay on the Isle of Bute where horse-trams operated from 1879 to be replaced by electric ones in 1902.

Tram mileage rapidly expanded in the first quarter of the century thanks to the efficiency and economy afforded by electric power; by the end of the First World War, horse-drawn trams had virtually been eliminated and there were only short sections of track still steam hauled. The 1920s represented the heyday of the tramway system, with route mileage peaking at 2,599 miles (4,158km) in 1923 and the number of tramcars in use at 14,416 in 1926.

There are two different types of tram track – the dedicated, or 'reserved', route restricted to them in the same way as a railway line would be; and those routes shared with other road users. Most of the Blackpool system, which opened in 1885 and survived the wholesale closures elsewhere, runs along the seafront in its own reserved track, though access to the main depot is through the streets and shared with other road users. Although the International Road Congress held in London just before the First World War recommended that trams be separated from other road users, this was seldom practicable in narrow and congested British town streets.

It was mainly the problems caused by the shared tracks that, ultimately, led to the demise of the tram. As early as 1923, the town-planning expert Stanley Adshead declared that 'Trams should be abolished altogether off traffic roads, and their place taken by the motor-bus' and recommended that separate tram tracks on the main arterial roads be encouraged instead, upgraded to light railways. Congestion, usually caused by other road users but exacerbated by the fact that the trams couldn't get round obstacles across their predetermined routes, worsened as the amount of motor cars and commercial vehicles increased dramatically after the Second World War. The trams also suffered from a chronic lack of investment, and as their condition deteriorated, they also were perceived as being old-fashioned and noisy. Official sanction to the demise of the tram was given in 1947 when a Ministry of Transport committee recommended the 'replacement of trams by vehicles of greater manoeuvrability'.

Trams were phased out fairly rapidly in the 1950s, often being replaced initially by trolleybuses but sometimes by buses. Trams were more respected in many major European cities and survived the often hurried and sometimes ill thought-out changes carried out in Britain; the trams of Amsterdam, for example, are famous for their efficiency and are part of the charm of that great city as well as one of the best ways of getting around it. With urban congestion continuing to increase in British towns, some far-minded planners eventually saw the possibility of bringing updated forms of trams back.

In a more sophisticated format, based mainly on the gradual improvements made on continental systems, the tram has returned to some urban areas in Britain, notably Sheffield, Manchester and the West Midlands. Modern trams in these areas either run on their own dedicated track bed – sometimes in the centre of a wide road and sometimes on former railway lines. The Black Country Tramway between Wolverhampton and Birmingham, for example, runs mainly on the route of the old Great Western Railway's Paddington-Birkenhead main line, partly on a new dedicated track and, for a short section, shares the main road.

Remains of older tramway systems are surprisingly common, but not usually protected. Seldom were there any major civil engineering requirements, but on a few inter-urban lines there would be a need for embankments and cuttings and some of those of the Burton & Ashby Light Railway survive. Their rapid demise, especially in the 1950s and early '60s, led to a massive nationwide campaign of ripping up tramlines and resurfacing streets so that very few tramlines now survive *in situ*. Occasionally, in a pedestrianised area, tramlines might be retained and restored in the cobbles as a feature – such as in the Wellgate in Dundee. Sometimes tramlines survive almost by accident – there is a short length of former horse-tram track off the Stockwell Road in Brixton probably dating to 1882, and another, of the Burton & Ashby Light Railway, in the yard of Ashby-de-la-Zouch railway station. However, most of the time the tracks were seen as a potential nuisance to traffic and pedestrians alike, and a useful source of scrap metal, and had to go.

Perhaps the longest redundant double tram tracks left are in central London – and mostly underground. During the redevelopment of the area around Aldwych and Holborn a new tram line was opened in 1906; to extend it, a long underpass, reserved for the trams, was opened between Southampton Row and Kingsway in 1906, complete with two 'stations'. The underpass originally took single-decker trams using a conduit pickup system; it was radically rebuilt in 1931 to take double-deckers but in the general decline of the capital's tram networks was closed in 1952. Part of the southern section was then reused for a car underpass, opened in 1964, and the rest for storage and other uses. The tracks are virtually intact in those sections and can be seen diving down from street level in Southampton Row.

The overhead wire systems could be adapted for the trolleybuses or in some cases used as lamp standards. Occasionally such a standard will survive in an unexpected place. Until recently there was a good collection of standards in Hastings, probably reused by the trolleybuses for a while but now removed. That town also has some surviving pole 'roses' on the walls of buildings where standards were not possible and angled poles had to be used instead high up on the adjacent walls.

The other requirement for trams was somewhere to house and maintain them. Initially, this accommodation consisted of buildings for the vehicles and separate stables for the horses, but obviously the latter were no longer required after the introduction of steam, and later electric, propulsion. A horse-tram depot survives on the Isle of Man tramway at Derby Castle, and in mainland Britain, just the

120 The unique tramway underpass in the middle of London was first built in 1906, rebuilt in 1931 and closed in 1952. Part has been rebuilt for motor vehicles, but the northern section ramp by Southampton Row survives and the tracks continue for hundreds of yards below the street beyond. Note the central conduit between the rails for the electrical pick-up

one tram depot is still in use for its original purpose in Blackpool. Their fairly high survival rate elsewhere since the decline of the trams is partly due to the fact that they were generally well-built structures of no great age with a great deal of covered space and good lighting, perfectly adaptable to the types of vehicles – trolleybuses and then buses – that displaced the trams. Hence the former Silverhill Tram Depot in Hastings was initially converted to take trolleybuses and then buses and is still a bus depot. There are several others that have survived in this way.

There are a handful of museums based in former tram sheds, but two of the more well-known sites have since closed. From 1964 the Glasgow Transport Museum used to be housed in the Coplawhill tram depot; that at one time had separate entrances for horse-drawn and electric powered trams before the former were withdrawn in 1901 when the museum relocated to the Kelvin Hall and the depot was converted into the Tramway Theatre, which opened in 1988. Clapham tram depot in London opened in 1910 and was converted for buses in 1951 before closing in 1958; it became the well-known Clapham Railway Museum until 1981 and has since been demolished.

In contrast, the former tramway depots at Tinsley, Sheffield, originally built in 1874 for horse trams and converted to electric trams in 1899, remained in use for trams until 1960 and was then converted into warehousing. The Sheffield Bus Museum Trust moved into part of the site in 1987. Another former tram depot at Whitton, Birmingham, has also recently become a museum. Other buildings have found other uses. An odd building in Brixton Hill, London, was constructed in 1923 to house the specially built double-decker trailer trams then being tried out by London County Council; these were considered to be too unstable and were withdrawn soon after the depot was built. It was then used for standard trams until being closed in 1950. It is now a car show room. In Cambridge, the former Dover Street Tram Depot is now a popular pub.

The electric tramways obviously required electricity and, in an age long before the ready availability of it, often had to supply their own. The power generating stations became a symbol of the new age of transport and many companies gave these utilitarian structures quite grand architectural treatment. Two of the earliest and best have survived and, curiously, their shells were designed by the same young architect, W. Curtis Green, who later specialised in transport-related and commercial buildings as well as his more usual domestic work. For the London United Electrical Tramway Company he designed a richly decorated building in a loose baroque style in Chiswick High Road between 1899–1901; this has, appropriately, figures representing 'Electricity' and 'Locomotion' on the facade. After the trams stopped working in 1952 it was used to power the replacement trolleybuses until the early 1960s. In 1985 the building was converted into flats and it now also has a recording studio. At the same time, Curtis Green also designed a vaguely classical power station for the Bristol Tramways, in brick with stone decorations and columns; he also designed this company's main Brislington Tram Depot and a power station for the Hove Tramways.

In contrast, Wolverhampton Borough Council had already opened a power station in 1895 before they began to operate a new municipal tramway system in 1902. The power station was extended and re-equipped as a result. Like most power stations of the date, it consisted of an office block, main turbine hall, and boiler house; coal for the furnaces was delivered on the adjacent canal wharf. Much of the complex, though stripped of its equipment, survives.

Cable tramways required power to haul the cables and the trams attached to them. This was initially usually steam power, requiring an engine house and winding room as well as the necessary stores. The complex that included the winding engine and the Rutland Street tram depot of the Matlock Cable Tramway survives at the top of what was one of the shortest and steepest cable-operated trams in the country, just over half a mile long with a gradient of more than 1 in 6, which opened in 1893 and closed in 1927.

CHAPTER 19

Trolleybuses & motor buses

Trams were obviously confined to specific routes by their overhead wires and by their fixed tracks. As road traffic in towns grew, particularly with the increasing numbers of motor vehicles, the tracks began to be perceived as a problem. Other road users had to cross them and as there was often only a single line, trams could lead to congestion. One logical development was a road vehicle that could benefit from the electric power from the overhead lines but not be restricted to the track. The result was the trolleybus – not be confused with the 'trolleys' of north America that are, in fact, trams.

TROLLEYBUSES

The trolleybus was a logical combination of the electric tram and the motor bus, theoretically combining the economy of the former and the flexibility of the latter whilst not requiring expensive track. Early experiments with the 'rail-less' electric vehicle were carried out by a German, Ernst von Siemens, who adapted a light-weight horse-drawn wagon to be powered by a small electric motor; its current came down a flexible boom joined to a small 'trolley' that ran along the twin power lines. Commercial application had to wait until 1901, in Germany, and the first application in Britain was 1909 in Birkenhead – the same town that had pioneered trams; the first major towns to run trolleybuses for public transport were Leeds and Bradford who began services in 1911.

Take up of the trolleybus was slow and erratic, and several systems were short-lived. Before the First World War, systems in Dundee and South Wales opened and closed quite quickly, and it was not really until the 1930s that the trolleybus began to make serious inroads into the work previously undertaken by the trams.

There was a further boom in trolleybus use after the Second World War as trams were considered to be noisy and unfashionable. Even though their route mileage increased from just 5 miles in 1911 to a peak of 828 miles in 1954 – by which time they had briefly overtaken the rapidly declining route mileage of trams – trolleybuses were only ever a relatively minor form of public transport in Britain.

For some reason, the trolleybus has never caught the public imagination in the same way as the trams did, for all their faults. The trolleybuses were quiet, efficient and comfortable – and perhaps it was their virtually silent running that meant that they were seen as characterless. In some towns they were known as 'whispering death', and in one of the few times they were ever enshrined in verse, in Philip Larkin's 1964 poem, *The Whitsun Weddings*, they were just seen part of unwanted suburban sprawl; the 'residents from raw estates brought down/ The dead straight miles by stealing flat-faced trolleys …'.

A sudden decline began at the start of the 1960s due to most towns deciding to expand their use of the even more versatile, if environmentally more damaging, motor bus. The last new route seems to have been a short extension in Teeside

121 These dark blue and cream trolleybuses on the South Shields system are of late 1940s vintage, with timber-framed bodywork from the Northern Coach Builders, Claremont Road, Newcastle-on-Tyne. The system opened in 1936 and closed in 1964

in 1968, by which time many of the larger networks, including London, had closed. The last commercial trolleybuses ran, appropriately enough, in Bradford in 1972.

In use, the trolleybus used much of the same basic infrastructure as the trams, including the electric supply system, and could also be maintained and stabled in the same depots. A handful of purpose-built trolley depots were constructed nevertheless. The trolleybuses did not, of course, require the tracks and those were usually ripped up once the trams were displaced completely.

THE MOTOR BUS

Although dealt with last, the omnibus was, by many years if not centuries, the earliest form of urban town transport; however, it was only a significant one at the end of the nineteenth century and the most important by the mid-twentieth century. Blaise Pascal began the earliest recognised, if short-lived, bus services in Paris during 1662, but these were for the wealthy and were barred from transporting peasants or soldiers.

A version of the modern 'bus' service was begun in Manchester in 1824 and other attempts were made in France in the early nineteenth, including one in Nantes. The name 'omnibus' is said to be derived from the name of a local shopkeeper, one M. Omnes – the shop being 'Omnes Omnibus'. The French experiments culminated in a company in Paris operating a service of 100 horse-drawn vehicles in Paris in 1828. Despite restrictions, that highly successful system was copied in London by George Shillibeer, a London carriage maker, in the following year and gradually spread to other main cities and towns in Britain.

The potential of steam-powered road-going passenger vehicles was established in the early nineteenth century but largely stifled by the development of the railways and the restrictions of the turnpike trusts. By the time the internal combustion engine was being developed, the potential for it as a replacement for horse-power could be tapped with a greater chance of success. Even so, the first motor-buses to be used in Britain, along Princes Street in Edinburgh by the Edinburgh Autocar Company Ltd in May 1898, were not a success and the venture folded in 1901. Several other ventures began in the same year in perhaps unexpected places such as Falkirk, Mansfield and Torquay. The first motor-buses in London began in 1899 and, like their Edinburgh predecessors, were unsuccessful and ceased in 1900. However, the reliability of motor vehicles was rapidly improving.

Buses were generally seen as being slightly superior to the trams and this distinction was generally reinforced by continuous campaigns of upgrading and investment sadly lacking in their railed counterparts. This was reflected also in the

122 Horse-drawn omnibuses were a common feature of major towns in the late nineteenth century before largely being replaced by trams. This is a typical example in Edinburgh, *c.*1900

longer-distance routes to the suburbs and between towns, the development of first the open-topped tripper *char-à-bancs* and then the luxury closed coach. The power, efficiency and size of the buses, and their comfort, gradually increased in the first half of the twentieth century and have continued to do so ever since. As the tram systems were gradually closed down, they were either replaced by trolleybuses or by motor buses; the trolleybus era was a relatively short one, and the motor buses inevitably took over their routes as well. The decline of the railway network through underinvestment and government apathy has, since the 1960s, seen the increase in fast, long-distance coach travel – and that despite, in turn, the rapid increase in the numbers of private motor cars.

As buses continue to be such important parts of urban transport, though seldom on a fully integrated level especially after their complete deregulation and opening up to purely commercial markets in the 1980s, much of their infrastructure is constantly being updated so that there are relatively few surviving structures. Their basic needs are for a large servicing and storage depot; a coach station in the larger towns; and bus stops.

Many of their early depots were simply taken-over and adapted tram or trolleybus sheds, and other suitable existing structures have also been used.

123 This 1951 Guy Arab double-decker bus is sharing a former tramway depot with the South Shields Corporation's trolley buses; the tram system began work in 1906 which is probably when the depot was built. Note the redundant tram tracks on the ground and the overhead wires running into the shed. By the time of this early 1960s photograph the trolley buses were also being phased out and the depot was about to deal with buses only

124 The South Croydon bus depot was built by the London & General Omnibus Company in 1915 but initially used by Thomas Tilling's buses, here seen lined up presumably soon after it opened

The recently demolished bus depot in Oswestry, Shropshire, for example, was a former drill hall that had actually been built in 1909 as a very unsuccessful roller skating rink. Few non-tram or non-trolleybus related buildings, however, were of sufficient size to be capable of being adapted in this way, and in most towns of sufficient size and bus traffic to warrant a bus station, a specially built complex was needed.

Most are fairly utilitarian structures, perhaps boasting a reasonably attractive brick facade to the large shed behind. One notable exception is the Stockwell Bus Garage, in south London, a particularly good and innovative designed by Adie, Button & Partners built between 1950 and 1954. It has a massive reinforced concrete roof of nine arches allowing a huge area of uninterrupted space within, capable of housing around 200 modern buses. A rare two-level bus depot of 1928 in New Street, Edinburgh, was also under threat at the time of writing.

In larger towns it became more convenient to provide a central bus station rather than to rely entirely on kerbside pick-up points. In some cases the bus station and bus depot are combined, or at least occupy different parts of the same site. In Britain, between the late 1920s and early 1960s, there were several examples of bus stations that were of good quality design – such as the neo-Georgian one of 1938 in Salisbury – and many more that were not. The increase in car numbers and steady decline in the relative importance of the motor bus in the last quarter of the twentieth century led to a decline in the numbers of bus stations of this type. Even some of the better examples are now being threatened with demolition and redevelopment. One of the most controversial sites, and one that warranted more national publicity in the media, was the very fine inter-war art deco bus station in Derby designed by Charles H. Aslin which appears, at the time of writing, to be doomed despite its innate architectural qualities and public opinion.

One coach station with a more likely chance of survival is in central London. The problems of providing facilities for long-distance bus and coach travellers in the city became acute as such travel became more common in the 1920s; up to 1,200 coaches left the Belgrave Square offices of the London Coastal Coaches

125 Charles Aslin's fine art deco bus station in Derby, built between the wars, is, at the time of writing, under threat of demolition. This is an important part of our transport heritage, and the local authorities of Derby should be ashamed of themselves for even considering the proposals. It is amazing that the buildings could not form the centrepiece of a new bus station in the same way that Wolverhampton managed to retain a former railway station gateway for its buses

126 The bus stop is usually a humble and fairly transient structure. Some urban authorities did build fairly grand ones to house styles in cast iron and, later, concrete, but few are as fine as this one in Pooley Bridge at the end of Ullswater in Cumbria's Lake District; it was a celebration of the 1953 coronation of Elizabeth II

Ltd in a single Easter weekend. To cope, a new purpose-built coach station was constructed on the corner of Buckingham Palace Road, Victoria, to the designs of Wallis, Gilbert & Partners and opened in 1932.

PART VII

TAILPIECE

CHAPTER 20

The rule of the road

Although only tenuously connected with the archaeology of the roads, one aspect of road travel that is often a matter of debate is the 'rule of the road' – especially now that Britain is a long-standing member of the European Union. As a country we still have not taken to two things that most of our fellow members take for granted – metrication and driving on the right.

Dante records that in 1300 traffic was regulated into two lanes across the bridge beneath the Castle of S. Angelo in Rome by a barrier, to improve the lot of pilgrims travelling to and from St Peter's. He does not, however, indicate whether people were asked to keep to the left or to the right. In Britain there are apparently no surviving medieval records of any rule of the road.

In 1722 an official attempt was made by the local authorities to enforce an existing rule of unknown vintage in which people kept to the left side as they crossed London bridge. An Act was subsequently passed in 1756 to enforce wagons to do so. In 1772, another Act applied the 'keep left' rule to all towns in Scotland, but it was not until 1835 that similar legislation applied in England and Wales – the same year, ironically, that the rule of keeping to the right was applied by law to all of France. Keeping to the left was clearly well established elsewhere in Britain by the later eighteenth century, as shown in this ditty by Henry Erskine (1746–1817):

> The rule of the road is a paradox quite,
> Both in riding and driving along;
> If you keep to the left, you are sure to be right,
> If you keep to the right you are wrong.

In the early years of the twentieth century, driving on the left was formerly more common in mainland Europe than it became, and part of the change to driving on the right is associated with the many changes made by Napoleon when emperor of France. Even so, at the start of the motor age, other European countries that initially drove on the left included Portugal, Sweden and the Austro-Hungarian Empire – even though the latter's German neighbours drove on the right.

Technically, the law in Britain was still not limiting drivers to keeping to one side of the road but, instead, making them keep to the left when meeting vehicles approaching in the opposite direction. Because of the often-precipitous camber of the road surfaces, it was more common for wheeled traffic to keep to the middle of the road if the way was clear, so that the vehicles and their loads could be kept level.

Even after the more scientific improvements in road surfaces following the work of Telford and MacAdam and the lessening of road profiles, there was still a tendency to use the middle of the road if possible. As late as 1923 an expert claimed that most motorists drove towards the centre of the road because of the tendency for the camber to make the steering of their vehicles difficult and to avoid the problem of skidding down the 'slope'. With the change over to right-hand driving by Sweden in September 1967, Britain and Ireland were the only remaining European countries to keep to the left; in other parts of the world, many of the former British Commonwealth countries, along with Japan, still drive on the left but most other countries drive on the right.

THE LAST WORD

This book started with a poem by the essayist and poet Edward Thomas who had a fascination with roads – amongst other things. Writing about the Pilgrim's Way in Kent in 1909 he summed up that attraction:

> For centuries these roads seemed to hundreds as necessary, and men set out upon them at dawn with hope and followed after joy ... And now they, as the sounds of their feet and the echoes, are dead, and the roads are but pleasant folds in the grassy chalk. Stay traveller ... and tread softly, because your way is over men's dreams ...

.

Index

If you are interested in purchasing other books published by Tempus,
or in case you have difficulty finding any Tempus books in your local bookshop,
you can also place orders directly through our website

www.tempus-publishing.com